Using the Bible Today

OTHER TITLES IN THE CANTERBURY PAPERS SERIES:
Series Editors Dan Cohn-Sherbok and Kenneth Wolfe

ESSAYS ON RELIGION AND SOCIETY
Edited by Dan Cohn-Sherbok

TRADITION AND UNITY:
Sermons Published in Honour of Robert Runcie
Edited by Dan Cohn-Sherbok
Foreword by Lord Hailsham

FUNDAMENTALISM AND TOLERANCE:
An Agenda for Theology and Society
Edited by Andrew Linzey and Peter Wexler

USING THE BIBLE TODAY

Contemporary Interpretations of Scripture

Edited by Dan Cohn-Sherbok

Bellew Publishing
London
1991

First published in Great Britain in 1991 by
Bellew Publishing Company Limited
7 Southampton Place, London WC1A 2DR

ISBN 0 947792 95 3 (cased)
ISBN 0 947792 94 5 (limp)

Phototypeset by Intype, London
Printed and bound in Great Britain by
Billings & Sons Ltd

Contents

Acknowledgements   vii

Foreword *John A. Simpson*   ix

Preface *Robert Runcie*   xi

Part I   Making Sense of the Bible ────────

1   The Bible and its Versions   3
Donald Coggan

2   The Bible and University Study   11
John M. Court

3   The Bible and Scholarship   18
Leslie Houlden

4   The Bible and Synoptic Difficulties   26
Enoch Powell

5   The Bible and the Secondary School   31
Kathleen M. Court

6   The Bible and Television   38
Angela Tilby

7   The Bible and Broadcasting   47
Kenneth Wolfe

Part II   Personal Discovery and Community ────────

8   The Bible and the God of Israel   71
Don Cupitt

9   The Bible and Jungian Depth Psychology   76
Leon Schlamm

10   The Bible and Human Suffering   87
     Lord Longford

11   The Bible and Ordinary People   93
     Christopher Lewis

12   The Bible and Ethics   101
     Peter Baelz

13   The Bible and Killing for Food   110
     Andrew Linzey

14   An Inner City Bible   121
     John J. Vincent

     Part III   **The Bible and the World**

15   The Bible and Scientific Discovery   137
     John Habgood

16   The Bible and Peace and War   145
     Ursula King

17   The Bible and Mission   162
     Geoffrey Parrinder

18   The Bible and Christian Witness   170
     Michael Nazir-Ali

19   The Bible and Inter-faith Relations   180
     H. D. Beeby and Lesslie Newbigin

20   The Bible and Paradise   188
     Rex Ambler

     Notes   196

     Biographical Notes on Contributors   203

Acknowledgements

I would like to thank all those who have contributed to this volume. Special thanks to *The Way* for allowing us to reprint Angela Tilby's chapter, which previously appeared as 'Like the Appearance of Lamps: Television and the Transcendent', *The Way*, Vol. 31, No. 2, April 1991. Thanks are also due to Deirdre McDonald and Susanna Burt for their help and encouragement with this book.

DAN COHN-SHERBOK
University of Kent,
Canterbury

Foreword

Since its formation in 1978, the Centre for the Study of Religion and Society has had close connections with Canterbury Cathedral. Two successive Deans have been Chairman of the Centre's Steering Committee; the Dean and Chapter, as a body, has given support and encouragement to the Centre's work; and, of recent years, the Cathedral and the Centre have together sponsored series of lectures in the Cathedral Library. Such a lecture series, given in the early months of 1990, forms the core of this present book. The fact that these lectures drew large audiences spanning all age groups, and by no means all of whom claimed religious alliance, has demonstrated the fact that even in a secular society such as present-day England, the Bible is still felt to have a relevance, and some understanding, both of what it says and how it can be used, is thought to be important. Each lecture resulted in lively discussion, and the issues raised have provided subjects for subsequent lectures, which it has been possible to deal with not just from a Judaeo-Christian viewpoint, but from a wider inter-religious stance.

Canterbury Cathedral is privileged to be associated with this project, and to provide a forum where the influence of religion in modern society – a still powerful influence, though perhaps differently exercised than in the past – can be explored.

JOHN A. SIMPSON
Dean of Canterbury

Preface

A story is told of the theologian Paul Tillich. He was about to preach a sermon when he was interrupted by a young man, holding up a Bible, at the back of the church.

'Professor, do you hold this book to be the Word of God?'

'When you hold it,' replied the preacher, 'I am not so sure; but when it holds you, it is.'

In some ways the misuse of the Bible is more damaging to faith than its disuse. It produces superstition in those who are persuaded by it and an aversion to the Bible in those who are exposed to it and not persuaded.

A proper use of the Bible will show the discerning reader that it is not one book but a whole library of books. In this way it is different from many other sacred texts. There is wisdom, narrative, poetry, preaching and prophecy. Its authors are people of power, or victims of oppression, ecstatic visionaries and sophisticated theologians, members of a priestly caste and opponents of institutional religion. There are other equally distinctive characters knowing themselves addressed by God, trying to fathom and express his dealings with us all.

The contributors to this book do not offer some artificial unity either in the composition of the Bible or among themselves. They illustrate how fruitful it is when we are prepared to 'stand under the Word' and discover for ourselves something of Coleridge's vivid experience of 'God marching up and down the pages of the Bible, bringing it to life magisterially wherever he will'.

ROBERT RUNCIE

Part I

MAKING SENSE OF
THE BIBLE

Chapter 1

The Bible and its Versions

Donald Coggan

The title of this chapter, taken by itself, would demand of the
writer that he should begin by introducing his readers to the ancient
translations of the original Hebrew, Aramaic and Greek texts of the
Bible. Thus he would have to give considerable space, for example,
to the great translation of the Hebrew Scriptures into Greek which
is known as the Septuagint and to the Vulgate which is associated
with Jerome and his translation of the Bible into Latin in the fourth
century AD.

But this chapter is part of a book entitled *Using the Bible Today*,
and its writer may assume that the 'Versions' referred to in its
heading are translations of the ancient texts into the English language. For the purpose of this essay we shall confine ourselves to
them – and that alone is a huge field.

But first, why versions, why translations *at all*? The answer is that
at the heart of the Christian religion is a story which, to the believer,
records the most momentous event in history and which he believes
it is incumbent on him to make known to the world. That event has
to do with the birth, ministry, death and resurrection of Jesus the
Messiah and with the interpretation of that event and with its consequences in the early decades of what came to be known as the
Christian era. The prelude to that event can only be understood by
a study of that extraordinary mixture of books which we call the
Old Testament – thirty-nine books in all, prophecy and proverbs,
poetry and prose, love lyrics and biography, apocalypse and myth.
The central figure who emerges in the four Gospels is given no
biography in the sense in which we use that word today. Rather,
those books present us with glimpses, snapshots as it were, of a
figure at once dynamic and gentle, sharp-spoken and tender, wound-
ing and wounded, healing and wooing. The fourth Gospel is best
regarded as an interpretative portrait of Way, Truth and Life. The
Acts of the Apostles (falsely so called, for most of them disappear
and the *Spirit* acts) gives an exciting story of the spread of the
Church, not devoid of failure and persecution. The Letters look back
on the event which was Jesus of Nazareth, relate that event to
life here and hereafter, and meditate on the significance of what

happened in that brief period when he walked, worked and suffered among us.

The story of the coming together of the twenty-seven books which constitute the New Testament cannot be told here. But it was not very long before the Church went to the world with a book in its hand much the same as what we have today. (There were a few books which were slower than others in obtaining 'canonical' status.) Indeed it could not do its missionary work without that book, nor could it offer its worship Sunday by Sunday without readings from it. It was an essential part both of its worship and of its outreach to the world.

Hence the need of translations. If Greek was the *lingua franca* of the Graeco-Roman world, then those books of the Bible which were written in Hebrew and Aramaic must be translated into that language. (That had been done some century and a half BC by those who gave us the Septuagint.) If there were corners of the world where only Syriac or some Egyptian language was understood, then it was a matter of urgency to provide the Scriptures in tongues 'understanded of the peoples' in those areas. It was a sad day for the ordinary Christian who could not read Latin when the only available text of the Scriptures or, indeed, of the liturgy of the Church was in a tongue he could not understand.

Where translations were not available or the people were illiterate, pictorial *art* proved to be one of the best ways of conveying the message of the Faith. Hence the wall paintings which adorn so many of our churches. *Poetry* and *music* contributed to the task. Caedmon, seventh-century labourer at the monastery at Whitby, discovered that he had a gift of composing verses and, as Bede tells us, 'sang the creation of the world, the origin of men, and all the history of Genesis . . . the incarnation, passion, resurrection of our Lord, and his ascension into heaven . . . He endeavoured to turn away all men from the love of vice, and to excite them in the love of, and application to, good actions.'[1]

It is impossible to say exactly to what extent the Venerable Bede (673–735) translated the Scriptures into the vernacular, but it would seem that that great man did much towards that end before completing his translation of St John's Gospel when, in 735, 'resting on the floor of his cell, he chanted the *Gloria*, and his soul immediately passed away while the name of the Holy Spirit was on his lips'.

It is a far cry from the days of Bede, of which we know little in regard to the translation of the Bible into the vernacular, to the days of the early seventeenth century and the birth of the King James Version which we shall consider in due course. In that long interval much was done to give the people the Scriptures in their own tongue. Certain figures are of such eminence that it would be wholly wrong to leave them unmentioned. There are at least two such.

John Wycliffe, 'the last of the Schoolmen and the first of the Reformers', Fellow and, for a short time, Master of Balliol College, Oxford, and Rector of Lutterworth in the County of Leicestershire, deserves first mention. The Bible which bears his name appeared near the end of his life and made a fitting climax to his career. The New Testament appeared about 1380, the whole Bible about 1382. It is truer to say of that volume that it bears his name than to say that he translated it. The project was due to his inspiration and had his assistance and support. We do not know precisely how much of it was his own work. We do know that the major part of the Old Testament was the work of Nicholas Hereford, and that the revision which appeared within four years of Wycliffe's death was made by a pupil of his, probably John Purvey. The translation owes its being to Wycliffe's horror at the ignorance of the clergy and to his conviction that the authority of the Church must be tested by the acids of Scripture. The fact that of the copies of the Wycliffe Bible which have survived, many are small, unadorned and closely written, points to Wycliffe's longing that the Bible should be open not only to the great and learned but to the ordinary people who could read. And if, as was mostly the case, they were illiterate, then they should hear the message from his 'poor priests'. The introduction of printing into England by Caxton came only some century later, but that, of course, speeded Wycliffe's plan in a way he could never have conceived.

Wycliffe died in peace in 1384. A posthumous condemnation by the Council of Constance in 1415 ordered that 'his bones were to be dug up and cast out of the consecrated ground'.[2] This eventually was done. Thomas Fuller quaintly commented, referring to the river Swift where the ashes were scattered: 'Thus this brook hath conveyed his ashes into Avon; Avon into Severn; Severn into the narrow seas; they into the main ocean. And thus the ashes of Wycliff [*sic*] are the emblem of his doctrine, which is now dispersed the world over.'

William Tyndale (?1494–1536). It would be almost impossible to exaggerate the importance of this great man's contribution, not only to the translation of the Bible into English but also to the development of Anglo-Saxon speech. Milton, Bunyan and a host of later English writers were deeply influenced by the language of the King James Version, and something between 70 and 90 per cent of that New Testament is wholly Tyndale's, not to mention his great contribution to the Old Testament.

He was a master in the use of simple, straightforward English. Note the power of the monosyllable in phrases like these, all of which we owe to Tyndale: 'In him we live and move and have our being'; 'until the day dawn and the daystar arise in your hearts'; 'the burden and heat of the day'; 'eat, drink and be merry'; 'the powers that be'; 'a prophet is not without honour, save in his own country'. The list is endless.

Tyndale worked from the Hebrew and Greek texts and, while he kept his eye on the Vulgate, on Luther's German Bible and on Erasmus's famous Greek Testament, he showed a sturdy independence and worked on sound principles of philology and grammar.

Like Wycliffe before him, he was horrified at the clerical ignorance which still abounded, and longed to make the Bible available for all to learn. In his Preface to the Pentateuch he wrote: 'I perceived . . . how that it was impossible to establish the lay people in any truth except the Scripture were plainly laid before their eyes in their mother tongue, that they might see the process, order and meaning of the text.' Foxe tells of his remark to a divine in Gloucestershire: 'If God spare my life, ere many years I will cause a boy that driveth the plough shall know more of the Scripture than thou dost.'[3]

That life, so nobly lived, met its end in 1536. Tyndale was strangled, then burnt, but not before he had prayed: 'Lord, open the King of England's eyes.' The following year that prayer was answered by the royal recognition of the Coverdale Bible which itself made abundant use of Tyndale's work. Coverdale's was the first *complete* printed Bible in English. (The Old Testament in the Tyndale Bible was incomplete.)

Pausing only to mention such versions as the Great Bible of 1539 (with which the name of Myles Coverdale will always be linked), the Geneva Bible (popularly known as the Breeches Bible), the Bishops' Bible (1568) and so on, we now come to the King James Version of 1611 (inaccurately called the Authorized Version, for there is no record of its having ever been officially authorized). It was in 1604, at the Hampton Court Conference, that a new translation of the Bible was decided on, with the full approval and encouragement of King James I. If we are sometimes tempted, in moments of cynicism, to doubt whether any good thing can come out of a committee, then the King James Version should give us pause. For it was the result of the work of *six* committees labouring at the same time – two in Oxford, two in Cambridge, two in Westminster. But behind these committees, and working with much success to keep them together, was the master-mind of Launcelot Andrewes, Bishop successively of Chichester, Ely and Winchester, of whom it was said that 'he might have been interpreter general at Babel . . . the world wanted learning to know how learned he was'.

The book appeared at the right time. It was the age of Shakespeare and Marlowe, of Spenser, Hooker and Bacon. Our language had reached what G. M. Trevelyan called 'its brief perfection'. In words which have become famous, Macaulay has described the 1611 version as 'a book which, if everything else in our language should perish, would alone suffice to show the whole extent of its beauty and power'. So it was that J. R. Green, in his *History of the English People*, was able to write of the time of Elizabeth I: 'England became the people of a book and that book was the Bible.'

The influence which this version of the Bible in up-to-date language exercised on the people in the years which followed its publication was immense. G. M. Trevelyan again: 'When Elizabeth came to the throne the Bible and Prayer Book formed the intellectual and spiritual foundation of a new social order. For every Englishman who had read Sidney or Spenser, or had seen Shakespeare acted at the Globe, there were hundreds who had read or heard the Bible with close attention as the word of God.'

The Authorized Version was to be followed in the next two and a half centuries by other attempts to 'English' the Bible, but they suffered by comparison with that of 1611 – their prolixity and floridity only serve to show up the majestic simplicity of the Authorized. The next event of real importance was the publication of the Revised Version (NT 1881, OT 1885, Apocrypha 1895). This was a landmark in the long story of the evolution of the English Bible. Some of the most able biblical scholars of the day gave of their best, doing their work mainly in two committees, one working on the Old Testament and the other on the New. Their number included B. F. Westcott and F. J. A. Hort, whose famous edition of the Greek text of the New Testament was to appear five days before the Revised New Testament. The revision was a cautious one, the translators showing great deference to the wording of the Authorized Version. But it was a great improvement on its predecessor, especially in obscure parts of the Old Testament, in the paragraphing according to the sense of the passage, and in the marginal notes which dealt with alternative renderings and variant readings. Though it never dislodged the Authorized from the affections of the people, it proved especially useful for students who needed a greater measure of accuracy in the text before them.

Yes: we may call the Revised Version a 'landmark'. But it was premature. As I have written elsewhere:[4]

> Shortly after the Revised Version came out, the dry sands of the Near East, and especially of Egypt, threw up thousands upon thousands of ostraca (old pieces of broken pots and vessels) and papyri (sheets, some fairly large and others no more than little scraps, of papyrus reeds glued together, rubbed smooth with pumice, and used as we should use bits of paper). On these ostraca and papyri were written, in the Greek of the street, the market-place and the home, all kinds of things, for example, lists of names or articles, and messages of all sorts. (One such, in

atrocious Greek, is from a schoolboy asking his father for money; another is from a husband on military service, writing to his wife who is expecting the birth of their child. 'If it is a boy,' he writes, 'well and good; if it is a girl, cast it out.') At first sight one would not think that such discoveries would have much bearing on Biblical scholarship. As a matter of fact, they were of the greatest importance. For, as these little scraps of writing were gathered together, deciphered, and compared with the Greek in which the New Testament was written, it became clear that the New Testament documents, so far from being written (as many had previously thought) in a kind of 'language of the Holy Ghost', were, as a matter of fact, written in the ordinary language used by the people of the first century Graeco-Roman world. True, the themes with which the documents dealt had an ennobling effect on the language and, as it were, lifted it out of the street on to a higher plane. True, the Hebraic thought of many of the writers and the use of the Greek Version of the Old Testament, the Septuagint, influenced the style of the Greek. True, some of the writers of the New Testament were men of culture and great literary skill – St Luke especially and the unknown author of the Epistle to the Hebrews. But *basically* the language was that of the *lingua franca* which was the chief means of intercourse among the peoples of the Mediterranean world of the time of Christ. Many of the discoveries were in themselves of no great importance. (For example, the Authorized Version of St Luke 15, v. 13, makes the Prodigal Son 'gather all together' before he goes into the far country. The papyri have shown that the verb can mean 'realise goods into ready cash'. This is precisely what he needed if he was to 'have a good time'!) But taken together, they opened up something of a new epoch in New Testament textual study.

The twentieth century was to see a flurry of new translations – some good, some bad, some like the curate's egg. Among pioneers who, acting as individuals, produced renderings of their own must be mentioned R. F. Weymouth who in 1902 produced his New Testament in Modern Speech and James Moffatt who in his solo effort (NT 1913, OT 1924, whole Bible finally revised 1935) tried to break away from old styles of translation, to give us the biblical books in modern English idiom, and to incorporate as best they could the results of modern scholarship. Nor should we forget Ronald Knox's translation of the Bible based on the Vulgate but showing evidence that he kept a careful eye on the original languages; nor J. B. Phillips whose New Testament in Modern English (1958) was to prove immensely popular.

Meanwhile, *groups* of scholars were at work. One such group in America put out the Revised Standard Version of the New Testament in 1946 and of the whole Bible in 1952. The American Bible Society was mainly responsible for the Good News Bible (Today's English Version) and Americans gave the impetus to the New International Version though they worked with the help of scholars from several other countries. A group of English-speaking Roman Catholics produced The Jerusalem Bible in 1966, thoroughly revised and produced as The New Jerusalem Bible in 1985. One could continue the list.

Why, then, was there a need for the New English Bible (NT 1961, OT and Apocrypha 1970, published by the University Presses of Oxford and Cambridge)? The fact that over four million copies of the NEB:NT were sold within a year of publication shows something of the intense interest which this translation aroused. The story has been told in Geoffrey Hunt's *About the New English Bible*.[5] Here we may mention certain special reasons for its production: people engaged in education were aware that the language of the Authorized Version was, for all its beauty, a hindrance to the understanding of its message. The same was true, to a lesser extent, of the Revised Version. Moreover, advances had been made in the realm of recent scholarship (for example, the finding of the Dead Sea scrolls) which needed to be incorporated in the translation. Again, there had been progress in the field of ecumenical co-operation which ought to be reflected in the composition of the panels of scholars who did the translating and of the Joint Committee who supervised the progress of the operation. Three panels (OT, NT and Apocrypha) did the work of translation and submitted their labours to a literary panel of scholars of English. The presiding genius from start to finish was Professor C. H. Dodd, whose sensitiveness to the nuances of language and theology was universally recognized. Professor (later Sir) Godfrey Driver (son of Professor G. R. Driver, who had taken a big share in the work of the Revised Version) was convenor of the Old Testament panel and Professor W. D. McHardy of the Apocrypha panel. Professor C. H. Dodd himself presided over the scholars concerned with the New Testament.

The reception accorded to the New English Bible convinced many that there was need for such a translation. Those who used it could be assured that they had before them a work of first-rate scholarship, which reflected no particular 'stance', and which had the approval of most of the main-line Churches in the British Isles.

But if some had asked in 1961 and 1970 what was the need for the New English Bible, it is probable that more asked a similar question when 1989 saw the production of the Revised English Bible. Only some twenty years, and yet another translation? They might have been surprised that, very soon after 1970, it became apparent to those most intimately concerned with translation matters that a revision would be called for, and in 1974 the Joint Committee met to approve nominations of scholars to the revising committees. This proved to be a much longer operation than they had anticipated – the story of its inception and progress is told by Roger Coleman in

New Light and Truth: The Making of the Revised English Bible (1989).[6]
The need became increasingly apparent as the years went by. The
fact that it was needed cast no shadow on the value of the New
English Bible though, naturally, there were certain emphases and
infelicities in it that called for attention. Under the guiding hand of
Professor McHardy, who took the place which C. H. Dodd had
occupied with the New English Bible, a book was produced firmly
in the tradition of the New English Bible, every verse of which
had been reviewed with an eye on the original languages – good
scholarship was assured.

We must mention some of the main issues which had to be considered: in the New English Bible 'thou' as the second person singu-
lar had been retained in the poetic sections. But the years since 1970
had seen much liturgical development, one aspect of which was
the frequent abandonment of 'thou' and the adoption of 'you' in
addressing God. In private prayer, too, 'you' was regarded as
natural and no less reverent than 'thou'. The Revised English Bible
was content to follow this pattern.

Again, C. H. Dodd and his colleagues who worked on the New
English Bible had not intended that it should be used in the *public*
reading of Scripture. In preparing the Revised English Bible, this use
was constantly borne in mind, as also its suitability for *congregational*
reading, for example, of the Psalms. The issue of inclusive language
was also considered with care and, where possible, appropriate
action was taken.

The Revised English Bible is an example of a unique and historic
co-operation between all the major Churches in the United Kingdom. No longer was the Roman Catholic Church represented by
observers on the Joint Committee, but by full members and by
participation in the actual revision work. It was a symbol of a coming
together of the Churches which augurs well for their future work of
joint evangelism and social commitment.

Language is fluid; it changes with the passing of the years. Liturgy
is fluid. Scholarship is fluid; years add to knowledge and the new
corrects the old. So long as these things are true, the work of
translation must go on. It is a work which calls for all that is best
in scholarship and devotion; and it is work which can always be
pursued in the confidence that God has yet new light and truth to
break forth from his word.

Chapter 2

The Bible and University Study

John M. Court

Academic Biblical Study

> Modern biblical scholarship arose in Western Europe as the old order crumbled in the late seventeenth and eighteenth centuries. Enlightened human reason emancipated itself from the authority of religious traditions and no longer took for granted that the Bible spoke reliably about God and the world. The biblical picture of the world was challenged by natural science, and the biblical story further undermined by moral criticism and historical study.[1]

It is inevitable that the academic study of the Bible, when it takes place in a modern secular university, should be coloured by this legacy of post-Enlightenment culture. The term 'criticism', however neutrally defined, has overtones of hostility. If the Bible is studied like any other book, there is no way of ensuring that only respectable religious conclusions can be drawn. It is appropriate to examine any presuppositions of the text or the interpreter, whether they are the dogmas of ancient faith or of modern philosophy. For this reason the results are unlikely to be uniform, not even uniformly negative. It is possible to evaluate what is meant if one says that a text is 'inspired' or 'authoritative'.

The nineteenth century was an exciting and creative era of academic scholarship on the Bible; the primary concern was to relate the biblical text to an evolving historical process. As with such processes in other academic fields (e.g. the natural sciences) what emerges at the end of the process may be quite at variance with the original state of things. So Catholic Christianity as an evolved phenomenon may be quite unlike the Galilean Springtime of the ministry of Jesus.

For the last forty years of the nineteenth century the collaborative work of three scholars in the New Testament field was particularly valued and celebrated in the English-speaking world. This triumvirate was J. B. Lightfoot, B. F. Westcott and F. J. A. Hort, who were all associated with Trinity College, Cambridge. They had much in common, but when they collaborated their individual concerns were complementary. According to Stephen Neill, 'Lightfoot was primarily the historian, Hort the philosopher, and Westcott the exegete'.[2]

John Robinson speculated in a delightful fantasy as to what St Paul would have made of Lightfoot, Westcott and Hort. In the person of Lightfoot, Paul

> would have recognized at once the Paulinist *par excellence*, contender like himself for the truth and progress of the gospel. Lightfoot's mental interests lay almost exclusively in the concrete facts or written words. He never seemed to care for any generalization. Lightfoot was essentially the historian and not primarily a theologian in Tillich's definition of one who takes rational trouble (*logos*) about a mystery (*theos*). But Westcott never ceased to wrestle at this, and it is significant that the only Pauline epistle on which he wrote a commentary, published posthumously, was Ephesians. Westcott's was the Paul that later appealed to Teilhard de Chardin: Paul the visionary, the mystic, the apostle of the cosmic Christ. Hort was not by temperament a Pauline man – he was more at home with Peter and James on whose Epistles he lectured and agonized for years without, characteristically, bringing any fruit to perfection. Yet in Hort I recognize, as I think the Apostle would, the Paul of Romans 1 and 2 and the speeches of Acts 13 and 17 – the Paul, that is, who could respond positively to the scientific humanism of his day, self-effacingly ready to be all things to all men, the Paul whose letters were powerful but his outward presence weak, the Paul who was buffeted by a continual thorn in the flesh given to check any confidence in his own powers.[3]

Twentieth-century Dilemmas

The nineteenth century of Lightfoot, Westcott and Hort might claim to be the golden age of academic Biblical Studies. The variety and richness of teaching opportunities in biblical languages and literature, Christian history doctrine and philosophy are now sadly diminished, towards the end of the twentieth century. Old and New Testament, Modern Christianity, Ethics, Systematic and Philosophical Theology seem to be still the most intensively taught subjects in English university departments of Theology and Religious Studies. In departments with a Religious Studies dimension the range of courses is broadened by other world religions, but the Christian content is often diluted. Early and medieval Church history, Patristic theology, and especially Liturgy have become much less prominent.

Ideally an academic course in Biblical Studies should begin with the resources of language (biblical Greek and Hebrew; with Aramaic, Syriac, and the other languages of biblical versions in support) and the techniques of Textual Criticism. Then the primary sources of the biblical texts can be studied with confidence from a variety of perspectives: literary, historical (including archaeological), exegetical, philosophical and theological. More recently these options have been supplemented by others: socio-anthropological, psychological, and the literary refinements of structuralism and deconstruction. But the languages and a balance of the original methodologies of criticism provide an indispensable prerequisite for reliable interpretation.

A recent degree course guide expresses the issue of the compulsory learning of biblical languages from the student's point of view:

> One difference is whether you have to learn Hebrew. The advantages of learning Hebrew are great. Not only are you able to come closer to the thought-world of the Old Testament, you are also in a better position to exercise an independent judgement in relation to many questions discussed by Old Testament (and sometimes New Testament) scholars. But it takes time to learn Hebrew, and the more the balance of studies changes, the more priorities change here.[4]

The final comment refers again to the influence of the Religious Studies perspective: 'Old Testament study may be one constituent of a history of religions survey of Judaism and Christianity that extends to contemporary expression of the two faiths.' The sheer breadth can be stimulating, but the element to be squeezed out because of pressure of time is the originally indispensable language resource.

Towards a Positive Solution

So far we have identified two major factors in the context of academic Biblical Studies, both brought about by large-scale cultural influences from outside. There is the hostile critical edge which, as the product of post-Enlightenment rationalism, may be destructive of the basic faith of a Christian believer. And there is the range of modern religious pluralism, often conceived in a supposedly 'neutral' environment of secularism, which by its very scale may well detract from the 'seriousness' of religious study. We need to consider if there are any remedies in our current situation, any means of at least compensating for these factors in our academic life without simply putting back the clock. It is my belief that there is a different way of teaching Biblical Studies which may prove to be a positive help in offsetting both these influences. This way of teaching can and should be used in parallel to the surviving academic programmes of Biblical Studies; it can also be used as a substitute which will fit within the constraints of a Religious Studies perspective.

While under the influence of the Religious Studies perspective I am struck by the similarity between this dilemma which I have identified in Christian Biblical Studies and the tensions which verge on incompatibility in modern Judaism (in the curriculum of the ultra-Orthodox yeshiva over against the 'liberal arts' programme on Reformed teaching).[5] Is there a way of concentrating on what one holds to be the essentials of faith, and studying these in a critical analysis which allows them to breathe in the relevant air of modern thought, without at the same time being choked or drowned in the flood of secular materialism?

The method I propose is the one which incidentally I have been pursuing in the writing of this article. We should study the Bible with all the seriousness at our command, but we should also do so with that element of distancing appropriate to the modern academic endeavour. We study the Bible by studying ourselves, or our contemporaries, or our predecessors, in the act of studying the Bible. From this process of study we can extrapolate the principles for study. This is what makes it more than an exercise in introspection.

Specimen Outline of Biblical Tradition Course

COURSE PROGRAMME:
First Term: Underlying presuppositions and modern perspectives
1 Introduction
2 Identifying the limits of the material: the Canon of Scripture Part Three?
3 The nature of an authoritative text: the concept of authority
4 Confessional and liturgical use of the text
5 What's in a translation? (Assessment of the Revised English Bible)
6 Different theories and methods of interpretation
7 Relationships between the Old and New Testaments
8 The relation of Scripture to Doctrine
9 Practical applications: the Bible in a living tradition

Second Term: Working examples – ancient and modern ways of reading the text
1 Allegory with Origen
2 Medieval exegesis
3 Latin and the vernacular
4 Ruling by Scripture: the divine right of kings
5 Rousseau – 'The Creed of a curate of Savoy'
6 Structural readings of the Song of Songs
7 How to write a Gospel (Form critical insights)
8 Narrative theology
9 The Bible in art (ancient and modern)

WRITTEN ASSIGNMENTS

The course requirement is three essays to be chosen from the following:

1 A 'written-up' seminar paper. Brief introductory seminar papers are invited for some sessions in the first term. After the seminar, write up a more reflective report on the topic which you chose to introduce.

2 A project of your choice on a significant historical instance of the interpretation of a biblical book or short text; the instance can be ancient or more modern, but not from the present day. This involves showing how the historical context affected the way the Bible was understood.

3 A comparison and evaluation of two contrasting readings of a particular biblical text.

4 Examine *one* modern literary rewriting of a biblical story. Compare it with the scriptural version and try to estimate what is gained and what is lost by the modern attempt. Some suggested examples are:

> Noah and the flood: Julian Barnes, *A History of the World in 10½ Chapters*, Cape, 1989;
>
> King David: Joseph Heller, *God Knows*, Cape, 1984;
>
> _____ Dan Jacobson, *The Rape of Tamar*, Secker, 1980.

5 Any independent proposal (subject to agreement).

Principles of Study

As Norman Perrin observed, 'The principles involved in the hermeneutical process are the same for any texts, sacred or secular, ancient or modern, literary or popular.'[6] This is to confirm the post-Enlightenment criterion that the Bible should be studied like any other book. But especially at this point there is an added dimension in studying the Bible as tradition. What is asserted is the principle of the Bible's contemporary relevance and its application at every stage in the history of the text.

This is going further than anything that can be said about most works of literature (apart from the universally celebrated) because they move in and out of fashionable acceptance. It also takes account of the whole spectrum of Bible study from the most academic literary processes, through the liturgical and kerygmatic applications, and up to and including the popular use of the Bible, as for example reclaimed by the Base Communities of Latin America. This whole spectrum can be subjected to academic scrutiny, and its various principles assessed and evaluated.

It is no longer a question of regarding rational academic methods and popular evangelism as belonging to separate enclaves and held apart as incompatible because of some ghetto mentality. Within the context of Biblical Tradition there is a proper space for seriousness in research, as required for linguistic, historical or socio-anthropological considerations. Study of the traditional use and application of the Bible should not therefore be reckoned as 'second-best' compared with academic Bible Study governed by rationalism, as Classical Civilization courses are often regarded in relation to academic Classical Studies.

It is hoped that from this wide-ranging exploration (or such sampling as time and resources permit) may emerge some reasonable guidelines, or a code of practice, for the study and exegesis of the Bible. Such guidelines could not be applied judgementally, to exclude this or that dimension of Bible study. Prejudice of this kind would be foreign to the whole nature of an open-ended enterprise. The last thing one wishes is to disregard the spontaneity of inspiration (applicable to the later stages of use as well as the first stages of creation of a scriptural text). Nor is revelation to be subjected to the ultimate criterion of reason, even if what revelation entails may be rationally considered. Rather there is a desire to create a sense of balance in the appreciation of all kinds of interpretation of the Bible, including those which go beyond verbal communication (e.g the use of other art forms or of mystical techniques of meditation).

It may be practical to categorize many aspects of Bible use by borrowing and applying terminology from the most recent methods of literary criticism (e.g. audience criticism and deconstruction).[7] Most regular techniques of exegesis involve the use of something like a mirror which reflects what a Bible text says on to the situation currently experienced by the reader (individual or group). There is a general recognition of the approximate nature of the reflection. But other techniques try to apply the text more directly, by constructing a window (rather than a mirror) through which one may look directly at the text. This classification brings together the methods of historical criticism in reconstructing the original situation, and also the broadly related methods of Patristic allegory and modern structuralism in causing a structure of meaning to emerge from the text.

But we must all include within our reckoning other techniques of exegesis which are not obviously literary. There is the highly activist use of formulae cut from the text; like the acclamation formulae which form critics recognized as important steps in the development of Christology, these phrases are shouted as slogans or paraded on banners. They are the political encouragement to Liberation Theology, but in different circumstances or earlier centuries such formulae are (or were) displayed on text boards, or illustrated in the murals or stained glass of churches. At the opposite end of the spectrum, in the passive reflection of meditation, there is a focus on biblical symbols which can transcend time and place. In the heights of mysticism one may arrive at a paradoxically negative way, where that which is of the greatest concern is the least possible to express in words. Our examples of Bible use should take seriously both the most articulate and demonstrable and the most allusive and hidden.

Chapter 3

The Bible and Scholarship

Leslie Houlden

The aim of this essay is to demonstrate the various ways in which the Gospels are and have been studied in the world of technical scholarship. The idea is basically simple. It is a matter of 'listening to' the text – hearing what it has to say. That nice way of putting it, which reminds us not to impose our own views and expectations on the text, neglects an important factor. Trying to understand a text is always a matter of a conversation, at least in the sense that we 'interrogate' the text. Of itself a text is inert, and we must take action if it is to yield us fruit. So we 'ask it' about itself: where do you come from? what is your setting? what do you wish to tell us? what do you really mean?

It can be tedious and even baffling to describe the various kinds of interrogation that have been used. To avoid abstraction, we select one passage and address our questions to it in turn.

The Healing of Blind Bartimaeus

> 46 And they came to Jericho; and as he was leaving Jericho with his disciples and a great multitude, Bartimaeus, a blind beggar, the son of Timaeus, was sitting by the roadside. 47 And when he heard that it was Jesus of Nazareth, he began to cry out and say, 'Jesus, Son of David, have mercy on me!' 48 And many rebuked him, telling him to be silent; but he cried out all the more, 'Son of David, have mercy on me!' 49 And Jesus stopped and said, 'Call him'. And they called the blind man, saying to him, 'Take heart; rise, he is calling you'. 50 And throwing off his mantle he sprang up and came to Jesus. 51 And Jesus said to him, 'What do you want me to do for you?' And the blind man said to him, 'Master, let me receive my sight'. 52 And Jesus said to him, 'Go your way; your faith has made you well'. And immediately he received his sight and followed him on the way (Mark 10:46–52).

We turn to the questions. The first ones are rather humdrum, setting out to establish facts – like the questions which open any interrogation. The others are of more general interest and, even when addressed to a rather simple (!) passage such as this, they open up fascinating prospects.

1 *What did the evangelist actually write?*

To be candid, we shall never know, for the original manuscript does not survive, and who knows what alterations occurred before the early manuscripts that survive were written (the oldest is from the fourth century)? But among those manuscripts there are not many significant variations, beyond a few attempts to improve the style. The reason? This was not a passage of any controversial interest, and even a copyist with theological prejudices could pass through it without feeling moved to 'improve' it. There is just one exception, a common one: the insertion of 'Lord' before 'Master' (equal teacher), ('And the blind man said to him, "Lord . . ." ') in v. 51. This term heightens the reverence with which Jesus is addressed, thus pushing the devotional and theological level up a notch.

2 *What sort of a passage is this?*

Technically, what is its genre? The answer affects the way a passage is heard. And we note that the Gospels were written to be read aloud, a circumstance in which we are particularly sensitive to genre. Thus, I heard Alec McCowen speak Mark's Gospel by heart. The style was anecdotal, as if each passage was prefaced by, 'I'll tell you another one'. Was that how Mark meant it?

Study of this Gospel indicates that its author was not without some training in rhetoric, the art of persuasive speech, one of the staple elements in education in his time (now virtually defunct). There are signs of careful writing in this passage, points that the hearer would pick up; for example, the movement from 'sitting by the way' (RSV has 'roadside', so not helping the demonstration) in v. 46 to 'followed him on the way' in v. 52. We shall see more clearly later that that makes for a most satisfying story. (RSV 'Go your *way*, v. 52, misleads: the Greek is 'go', simply.)

If the author (Mark, we call him, though there is no plain early evidence) knew some of the tricks of his art, was he aware of using them in a religious cause? Was he writing a work that he already felt as 'scripture'? Probably not, in any formal way – that status was reserved for the books that Christians came to call and use as 'the *Old* Testament', books inherited from their Jewish roots. Yet Mark's little book was about Jesus, already the object of Christian worship, and was read in Christian gatherings, surely as religious a context as you could imagine. Moreover, the way later Gospel-writers, like Matthew and Luke, used Mark, while showing readiness to adjust his meaning to their ideas, also shows a measure of reverence for Mark – his work is in some sense authoritative. In these ways, this was from the start a 'holy book'.

3 *How does this passage relate to its parallels elsewhere?*

This story occurs not only in the Gospel of Mark, but also in those of Matthew and Luke. The positioning is the same in all three cases, and the wording is close. The passage then plays its part in building up the case for seeing the three books as literarily dependent on each other – in some way. In what way they are dependent cannot be decided without a consideration of all of the three books, and even then 'deciding' may be too far-reaching an ambition. (See Matt. 20:29–34 and Luke 18:35–43.)

But this passage can make a small contribution towards that end. It does not necessarily work in only one direction. On the one hand, both Matthew and Luke present a more orderly and reasonable picture at one point in the story – the very beginning, Jesus's movements in relation to Jericho. Perhaps for a reason that will emerge later, Mark writes, strangely, of Jesus coming to Jericho only to leave it. Matthew and Luke both rationalize this: Matthew drops the coming to Jericho, thereby starting the story with 'And as they went out of Jericho . . .'; Luke chooses the other option, having 'As he drew near to Jericho . . .' (and then exploits Jesus's presence at Jericho in the story's sequel, his own special addition to the narrative, which starts, 19:1, 'He entered Jericho and was passing through', leading into the story of Zacchaeus). In so far as both alterations are to be seen as rationalizations of the story line, they support the view that Matthew and Luke were later than Mark and smoothed out his narrative where they felt such treatment to be necessary.

On the other hand, Matthew's version at this point could be seen as so awkward (raising the question for us: We didn't know that Jesus was in Jericho in the first place, did we?) that we might suppose Mark to be making an admittedly rough attempt to rationalize it. The view that Mark may be the successor and not the precursor of Matthew can also be seen as supported by the inclusion in Mark of the blind man's name (or at least a name for the blind man) – on the basis of a theory that stories tend to develop names when told over a period. (An Englishman, an Irishman and a Scotsman become Brown, Murphy and Campbell.) But the theory is inconclusive (stories can also be shown to lose names in the telling) and perhaps irrelevant. It is not hard to imagine other reasons for Bartimaeus's becoming anonymous (assuming the name was indeed in Mark – there is slight manuscript evidence to the contrary): he was a figure known to Mark's Christian group, but not more widely.

The other important difference in the three versions is that in Matthew the story is about two blind men, a doubling up which Matthew engages in elsewhere: in the story of the demoniac (Matt. 8:28–34; cf. Mark 5:1–20); in that of Jesus's entry into Jerusalem on two beasts (21:7; cf. Mark 11:7); and indeed in a further story of the healing of the blind which those who see Matthew as freely creative in places, take to be simply a repeat of our present story (9:27–31). Can we explain this making of two from one? Possibly it was done on the basis of the Jewish concern to present testimony on the word of 'two or three witnesses' (Deut. 19:15) – a principle Matthew shows his support for (18:16).

4 *What would the story have conveyed when originally told?*

We can only guess, but at least our guessing can be intelligent! Let us suppose that Mark did not invent this story but that the text has a pre-history. (Strictly, this *is* a supposition because all we have is the book, which says nothing of its own background.) Let us suppose further that, just as the book was for reading aloud, so the stories which go to make it up were originally told – aloud, to Christian (and perhaps other) audiences. In other words, the present use in churches of this story was very like its earliest use: to be read in isolation, in the setting of worship – the gospel for the day. (The awkward beginning may point to rough 'stitching' into the narrative.) What would it then have meant to those who heard it, assuming its wording to be that which Mark in due course transcribed (a large assumption, admittedly), assuming too that in a much more oral culture than ours ears as well as tongues were better tuned?

We trace the story in this light, and find it to be a story about conversion and baptism:

v. 46: Jesus is not a lone operator, but is surrounded by companions – in whom the audience (in, say, AD 50) may see itself. But (moving to the individual perspective) they may also see themselves as formerly outside this precious community in which they have found truth and life, and among them and their friends are people who have still not made the transition (1 Cor. 6:11). They cannot 'see' and are destitute both spiritually and socially – for the Church offers not just a new truth but a new sphere of life. They are 'by the roadside' ('off the track').

v.47: But the key first move is awareness of need, and then the urgent expression of need; in terms that show recognition of the source from which it can be met (Jesus), his credentials (Son of David) and the divine, saving gift which is at his disposal (have mercy).

v. 48: There are obstacles and discouragements which hinder faith; persistence is required – and will be rewarded.

v. 49: The word rendered 'call' is not that which Paul had already made much use of to speak of God's summons to people through Christ (e.g. 1 Cor. 1:1f., 24; 7:20–4), but it finds significant use in this sense in the later Gospel of John, e.g. in 1:49; 10:3; 11:28. Here, Jesus's 'call' is readily available. And the community of faith offers its aid. They point to Jesus, the one source of the 'call' ('he is calling you'); and they urge movement in a word full of echoes in Christian speech: 'rise', the word of resurrection. Paul had already established the idea of baptism (conversion) as dying with Christ and entering upon the resurrection life (Rom. 6:3–11). The convert must come to that point of crisis.

v. 50: In Gal. 3:27, Paul used the image of donning fresh clothes for coming into the Christian life ('put on Christ'; and cf. 2 Cor. 5:1–5). Here too there is the motion into commitment.

v. 51: There is (as still in baptismal rites) the moment of formality: the question, asked and complied with. In his answer, the blind man uses (and the narrator repeats it in v. 52) a term which is likely to carry overtones for Mark's audience: 'let me be enlightened'; in any case, the metaphor of 'sight' for 'truth' pervades this story.

v. 52: 'made you well' conceals ambiguity (like 'receive my sight'). The word means both 'save' and 'heal' – and the unfortunate translator is compelled (as the original writer was not) to choose the level at which he will present the story: as an event to visualize or as a spiritual message to receive? (The RSV renders this very same sentence – 'your faith has ? you' – by 'made well' in Luke 18:43, but 'saved' in Luke 7:50, perhaps indicating a modern tendency to over-spiritualize sins and over-materialize diseases.) The saved/healed man becomes a 'follower' of Jesus, for that is what salvation means. And the trigger is 'faith', as Paul had already emphasized. (Acts 24:14 seems to indicate that 'the Way' was at one stage a name for the Christian Church.)

The modern literalist at first recoils from such a 'hearing' of this story, which presents it as an extended metaphor for conversion, but we have only to put ourselves into the religious – and verbal – shoes of those who heard it in the early decades of Christianity to realize that it can hardly have meant anything else (though the details are of course open to discussion).

5 What does the story mean within the Gospel as a whole?

The form and use of the story before it was put into the Gospel are strictly a matter of speculation. However likely such use in the setting of oral tradition may be, we have no direct evidence of it. What we do have is the Gospel of Mark, and that is where the story belongs and where we meet it. But what is the relation of a particular story to the Gospel as a whole? We cannot be sure – Mark nowhere lays out his intentions in composing his book – but we can consider possibilities.

It may be, for example, that Mark simply assembled stories and sayings from the tradition of Jesus's words and deeds, placing them in a convenient but not otherwise significant framework. In that case, subtle (or even unsubtle) links between one passage and another would be in the eye of the beholder, not in the mind of Mark. They would not represent Mark's meaning, but only ours. Whether we attended to them would depend on whether we felt free to draw out 'our' meaning, regardless of Mark's intentions. A knowledge of rhetorical procedures in the first century might encourage us to suppose that links and patterns of word and idea running through the Gospel are not improbable: not improbable, that is, as intended by Mark. They would be elements in his persuasive art. But we might decide that we were entitled to discern such links and patterns off our own bat – provided they are really there in the text.

This way of looking at the Gospel certainly moves away from seeing Mark as *editor* and towards seeing him as *author*, and away from seeing the book as a collection of items and towards seeing it as a single, whole work. If we go in the direction indicated at the end of the last paragraph, this way of looking at the Gospel also entails a choice between focusing on the book-plus-its-author (with a real-life setting in the first century) and focusing on the text-in-itself – words on the page – which might have been written anytime-anywhere for all that it matters. This choice seems to some to be harsh, unnecessary and unrealistic; to others it offers a kind of release, liberty to attend to the text as it is and for its own sake. Without necessarily making the choice, we turn to some of the links between our story and the rest of the Gospel. In any event they may prove illuminating. They will certainly shift our attention from the episode in isolation (the gospel for the day) to the book as a single whole; and we may wonder whether Mark can have meant his book to be read out at a sitting. If it were not, would not much of his meaning (supposing it to have been *his* meaning) have been missed? One cannot keep patterns of words in one's head from one week to the next, and there was no pocket edition to take home and ponder for oneself.

(a) Stories of the healing of a blind man bracket Mark's account of Jesus's journey with his disciples to Jerusalem, foreseen as leading to his death (8:31; 9:31; 10:32–4). There is the story in 8:22–6, and there is our story. Should we then regard that journey as the path to 'sight', the kind of seeing which Jesus bestows on Bartimaeus?

(b) Calling Jesus 'Son of David', thus reflecting his role as Messiah, looks on to 11:1–10, where the crowds effectively take up the blind man's recognition (even while blind, as the crowds, alas, show themselves to be). The idea of Jesus as the one greater than David was established by Mark early, at 2:23–8, and the doctrine is repeated at 12:35–7.

(c) We have already referred to the part played by the term 'way' or 'road' in vv. 46 and 52. But it pervades this Gospel. Jesus's whole mission concerns 'the way of the Lord', 1:2–3, and his journey to death in Jerusalem is 'in the way' (e.g. 10:32). The phrase, 'by the way', in v. 46 has already been used at 4.4 and 15 (RSV 'along the path', unhelpfully for our present purpose). The seed sown there was fruitless; it represents the fate of the message in those whom Satan attacks. That is what awaited Bartimaeus, had Jesus not called him and had he not risen up in response to the call. In terms of the parable of the sower, Bartimaeus, like almost all the 'small characters' in Mark, making a single brief appearance in the narrative, comes to represent 'those who hear the word and accept it and bear fruit' (4:20).

(d) But seeing and sight are the central ideas in our story, and they are central throughout this Gospel. 4:12 indicates how vital yet how difficult and precarious seeing is. Above all, it is something 'given' (4:10), as our story shows. Even for believers it remains precarious and fragile (8:14–21); yet sight is the ultimate promise to Jesus's disciples (16:7). And it is 'seeing' Jesus's death which elicits the crowning move to faith in the whole book, that of the centurion, the executioner who most directly brought about that death (15:38). So Mark's great point is most dramatically made: that the route to faith ('seeing') is the 'seeing' of Jesus's death. It was a point Paul had already hammered home (e.g. 1 Cor. 1:23; Gal. 6:14). and Mark makes it using a variety of images in relation to discipleship (e.g. 8:34; 10:38; 14:22–5), that of 'seeing' being the most pervasive. Mark presents a picture of faith which combines realism about its hardness with delight in its simplicity and directness. That which is its stumbling-block (centred on the crucifixion) is also the key to God's purposes.

This collection of questions to which Mark may be subjected is not exhaustive. It represents most of those currently asked, but there is no sign that new interlocutors will not produce new questions. Some indeed are already over the horizon. Liberationists, with their eye on Christianity as life before it is thought, rather than the reverse, will see in Bartimaeus and his story a perfect example of their priorities. His movement towards Jesus was the door to his salvation, and his following of Jesus was its fruit. Feminists can have no special view of this story, but they can see Mark's whole Gospel coloured by the story, told with unique emphasis, of the women who anointed Jesus on the eve of his passion (14:3–9). Both detached scholars and the various groups of the committed (the two may coincide in persons, but they are distinguishable roles) engage necessarily in conversation with the stories they interpret. They construct a picture in terms of which their enquiry is then formulated. In that sense, the text itself is both inert, awaiting the enquirer, and open, awaiting all kinds of enquirer.

Once, questions of date and place of writing and of the author's identity dominated the scene. They have faded for lack of evidence, though there are old legends and there are surmises. They do not take us far. Rome or Galilee, about AD 70, may be the best bet. In conclusion, it may be helpful to label the questions we have asked with their technical names:

1 Textual criticism, in the strict sense, though the term is often more widely (and wrongly? unhelpfully?) used.
2 Genre criticism.
3 Source criticism.
4 Form criticism (or at any rate some aspects of it).
5 Redaction criticism, where the activity of the author is in mind, but moving into literary or narrative criticism (and verging on structuralism) where the focus is exclusively on the text. Sociological questions may be asked as a development of redaction criticism and enter into some kinds of form-critical enquiry, for example when the social character of the setting in which the story was used is brought into view. In relation to our passage this approach seemed marginal.

Finally, there has been no attempt to answer (or even ask) the one question which many modern readers ask: did it happen? is it true? With regard to a story such as we have looked at, the scholarly enquirer has no privileged access, no evidence hidden from others. He or she can only bring out meaning from the story presented to us by Mark and suggest its background. A responsible decision on the question of historicity must depend on matters that go beyond the story itself (the object of our study) and indeed beyond the Gospels; such as the credibility of miracles in general and of acts such as this in particular; the status and nature of Jesus; the activity of God in the world. In diverse times and places various ideas and theories and assumptions on all these matters have commended themselves, sometimes by way of rigorous argument, more often by way of predilections that were simply 'in the air'. Any student of the Gospels will have ways of thinking about them. But perhaps different and even contrary ways allow the possibility of deriving great fruit from the study of the Gospels and their constituent elements, fruit that goes well beyond technical knowledge and into the nourishing of the spirit.

Chapter 4

The Bible and Synoptic Difficulties

Enoch Powell

I am going to examine with you an episode in the Gospel according to Matthew. We shall travel through some pretty rough country and end at a crossroads where the direction posts have been removed; but I hope our journey will be none the less fruitful on that account.

The episode occurs on the journey which immediately after it is to bring Jesus to Jerusalem and to his passion. It begins with the words: 'and when they were leaving Jericho'. As Faust exclaims when in Goethe's drama he opens St John's Gospel and reads the first sentence, 'I am in difficulties here straightaway'. Nobody has yet informed us that Jesus ever came to Jericho in the first place. So on reading the words 'and when they were leaving Jericho' a little twinge of dismay passes through us if we are candid with ourselves, as I hope we intend to be.

A report of the same episode is to be found in the Gospels of Mark and Luke. So we look them up for help. There is no trace in them of our difficulty. Mark writes (10:46): 'And they came to Jericho. And as he was leaving Jericho', etc., etc. In Luke (18:33) the episode occurs when Jesus 'drew nigh to Jericho' and is followed by another event, found only in Luke, which happened while he 'was passing through Jericho'.

We can read Mark and Luke without the slightest bother: our difficulty in Matthew does not assail us there. But its removal has left us face to face with a real problem, which we would dearly love to dodge. One of two things must have happened. Either Matthew left the arrival of Jesus at Jericho out, or – yes, go on, *or* – Mark put the words 'and they came to Jericho' in because he was finding the same difficulty as we do in Matthew. Now, I know – and you can know, unless you are frightened – which of those two things actually did happen. It was Mark who put the problem-solving sentence in. How do I know? Because the words 'and they came to Jericho' in Mark absolutely require that something happened at Jericho, whereas nothing does.

We are in deep water. Mark read the Matthew that we read, and when he found a problem, he edited it out. That is going to worry us when we read on, and Mark tells us the name of the blind man who features in the episode. But the water is deeper still; for Luke too has edited our problem out. Only he does happen to provide something which occurred inside Jericho, besides the incident just outside it, which he has switched from departure to arrival. We have been driven to an unwelcome but obviously important conclusion. Put brutally, the original was Matthew, warts and all, which Mark and Luke felt themselves at liberty to correct and improve.

In case anybody is worried about extrapolating so important a statement from a single piece of evidence, however cogent, this is probably the place for me to make an assertion which would require, and I hope will receive, a whole book to demonstrate it at length. The case we have examined is only one of hundreds where the wording of Mark and Luke, compared with that of Matthew, can be rationally explained only on one hypothesis – that they were using Matthew. This being so, we must evidently treat Matthew with massive respect, when we endeavour to understand the reasons for the difficulties we encounter in reading him. They perhaps have causes deeper than accident or incompetence. If so, they will lead us far into the history of the evolution of the gospel, even of the origins of the Church. But it is more than time for me to come to grips with the incident itself which happened 'when they were leaving Jericho'.

Two blind men seated by the road hear that Jesus is going by. They call out 'Lord, have mercy upon us, son of David', which, despite the attempt of the crowd to silence them, they continue to repeat. Jesus stops and calls them. 'What,' he asks, 'do you want me to do for you?' 'Lord,' they reply, 'we want our eyes to be opened.' Jesus takes pity on them and touches their eyes, whereupon they recover their sight and follow him. It is a coherent and straightforward narrative; but we remember having read it already somewhere else. Immediately after the raising of the dead girl (9:27), two blind men followed Jesus, shouting out, 'Have mercy upon us, son of David'. The narrative continues: 'And when he came into the house, the blind men came to him, and Jesus said to them: "Have you faith that I can do this thing?" They said "Yes," whereupon he touched their eyes, with the words "Let it be as you had faith," and their eyes were opened. Then Jesus impressed upon them, "see that nobody knows". They however went out and published it abroad in all that land.'

That episode is found in neither Mark nor Luke. You must decide whether they omitted it as a duplicate of the other; but that a duplicate it is, you will deny only if you are determined to do so in order to avoid being forced to conclude that Matthew is a book which contains duplicates. That would be a very peculiar book indeed, a book which must have a peculiar origin, a point to which I shall return.

Meanwhile, comparing the duplicates, of which for convenience I will call one A (the Jericho event) and the other B, we notice something highly remarkable. A, you remember, was all plain sailing, no problems at all. B on the other hand presents several severe problems. There is suddenly a house, inside which the dialogue and the healing take place. Before they come out of it again, Jesus tells the blind men to keep everything quiet, a request which they not only flagrantly ignore but which was inherently absurd: it could hardly escape notice if blind persons, especially after having drawn public attention to their plight, were walking about fully sighted!

So which of the two alternatives was the original, from which the other was derived? There is one naggingly irrational touch in the Jericho alternative. That is when Jesus asks blind men begging for compassion what they would like him to do. That rather absurd touch betrays an author who has studied alternative B, with its striking challenge, 'do you believe I can do this thing?' which takes for granted the nature of the mercy for which the blind men long. Moreover, the behaviour of the crowd, inexplicably telling the blind men to shut up, plagiarizes the problematic and disobeyed injunction of Jesus to secrecy in alternative B: the feature has been reused in alternative A but simply to enhance the drama of the scene. A curious verbal point is perhaps worth a moment's delay. The transition which introduces alternative B, 'as Jesus passed on from there (*paragonti ekeithen*)' uses a word (*paragein*) which normally means 'pass by'. Evidently this is the hint exploited by the author of alternative A to situate the blind men by the roadside when Jesus was to pass by.

In exploring the relationship between the two alternatives A and B, we have incidentally answered the fundamentalist objection that there could have been two events, similar but separate, each of which is faithfully recorded in Matthew. What we have found is a deliberate rewriting of a passage, which removes its difficulties – and, as we shall presently see, removes other things as well. There cannot be two actual events, one of which remedies the literary deficiencies of a description of the other. What we are reading is literature, not history; but that very fact confronts us with three demands.

We have to explain why a narrative was composed which visibly involved the difficulties, if not absurdities, of alternative B. We have to explain why it was rewritten without those difficulties as alternative A; and finally we have to explain why two alternatives, one designed to replace the other, were both put into the same book, Matthew, but for which Mark and Luke would have withheld from us the knowledge that they ever existed.

It will be convenient to tackle those three challenges, which I have set out in chronological order, by starting with the reason for alternative A. Quite striking in alternative A was that it omitted 'faith' which played such an operative part in the original alternative B. Why delete 'faith'? Answer: because the alternatives are point and counterpoint in a profound theological debate, present at the inception of the Church and traceable throughout its history: by what are we saved, or admitted to God's Kingdom, by faith – faith, that is, in the atoning efficacy of Jesus's sacrifice – or by works? By faith or by fulfilment of the Law? It was the former answer, 'by faith', which threw the Church open to the Gentiles; and around it raged, especially after the destruction of the Temple had made the Law literally unfulfillable, a dangerous division which separated gentilizers and judaizers (if the barbarous terminology can be pardoned).

Alternative A expurgated and disarmed in a judaizing sense whatever it was that alternative B had been saying, saying in a fashion so elaborately encoded as to be indifferent to dramatic credibility yet able to be read, by those who did not know what was going on, as straight narrative. Take the words 'into the house'. As narrative they raise intolerable difficulty. It cannot be the house where Jesus has just raised the girl, because then he would be going round in circles. It cannot be *his* house, because he does not have a house. A house was for some reason necessary; so it was put in, regardless of the trouble it caused.

The principal, code words involved are 'mercy', which signifies God's mercy, preferred by Him to 'sacrifice', in admitting sinners (including Gentiles) to salvation; 'healing', which signifies conversion, especially from paganism, in the form of enlightenment, the giving of sight; and 'faith', the crucial acceptance of Jesus's atonement. The narrative of alternative B asserted, for initiates armed with its vocabulary, upon the authority of Jesus himself, that the Gentiles cry to Israel for the message of the saving act which has rescued them. However privately communicated ('in the house') in the Gentile mission field, nothing can prevent it spreading throughout the world. No wonder if such an incident called in a judaizing version of the Gospel for expurgatory replacement.

That brings us to the last challenge: why then are both alternatives now in the same book? And to the logical answer: because that book represents a conflation or reconciliation – call it which you will – of the two theologies which had threatened to tear the Church apart. If Jesus was going up to Jerusalem, where better to insert the alternative narrative than somewhere on the road, and why not Jericho?

The remarkable salutation 'son of David' is fraught with signifi-cance. This incident in both alternatives A and B is the only place except one in Matthew where Jesus is so described. The exception is the incident of the Canaanite woman, whose appeal to feed the dogs (the Gentiles) with the sacramental bread that falls from Israel's table, is prefaced as here with the hauntingly familiar 'Lord, have mercy' (*Kyrie eleison*) and the description of Jesus as 'son of David'. Since Jesus himself is presently in Jerusalem (22:42) to deny the proposition that he, the Messiah, is 'the son of David', the placing of that appellation in the mouths of suppliant Gentiles could hardly have been accidental or meaningless. The Gentile church acknowl-edges the parentage, if not the primacy, of the Jewish church: the world kingdom of the Messiah is the glorified and infinitely expanded kingdom of Israel which was promised to the house of David. If Matthew was a work of reconciliatory conflation, the kiss of reconciliation was here in these words. Greatly daring, we may also wonder if the liturgical *Kyrie eleison*, the cry of the Gentile world for that mercy (*eleos*) which God put higher than sacrifice (*thysia*), is older than the Gospel – as old, may one venture, as the Mass itself.

We have come a long way from those words 'and when they were leaving Jericho'. If the end result is a reconstruction, we came to it by being led to concentrate upon the text of Matthew, by refusing to ignore the signals of some previous textual event, and by insisting on finding if not *the*, at least *an*, explanation of words which men wrote in order that other men might read them. I conclude with a suggested exercise for those whom it may interest. Both Mark and Luke reduce the two blind men to one blind man – a blind *beggar*, actually, because that would account for his being beside the road-side near the exit from a city. The picture which the 'Jericho' recen-sion (if I may so describe it) created made a deep impression. In John (chapter 9) the incident has become a major event, narrated with detail and dialogue which are no more to be found in the original source than are the colours and movement and personages of a great Renaissance artistic evocation of, say, the Annunciation or the Nativity. The critic stands in awestruck amazement before the creative potentialities of a textual event which he believes he has been led to uncover. He may be put in mind of Matthew 9:8: 'And the multitude when they saw were afraid and glorified God, who had given such authority to men.'

Chapter 5

The Bible and the Secondary School

Kathleen M. Court

'There is a book who runs may read' we used to sing in assembly in my schooldays. I wonder if anyone sings that hymn any more, or more pertinently, how many people in education regard the Bible as the invaluable asset and guide to daily living that our hymn-writer did?

We have plenty of evidence that study of the Scripture was an essential part of the curriculum in the nineteenth century, along with the 3 Rs. For example:

> Every morning at ten o'clock the Rector arrived to take the older children for Scripture . . . His lesson consisted of Bible reading, turn and turn about round the class, of reciting from memory the names of the Kings of Israel and repeating the Church Catechism . . . From his lips the children heard nothing of that God who is Truth and Beauty and Love; but they learned from him and repeated to him long passages from the Authorized Version, thus laying up treasure for themselves; so the lessons, in spite of much aridity, were valuable.[1]

Children were also drilled and examined in the minutiae of the doings of Bible characters. The situation today, however, has been felt to be so different in terms of the grounding children receive in the Bible that one contemporary literary critic, George Steiner, admittedly writing on the American educational scene, claimed:

> As any high-school or college teacher will testify, allusions to even the most celebrated Biblical texts now draw a blank. One is, indeed, tempted to define modernism in Western culture in terms of the recession of the Old and New Testaments from the common currency of recognition.[2]

We are of course far removed from the days of Milton when the AV/KJV Bible was the main book – stories, laws, histories, poetry and entertainment – of Everyman, and its cadences informed our national literature. The growing tide of secularism and decline in churchgoing mean that many children come to school without that basic knowledge of the Bible that most enjoyed in the past; not all primary schools even use Bible stories. Where do we begin at age eleven? It may well be that we cannot begin with the Bible at all, because there is no perceptual groundwork ready for it. It may well be that we have to prepare first, get children tuned in to a spiritual and religious wavelength, before the Bible begins to have any relevance at all.

'Experiential' RE expects the teacher to begin with Plato's conception of the teacher as 'someone who helps pupils to recognize what they already potentially know', also 'Religious educators are sometimes accused of attempting to indoctrinate their pupils. But when religious education is correctly understood, it becomes clear that it is the reverse of indoctrination. What it does is to demonstrate that there is more than one perspective on reality. It enlarges, rather than diminishes freedom.' So the teacher has two tasks:

1   'To help pupils to learn to be aware of and to take seriously their own inner experiences and their potential to be aware. Hence, learning to respect the inner experience of other people.'
2   'To help pupils to be aware of the power of language and intention to structure our experience, but not by entering into religious practice in a "confessional" sense.'[3]

Now whereas this approach sharply divides itself off from the confessional and world religions approaches, I suspect that one needs to be more eclectic in a state school, and use the best that this method can offer before turning to other ways of Religious Education.

There are of course many other demands on the RE teacher than just being the purveyor of scriptural texts for all seasons. I wonder what my early predecessors would have made of the boundaries of the subject today? The Educational Reform Act 1988 requires that education 'promotes the spiritual, moral, cultural and physical development of pupils at the school' and 'prepares such pupils for the opportunities and experiences of adult life'.

The new Agreed Syllabuses we shall have to work with 'must reflect the fact that religious traditions in Britain are mainly Christian, whilst taking account of the teaching and practices of other principal religions'.[4] The latter must be done in such a way as to 'ensure that it promotes respect, understanding and tolerance for those who adhere to different faiths'.[5] In practice, what does modern RE amount to?

1   An approach to other major world faiths.
    (a) We live in a multi-cultural Britain: few schools outside rural communities have no pupils at all from different faiths; some have large numbers – be they Sikhs, Muslims or . . . It is absolutely vital that education on the particular and distinctive practices and beliefs of other faiths should take place. Apart from harmony in the classroom, e.g. why Ranjit wears a turban, we

are hopefully fostering adult toleration and understanding in the next generation, which has been woefully lacking in the past. Ignorance leads to fear and hatred; knowledge and the jargon word 'empathy' can take them away.

(b) No child at all aware of world news can doubt the need to understand the role that religion and culture play in shaping world events, e.g. the rise of Islamic fundamentalism and the recent history of the Middle East. This needs time to explore and explain.

2   An appreciation of the needs of others.
     Basic Christianity demands that we study the situations of e.g.
        — the homeless in cardboard city
        — the starving in Ethiopia/Sudan
        — the orphans in Rumania
        — the plight of the Kurds
            . . . the list is endless.

We also need to assess our responsibility for these people and look at the response made by various role-models. From Mother Teresa to the Brandt Report, although there is a Bible-based dynamic in the Good Samaritan, and the need to love your neighbour cannot be stressed too much, this is not Bible teaching *per se*.

3   An approach to moral issues.
     Debate in a Christian context on everything from shoplifting in Woolworths to the rights and wrongs of embryo research, may take on board some well-worn Bible texts, but the arguments range more widely than these. In a debate on the Gulf War in my classroom the texts were left far behind, as we pursued Aquinas and subsequent contributions to the Just War Theory. The big issues of Life and Death (neatly encapsulated in a recent publisher's hand-out as 'Abortion to Work'!) via sexual relationships, Aids, etc., all belong here.
     If all the above is 'loving your neighbour' by the back door, what happened to the first of the two great Commandments, 'You shall love the Lord your God'?

4   More of a philosophical approach.
     After a decade or so of preoccupation with moral and social issues, I am happy to report that He is making a comeback with RE; but before accepting stories of His doings, a sceptical audience needs convincing of His existence. Philosophy of Religion, which seems to be doing well in the A-Level syllabuses, is spreading down the school. What Thomas Aquinas, Pascal and others would have made of the watered-down and simplified

versions of their classic arguments for the existence of God, produced with amusing cartoon illustrations, I cannot imagine![6]

So far our use of the Bible in RE has been marginal, so where does this leave it? Well it will not get anywhere if it is represented by a chalky pile of dog-eared, coverless RV Bibles lurking in the corner. Sadly, this may well be a fair description of many school Bibles, given the resources available for RE, a hard-pressed subject in the limbo of being neither a core nor a foundation subject in the National Curriculum, and bearing in mind under-funding of schools.

The problems with using the Bible in class are:

1 The language
   When I was at school in the 1950s and 1960s we used the RV and latterly the RSV. Nowadays even quite bright children reading St Luke for GCSE stumble on the just-post-war language of the RSV; why should one translate both from Hebrew/Greek and forty-year-old English? The NIV and better still the Good News Bible are far more accessible, and the 'message' is far more important than the beauties of archaic prose (and I speak advisedly as one who still worships frequently in the cadences of the Book of Common Prayer).

2 The packaging
   (a) Textbooks today across the subjects are bright and attractive; there is ample use of colour and illustration and a well-thought-through layout. They are light-years away from their dull predecessors. We cannot afford the Bibles we use to be any different, paradoxical though this may seem; the appearance can engage the interest or be a complete 'switch-off'. Bibles with relevant or thought-provoking coloured photographs inserted in the text, line drawings or simple cartoons, can break up the blocks of text and be visually appealing to the pupils. The binding also matters; although some compromise between the durability demanded by a restricted budget, and the cheaper price of the paperback editions is hard to find. That compromise found by some publishers in reducing the print size is not so helpful for classroom situations. It is worth adding that we have also found flexi-covered pocket-diary-sized New Testaments (with reasonable print) to be popular.
   (b) Long runs of solid print are totally unfamiliar to many children, and when you add in columns, and the problems afforded by chapter and verse divisions (the brother of our school's founder, Stephen Langton, Archbishop of Canterbury, has a lot to answer for) even after the child has located the right book, you have to surmount quite a number of obstacles before

engaging the child's interest in the text. Ideally then one is looking for a Bible broken down into sections under sub-headings, with a great deal of clear sign-posting. The Bible Society have answered this need with a New Testament in magazine format text,[7] and some textbooks nowadays print out the relevant excerpt as a shortcut round this problem. Younger pupils and those of lower ability profit from specially adapted and simplified stories, perhaps in cartoon format, or videos and computer programmes. The use of audiotapes has been around for some time, and allows for dramatic performance of stories, and discussion by 'experts' in the format of a Radio 4 news programme.

So we are equipped with a bright, attractive set of Bibles with up-to-date text, colour photos and clear sub-headings complete, for classroom use only of course (the tatty old Bibles can go home for homework as necessary, though, thanks to the Gideons, every child in my school at least has a New Testament and Psalms of their own). How do we use the Bible – when we are not employed teaching the 5 Ks of Sikhism and embryology? (I stress that the following is my individual view; I have no means of knowing how representative this is nationwide.)

Old Testament

This falls under four headings:

1 Founders
   We look at the lives and work of the Patriarchs and Moses; they also provide a valuable resource for discussing religious experience and our response to it. Other Founders include Nanak, the Buddha, etc.

2 Stories about creation and our care for it
   Genesis 1–3 and Noah's Flood, along with the poetry of Psalm 104, are part of our looking at the religious response both to how the world began, and the stewardship entrusted to mankind, which is at the heart of the conservationists versus the multi-nationals debate, animal rights, etc. These stories also appear in our 'great religious stories of the world' lessons, where Gilgamesh's quest for immortality brings him into contact with Utnapishtim, the survivor of a parallel flood to Noah's.

3 Moral teaching
   This would not be possible without consideration both of the Ten Commandments and the ethical teaching of the classical

prophets like Amos, with his strictures on those who abuse human rights.

4   Background to Judaism
The power of the Torah to regulate the lives of adherents is seen in the daily recital of the Shema, the wearing of the phylacteries with their sacred texts, and the dietary laws or Kashruth. The Passover most clearly, and other festivals, receive their rationale from scriptural reference.

New Testament

Here the concentration lies more heavily on the first two headings:

1   Jesus as Founder
With more emphasis on the infancy narratives and the events of Holy Week and Easter, we try to give some basic grasp of the life of Christ.

2   Jesus as Teacher
As with 'Moral teaching' above, it would be impossible to tackle moral issues without reference to Jesus as ethical guide (I hesitate to say law-giver), e.g.
(a) Jesus's parables, etc., on the right and wrong uses of wealth when considering Third World issues.
(b) Jesus's teaching on turning the other cheek, whether considering personal violence or something like the Just War theory.
(c) Jesus on divorce, etc.
Jesus was of course also an incomparable storyteller; how better to learn of the compassionate forgiveness of God than from the father in the Prodigal Son? With a bit of help many of Jesus's parables may be made to speak to the present day.

3   The early Church
How it all began, the link between the Galilean preacher and the parish church down the road, can only really be told from Acts with the back-up of selected passages from the epistles of Paul. I doubt, however, whether anyone was ever the better for spending hours drawing maps of the various journeys of St Paul!

This list seems pitifully small, but given the joint constraints of available time and the extent of the syllabus, it is all that we can do. It is probably more than is covered in some schools, and much less than is undertaken in others. On analysis it is plain that we see and use the Bible as a valued and valuable teaching resource, but that is all; it is a contributor to a larger picture, a means and not an end in itself. The days when the lesson could be called 'Scripture' in schools are long gone; Religious Education is a broader subject, covering a wider range of topics. It is no longer a knowledge-based subject pure and simple.

Some children, thankfully, are encouraged to read on and further, but family and peer group support are usually necessary to encourage this. In a recent survey of youngsters 60 per cent rejected the idea that the Bible was out of date, but 35 per cent found it boring to listen to.[8] These are not totally dispiriting figures and I hope that in the Bible they find more than a textbook, in fact a guide for life. I also hope that they will progress to find Bible study as rewarding as I have, both in a spiritual and in an academic sense; but for some it is an achievement to see them reading this book at all. The Bible is at the margins of their home culture. It would be unrealistic to expect that school alone could make a fundamental difference in this.

Thus it is that for many pupils incredulity is the reaction to stories of the courage of the twentieth-century Bible smugglers – 'Why should they risk their lives for the book on my desk?' 'Why should a Life prisoner be converted reading this book, and why should he change from a murderer to a minister inside a few years?' We hope we can provide some answers, but with the best we can do they may be left with a mystery, and may only 'see through a glass darkly'.

Chapter 6

The Bible and Television

Angela Tilby

The BBC's Television Centre in west London is a round low funnel of a building flanked to the north and west by twin spurs and to the south by a white tower. It is set a few hundred yards from a motorway in a square whose other edges are a poor housing estate, a football stadium and an industrial park. On summer mornings you can see the sun rise over the heart of London, on chilly afternoons you look out on the silhouetted skyline of factories, churches and mosques stretching away to the west.

I have worked at or near Television Centre for over ten years. At night with its lights on it resembles a space station set in a wilderness as bleak and barren as the moon. Sometimes I feel that the landscape is so scarred that it is impossible for any improvement or addition (and there have been many over my ten years) to make much of a mark on the place.

Within the complex a one-way service road bears lorries laden with props to be delivered to the mouths of studios at various points on the funnel's perimeter. Pedestrians are in constant danger, often having to duck in and out of slow heavy traffic, in an attempt to reach a path of safety. The traffic is endless. Sometimes the complex barely seems to sleep. Look down from a studio gallery at night or day and the chances are you will see activity. Lights being rigged, cameras moving into position, monitors blinking, the endless murmur of the director's talkback filtered through a hundred headphones. Here you may see a paint-and-plaster model of the world. Here, a telephone box lying on its side. There, a Roman statue. Here a jungle of green house-plants. There, a water carafe and glasses.

This round building, if it had a soul, might well imagine that it encircled the world. Images come in by satellite, messages by fax and phone. They are received and discussed and interrogated and processed and packaged and edited and transmitted as *stories*. News bulletin after news bulletin is fed on stories, selected from the mass of information that laps at the system like an endless chaotic sea. There is constant sifting and changing, a taking in and a giving out, which never ends. Some stories never come home. Some have their moment and disappear like fireworks. Others run for a few days and fade. And there are those which rumble on for months or years, breaking from time to time like froth on the sea's surface.

The stories that come to places like Television Centre are doomed for two destinations. They either become junk or archives. Either way the little narratives that flood in with each day's tide of gossip and information help to build up the bigger stories which endure; the narratives of power and displacement within which we are all, somehow, located. Few of the individual stories that television handles become a permanent part of our communal history. They are of their nature fragile and ephemeral. Yet all carry the possibility of becoming part of the big stories which are shaping our lives and the life of the world. Small incidents add up to make immense sagas of war and peace, of greed and generosity, of injustice and the struggle for change.

As I drive daily to Television Centre I realize that it has become for me more than a working environment. It is a symbol of human transience and fragility, of human ingenuity and passion, of human despair and endurance. There is no sign of transcendence, yet the ache of God's absence is nowhere more real to me. Even the technology speaks of a missing God: 'I have watched the wheels go round in case I might see the living creatures like the appearance of lamps, in case I might see the Living God projected from the machine.'[1]

The Christian Church has a part in the narratives that radiate from places like Television Centre. It is a minor part, but not an insignificant one. It is not, however, the part we would necessarily choose to be reflected by. It is mostly about personalities: popes and archbishops, sung and unsung heroes and heroines. As viewers and listeners we rather like our saints, and we like them either big and powerful or innocent and ignorant. The stories about the Church which get on television are also about scandal. Church gossip is juicy gossip, and we like to knock down the self-righteous from their seats and exalt at least some of the humble and meek. As viewers we are also crucifiers and there are times when we cheer on as reporters and interviewers make martyrs. Perhaps most significantly there are stories that come through television about the moments when the vocation of the Church makes sudden sense 'to those who are outside'. This is when it is simply doing its job at the time of tragedy and disaster; saying the words of grief and consolation that everyone else is too stunned to say.

There are a rich selection of Church stories which the world can receive and they are true, though they are not the whole truth. They may be truer, though, than the Church's stories about itself, which have a tendency to be grandiose or bland, though both the grandiosity and the blandness contain a secret bitterness.

Television as a Cradle of Meaning

Television is becoming a vital cradle of meaning for most of Western society. This is enormously interesting and important. It is important for our spirituality and important for our theology because: 'It is easy to miss Him at the turn of a civilization.'[2]

Television is changing the way in which we relate to each other, to ourselves and God. As a programme maker and a believer I am not prepared yet to evaluate this change. I see ambiguity on every side. Television can do dreadful things. It can also inform, illuminate and empower. Unlike many church people I am hopeful for television in the long run. I believe that it is at least possible that it has been given to us by God as a major instrument in the forging of a new global community. It will give us a new language of images in which some of our ancient and intractable differences can be overcome. This will not be easy. Television is very new and new gifts have to be handled with care. Its ability to flood us with universal images may help exacerbate local crises of identity in which religious fundamentalism is a first line of defence. Nevertheless television may yet help us both to discover and promote the first ever global culture, while at the same time preserving and honouring local memories and traditions. Though abuses occur all over the world the potential remains in television for seeing one another without labels, simply on the basis of our common humanity.

At the same time television offers us a sober reminder of the transience and flawedness of our common humanity. A sense of common humanity will not save us (the mistake of theological liberalism), though it may make us aware of what we need saving from. Television is a sign of the kind of God we are missing. Like the darkness of Advent, the saturation of images on our screen forms a mute cry for the clarity of uncreated light.

Yet the Church is not attempting to understand this and to recognize how deeply it alters the context in which the Gospel story can be told. On the contrary the Church is aggressive and fearful towards the mass media, and its deepest thoughts impress me as a litany of envious sulks. The problem is that the Church assumes that the only relationship it can have with the mass media is one of power and influence. 'We must get ideas into people's heads!', one delegate cried at a Christian Conference on the media I attended recently, as though the media existed in the divine dispensation only for the purpose of correct brain programming.

If the Church cannot have control, it has to be critical and judgemental. This is a pity. For the mass media are not *things* which the Church can direct or advise or make judgements about. Nor for that matter can anyone else. They are not things so much as a whole new context of communication which is changing the way we see and are. It is as radical as printing and has about as much capacity to educate and corrupt. Printing speeded the Reformation and brought to reality the possibility that every person could read the Word of God in their own language. Television is even more democratic. It locates us in a reality which is even more widely accessible, because it is visual and not verbal. We do not yet see what it is making of us, but it will be something different from what we are now. There is a great deal that the Church could learn from the mass media if it only took the trouble to listen and watch.

Television, Christianity and Narrative

One thing is clear, though. Television does not only communicate through images. It is in its very essence a narrative medium. It is at its best when it tells stories. Christians should understand this. After all Christianity comes in the form of a story. The story of Jesus Christ, the Word made flesh, who was born, crucified and rose from the dead, is the core story of our faith. It is also the story in which every Christian soul participates. Stories have always been an essential part of religious communication. They are the most primitive form of mass media. Why stories fascinate us is that they come to us as entertainment, as leisure. They engage rather than proclaim. They invite rather than dictate. They are the medium that Jesus used. What Jesus meant is very often far from clear. The meaning is in the encounter with the story but, in spite of the efforts of theologians, the power of the stories of Jesus cannot be reduced to a single, theologically sound meaning. In fact the strength of the stories of Jesus is that they travel with us, interpreting their author in different ways to us at different times.

Though Christianity is based on a story, Christian theology is ambiguous about stories. It prefers to deal in timeless truths. Stories are too ambiguous for the weighty, word-based proclamatory style of communication which the Church wants to sustain. Why the Church distrusts stories is that they are forms of communication which are not controlled by the didactic rational functions. They are beyond the grasp of clergy and are more powerful than their dicta are. This is because stories do not set out to teach or improve or to compel decisions. On the contrary stories are there because people tell them. Stories are about heroism, flights of fancy, laughter, tragedy and sex. Stories are not necessarily true. Their purpose is not to communicate detail so much as meaning. But they are not above criticism. The whole point of stories is that they are powerful without being dogmatic. They can be subverted by counter-stories as they often are, even within the Bible.

In the mass media many stories meet and illuminate, conflict and subvert one another. Our mass media are pluralistic and reflect the fact that our society has many sources of value. To some this is in itself a cause of alarm. A Muslim critic claims that 'the media distort and corrupt. They do so with an exuberant neutrality being no respecters of persons.'

That 'exuberant neutrality' is a well which can be construed either as a fecund darkness, or an empty void. From the Islamic perspective, and I suspect from some Christian points of view, such 'neutral' containers are dangerous. The very claim to neutrality is an offence, because in religions of proclamation and decision neutrality is taken to be at best an impossibility and at worst a disguised decision *against*. So Christians have been among those in recent years who have assaulted media notions of neutrality, impartiality and balance. Instead of struggling to preserve a serious level of public investment in broadcasting Christians have weighed in with heavy guns against television's fascination with sex, violence and materialism. The result is that television is in real danger of passing into the hands of fewer and fewer people whose sole passion is to make money out of it, while restricting the range and depth of the stories it can tell.

Faced with this, anxious and naïve Christians have indulged in grandiose schemes to set up their own little stations, and preserve their own little time slots against the dark and dangerous world. Too many Christians have assumed that the mass media need Christian proclaimers in order to contain the illumination of the transcendent. As though their *presence* guaranteed God. There are of course Christian TV stations. Mother Angelica has her Eternal Word network in which improving Christianity is the jewel in the crown of broad-based inoffensive 'family' entertainment. There are forms of religious broadcasting in Europe and America that are controlled by Church bodies.

But an irony comes in here. Where these ventures work and gain audiences it is because they do what everyone else does. They provide a space for shared stories. They concentrate on charismatic personalities; on romance, disaster and conflict. They dramatize the battle of right and wrong in ways that thrill and persuade.

Yet they are not invulnerable to the ambiguities that surround the whole medium. The story of the American televangelists is a wonderful, if pathetic, example of how the Christian enterprise is hoist with its own mythical petard of the corruption of public life. Looking for evil *out there* they become it *here*, and in public, to the sorrow, shame and fascination of their followers.

It is true of course that some would see any Christian involvement in television as a betrayal of that ascetic rejection of the world's values which informs the Christian story. Yet there is even another irony here. Glamour is not foreign to the Christian story even in its ascetic strand. The lonely ascetic, the prophet, the compassionate nun, the Merton figure assailing the powers of this world, form aspects of a shared, and not necessarily Christian, mythology out of which all our identities are built. To attack the stories that arise out of the neutrality of television, while being insensitive to the narrative character of almost all Christian discourse, is to demonstrate an extraordinary degree of psychological and theological naïveté. Anyone who condemns *Dallas* has not understood the Old Testament. I sometimes wonder if Church critics are attacking in television what they cannot endure about their own history.

One prong of the Christian critique of television concentrates on sex, violence and materialism. The other assaults television because it is a medium of consensus and is therefore thought to exalt the status quo at the expense of social criticism. Critics go on to claim that television acts as a drug, dulling dissent and quelling the need for social struggle and change.

This is simply untrue. There have been many occasions when television has shown a capacity to arouse discontent and to focus the will for change. Careful, well-documented investigative television journalism has an extraordinary power to reveal corruption and promote peaceful change. On a more dramatic level it is at least arguable that it was television which made the Vietnam War unwinnable, and will continue to undermine any lengthy military conflict in which the Western powers are engaged. The British government just about held the national consensus in the Falklands War because the campaign was short. It would have been impossible to maintain the momentum over months and years. Hostages and body-bags on television are intolerable over time and governments know it. If the Western alliance is ever destroyed it will be by enemies who use television merely as a tool of ideology, who have an undemocratic control and censorship of television, and can therefore prevent the damage being seen. In spite of the carpings of the Church the 'exuberant neutrality' of the Western mass media turns out to have hidden moral teeth located in unexpected places.

Seeing God's World

Where is God in all this? Television does not reflect God, but it does see and hear God's world. The world television sees is fragile, sometimes empty, sometimes aching, always incomplete and in need. It is what the Christian story has always told us, a vale of tears crying for redemption. God is not in the box. He does not have privilege, he does not 'project from the machine', however much the lamps attempt to scrutinize him.

Wandering around Television Centre at night I sense not the presence of God, but God's absence and distance. Yet it is not an empty absence or a cold distance. It drives me to prayer. It is the distance of a waiting and purifying darkness. God will not be our idol, and refuses our invitation to become enshrined as our tribal god. He does however choose to be incarnate, to become part of the human story.

At the beginning of the second week of the Spiritual Exercises, St Ignatius Loyola presents a contemplation on the incarnation.[3] He imagines how 'the Three Divine Persons look down upon the whole expanse or circuit of all the earth, filled with human beings. Since they see that all are going down to hell, they decree in their eternity that the second person should become man to save the human race.'

The exercitant is invited to look both down and up. Down on the variety and diversity of this world: 'Some are white, some black; some at peace and some at war; some weeping, some laughing; some well, some sick; some coming into the world and some dying, etc.' Then he or she is to look up to where the Divine Persons are seated on the throne of majesty: 'They look down upon the whole surface of the earth, and behold all nations in great blindness, going down to death and descending into hell.'

What fascinates me about this passage is that it begins with visionary imagination. The exercitant is encouraged to see as widely as the world and as deep as the heavens. He or she is to see the world in its transience and despair, in its fragility and endurance, condemned and yet continuing under the divine gaze. God is not present in the world. God looks on the world from outside.

The exercitant is then invited to look at the Divine Persons looking on the world. In the divine vision all are condemned. The condemnation does not arise from God. God looks on it from outside as though it has arisen entirely from within the human context. There is no divine judgment, no separation between the righteous and the sinners. Hell is the destiny that all share.

Next the exercitant is encouraged to listen. First to the variety of human speech, to the messages that pass from person to person. These may be legitimate messages of information, hope, encouragement or warning. But he or she is also to listen to swearing and blasphemy; expressions of frustration and anxiety. Then they listen to the Divine Persons who say, 'Let us work the redemption of the human race'. Just as all stand condemned, all humanity is included in the divine purpose to save.

The Christian Story

At the heart of the faith of the Church is the doctrine of the incarnation. Jesus Christ the Word made flesh, the true image of the Father, is born and dies and rises again among us. Because he is incarnate he is part of the human story. The incarnation is the way in which God engages with us. He is not simply a presence, he does not simply identify with our condition. He engages with us in order to suffer and die on the cross for our redemption. He does not enter human space and time in order to possess it, to secure his slot in the human story and go away again, leaving a shrine with his image in it. He is not content to dominate or reject the human story. Instead he serves it, being himself rejected. He remains ambiguous in his very being. God and man; glory and fragility; spirit and flesh. Much as we hate dualism in the trendy holistic perspective that has become popular in the last decade or so, Jesus Christ is always an issue of two-ness as well as one-ness.[4]

He does not turn man into God or God into man. Our salvation depends on the integrity of the two natures as much as on their indivisible unity: 'For the right faith is, that we believe and confess: that our Lord Jesus Christ, the Son of God, is God and man . . . Perfect God, and perfect Man: or a reasonable soul and human flesh subsisting One . . . not by conversion of the Godhead into flesh: but by the taking of manhood into God; One altogether; not by confusion of substance: but by unity of person.'[5]

The difficult process by which this 'unity of person' was achieved is outlined in the New Testament. Christ holds together the tense opposites of Godness and humanity, and resolves them for a little while within the human story, until we cannot stand it any more and arrange for him to be destroyed. Nevertheless, according to our Christian story the strategies of destruction do not ultimately work. The obvious and tragic story of the death of Jesus is met by an unexpected counter-story. This is the resurrection. Christ is alive and lives for ever more. Christ has harrowed hell and led captivity captive. None of this can be proved. It is discovered not in the glare of public lights, but in common human places where the memory of Jesus is treasured: in a cemetery, on a road, by a lake, and in an upper room.

The resurrection story must always be vulnerable to human doubt. It is not perceived by the camera and the tape recorder. The resurrected Christ cannot be held or enshrined. He ascends 'to my God and to your God'.

Yet the Word and imagery that the resurrection leaves us with constitutes a dramatic script that we will be working with for ever. We know it in our created nature as much as we do in the Gospel.

Death ends us, yet it is not the end. God's life is inexhaustible and has its meaning in compassion. Even the armoured tomb in an ancient church can be a testimony that comes close to proving:

> Our almost-instinct almost true
> What will survive of us is love.[6]

Ultimately the resurrection is the ground of human faith and hope. It is the basis for any positive estimate of culture and history as well as for the judgment that falls on all human efforts to be human. It is the first fruits of the Spirit and it suggests to us, rather delicately, that gifts of God are given for our good and not for our confusion and destruction.

Among these gifts is the technology that has produced television, and we could at least learn to give thanks for it before we take it apart with our crude and mechanical theological scalpels, remembering that, for all our suspicions, Babel was reversed at Pentecost. The word made flesh will not be 'made word again'[7] however many bleak and despairing Calvinists of the spirit require that this should be done.

Chapter 7

The Bible and Broadcasting

Kenneth Wolfe

> In order to make any advance in religious matters, it behoves those theologians who are above professional prejudices to brave the singularity of extending their hand to the thoughtful among the laity.[1]

> This is a big and difficult subject; but it is too important to leave it to the specialists. The ordinary person wants to know what Jesus was really like and how to read the Gospels.[2]

> Public Service Broadcasting recognizes the universal desire to be entertained, but it also has regard to other equally universal desires: to be honestly informed and enabled to think for oneself.[3]

Well over a century separates the first of these observations from the other two: David Friedrich Strauss in 1864 tried hard to help a wider public grasp some of the new complex questions about Jesus and the New Testament emerging from the slowly burgeoning scientific study of the Gospels; in 1977, Don Cupitt and Peter Armstrong were doing roughly the same – this time on television; in 1990, the then Archbishop of Canterbury, Robert Runcie, brought both concepts together in the language of deregulation on the agenda of modern broadcasting. All three utterances brought out the worst in some people and the best in others. All three utterances in their turn wrung a measure of wrath from those in the ecclesiastical establishment (in Strauss's view, not above 'professional prejudices'); again, in 1977, from that substantial clutch of 'specialists' to whom, in Armstrong's view, such 'important' matters should certainly not be left; and again last year, by which time public service broadcasting was a highly-charged subject, which evoked widespread comment from those who saw its days being numbered.

These three utterances raise crucial issues about knowledge, academia and the clerical management of the ever-developing results of scholarly endeavour in the study of the Bible. Specifically, its perception in the public, rather than the ecclesial, domain. Today, that means the mass media and, particularly, television.

Strauss wrote for a literate laity and one which, while not tutored in these specialist areas, nevertheless was at home with books in general and theological learning in particular. This modest lay stratum might have comprised perhaps a thousand or two – there are no figures of his publisher's print runs – but probably not many more, in spite of the furore caused by his notorious 1835 book, *The Life of Jesus*, and a second version 'for the German People' more than a generation later. By contrast, Cupitt and Armstrong in 1977 in a two-hour marathon on BBC2 asked 'Who was Jesus?' at the very moment when Sir Lew Grade's ITV epic *Jesus of Nazareth* was giving a long and very firm answer: 'Who was Jesus?' – clearly 'What the Bible said he was!' Undaunted, Cupitt and Armstrong asked their question as had David Strauss before them; they knew that too many were no longer happy with the old answers; by no means. They addressed more or less the same issues not so much this time to a *readership* but to a literate *audience*, comprising many tens of thousands, some of whom would be quite at home with books as most were with the television. Most of the viewing audience, however, would not be especially committed readers but doubtless familiar with the popular verses and oft-told stories of the English Bible.

In Strauss's time, it had been in the vernacular for almost three centuries and thus perfectly accessible to the literate – however few – along with those who merely had ears to hear. In 1977, there were vernacular versions of all kinds and for all tastes. Whether they could read or not, those before their altars, and later, those before their screens, were happy to have the familiar words of Holy Writ read, expounded, narrated, illustrated and affirmed; but not dismantled. Strauss and Cupitt, however, thought it was time to do so!

The efforts of the Gideons to have a Bible by every hotel bedside might be a joke to some but, as many well know, it has for a long time been a charming effort to put the English prose of the King James translation at the disposal of the uncommitted, the untutored and the unchurched and to bring comfort, consolation and perhaps the seeds of enlightenment. That it has been superseded by what are regarded as more 'relevant' and 'intelligible' translations once provoked the late A. J. P. Taylor to lament that, together, they 'struck perhaps a mortal blow against the English language'.[4] Perhaps.

Few would deny that the widespread appreciation of the Bible is part and parcel of folklore; it sells in huge numbers and in every major language of the world. Efforts continue in obscure academic corners to translate it into even more obscure tongues familiar perhaps less to missionaries than to anthropologists. Generous evangelists, when they are not giving it away free, are naturally free with their quotations! Repetition, recital and re-enactment of biblical text in poetry, theatre, liturgical music and hymnody are deeply embedded in Western culture. On railway stations, there are extracts ten feet high, voiceless wayside pulpits which expose the sacred sayings and worthy sentiments to the passer-by in hope that the textual pollen of Holy Writ will attract some response, however flimsy, temporary or shallow. Do not pithy biblical sayings, tender stories and sculptured images adorn everyday language and inform a popular understanding of human nature, of right and wrong, neighbourly ethics; and for many, the sacredness of all life, everything material and even time itself? Mess with it at your peril.

Which is exactly what Strauss and Cupitt dared to do in their respective times for their contemporaries. Theirs was clearly seen as most certainly NOT a 'Use of the Bible Today' which would help a troubled world, comfort perplexed souls and guide the seeking convert. The Bible – the legacy of Western culture – was, moreover, a crucial component in the Churches' pastoral equipment which, along with many others, revolved around their central liturgical pivots in their sacred space, their places of excitement, inspiration and haven. In those spaces, the Bible was more than the sum of its parts; more than literature or the history of religion – it was an icon. In the sacred place it became an image of the truth, an artefact of utter certainty and a casement in the cavities of holiness through which all manner of folk, however humble or elevated, tutored or superstitious, pharisee or publican, might be led by their holy men towards the hope of enlightenment, consolation and assurance.

In the liturgical conservatory, the biblical witness was infused with a vapour of sacred unworldliness and insulated by an aesthetic superstructure both positive and celebratory. Both gave it a sublime and untouchable reality and kept it at arm's length from those massing at the doors clamouring for answers to their increasingly well-informed questions. For the moment, forget the aesthetics, they said; just for a while, forget the celebrations, they urged; forget the sacrality: don't get us wrong, they said, but what actually is the truth of it? The very question itself, let alone any of the answers, was considered vulgar and properly belonged elsewhere in the worlds of doubt and dispute; it was cast beyond the pale in those realms of secularity where science and objectivity, in the nature of things, did their best and worst. The vast majority, it was said, had no notion of such things and were best protected from questioning endeavour; it could only harm the faithful, erode their certainty and deplete both attendances and sales.

So thought the custodians, the ministers, the servants, the mediators, the priests and the dispensers: these are our questions, they said, not theirs. It was the sad gulf between town and gown, between those who knew and those who did not; those at ease with the mysteries and those alarmed by them. More exactly, those who had been through a theological and critical education in the course of their priestly or ministerial training and were well versed in the technicalities; unlike – to put it quaintly – 'the souls committed to their charge' who had no such luxuries. The mediators kept the technicalities to themselves; the untutored put belief into action; that was their job.

However, for Strauss in the nineteenth century and Cupitt and Armstrong in the twentieth, these were fast becoming everybody's questions: Christian non-specialists in these matters were increasingly well informed and a good deal less certain than ever before that the questions about the life of Jesus being asked by their intelligent contemporaries were being adequately answered by those appointed to do so. Disenchantment with the institutions of mainstream Christianity was increasingly quickened by a mismanagement of ideology: those outside the pale were both asking and – for want of a sympathetic hearing – dismissing them; or they simply decided that no confident answers would be forthcoming. They had a way of shaking off the dust and voting with their feet, especially in the second half of this century. Strauss, in his time, lost his job because he heard these questions being asked and did his best to make an intelligent response with scientific integrity. So likewise did many others whose pains for their troubles gave shape to a new definition of the old heretic: modernist and liberal. From Strauss onwards, there have been many: Loisy in France, Briggs in America, Tyrrell in Britain, to name but three. The most notorious was John Robinson. There were and are many, many more who listened to the questions from across the divide and stood shoulder to shoulder with those who were asking them.

Modern divinity studies began with Strauss's notorious *Life of Jesus* in 1835.[5] Nineteenth-century Europe and Victorian Britain were in the throes of volcanic social change and monumental revolution in just about every area of thought-making, policy-making, money-making and indeed, the business of making anything out of anything else. Science was turning its hand to technology and finding means of mobilizing all sorts of things, people and ideas with quite revolutionary consequences: people were beginning to know. Widening the franchise was not only about politics but education, human rights and access by the rank and file to formerly privileged reserves, financial, environmental and literary. By the end of the last century, an increasingly sizeable rank and file was thinking, demonstrating, demanding, asking, reading the newspapers (if they could afford them) and forming opinions about matters of which only a generation before they would have had no notion. A few establishment voices were calling for more involvement; after all they might be going to war! Which is exactly what they did – again and again.

*

When the century was over, the men went to yet another war; and then they came back. In 1922, to their astonishment and everyone else's, with the guns long since silenced and the fighting well and truly over – bar the hurt, the disillusion and the destruction of body and property – there was something utterly new and quite miraculous in their lives, if they could afford it. Its like had never been seen before; it was as startling an innovation as flying – and almost as unnatural. The ingenious telegraphic trickery which all had known in wartime was suddenly domesticated and achieved this time, without wires: broadcasting in Britain began, and overnight, not only geographical boundaries were scaled; if you had ears to hear, you could do simply that: hear! It was thoroughly astonishing.

Whatever enfranchising of the rank and file education had achieved by then, it was nothing to what broadcasting could and would do. Few could believe it; few took it seriously; few thought it anything but another 'stunt'; few had the imagination for it; few could envisage the implications for culture and society and few remembered the two ladies on the Clapham omnibus: 'What'll I get my 'usband for Xmas?' she asked. 'Why don't you buy 'im a nice book?' . . . 'No – he's got a book.' Above all, broadcasting could do without them and it was thus no surprise that the common people heard it gladly.

John Reith, the son of a Scottish Presbyterian divine, was in charge of the new BBC and was to start the ball rolling for religion in the broadcast output, naturally on Sunday evenings. First there were talks in the concert intervals and then some asked, why not readings from the Bible? It did not belong, answered others, and besides, the wireless was hardly a sacred medium for Holy Writ, surely?! Reith appointed a committee to tell him about what he informed William Temple was the most delicate BBC policy area, religion.[6]

Soon enough, however, this precious conscientious objection evaporated and increasing numbers heard the Book on the air; many never before. Then, why not actual services from churches? The demands progressed with what some thought rather rash boldness and in a few years, the Mary Whitehouse of the 1920s clamoured for – and got – a daily quarter-hour service neatly designed for every weekday morning: a hymn or two, a collect and, of course, a portion of the lectionary; the Bible would be heard, the stories would be told, traditions would be confirmed.

Yet another push by the public and the BBC began the Epilogues which persisted through all manner of changes into the television age and only finally gave out when all-night programmes were introduced in 1988. One way and another there had mostly been something at the end of the broadcasting day.[7]

More important was the BBC's venture into what is called adult education and its Talks initiative. Religion was a singularly interesting subject and would surely make excellent broadcasting, in the light of the advances in academic and intellectual circles concerned with the persistent dialogues between scientific and religious world-views. After all, now that there were so many church services, it was time for exploration and investigation into the grounds of belief and the character of Holy Writ. This was all the more exciting to the broadcasters because the talks were from their own studios whereas sermons were from other chaps' churches; it was a matter of authority. It was, of course, also a matter of content. From the outset, there were always those with vision and imagination in the Churches' leadership who thought that through broadcasting, the rank and file could at last be enfranchised in the rudiments of religion in general and the relevances in the modern world of Christianity in particular, normally the preserve of the Churches' middle management, the clergy.

It was soon clear, not only to the BBC but to the eminent clerical minds that advised it, that the general quality of sermons submitted for broadcasting was poor. Above all, it was this fact that pushed Reith into getting a cleric on to the payroll specifically to look after the religious output. Thus began a tradition which would pervade the BBC until the late 1960s: religious programmes were to be conceived, organized, produced and even defended by propagandists for the Christian faith, i.e. the clergy. Imaginative, talented, energetic, and highly sophisticated as most of them were, they were clerics nevertheless. (When ITV began in the mid-1950s, the Independent Television Authority advised the companies that they would do better to have clerics as advisers, not as producers. The debate continues.) The more religious affirmation on the air, the more clamour from the ground: an increasingly non-believing majority wanted to ask a few questions. Not on the air they said; that was 'controversial broadcasting' and the Postmaster General had forbidden it!

Thus, the whole weight of endeavour in broadcasting policy was directed towards making religious assertion more intelligible, church services more accessible and the Christian faith more relevant. There were series of religious talks which sparkled like jewels but were set in what was, to some, an ungainly and inappropriate liturgical space; simply because this was an 'educational' rather more than a hortatory exercise. The bulk of broadcast religion then and now has rightly been committed to presenting the nature of religion in the West and its relevance to modern society and its changing shades of thought. It was perfectly clear to the leadership of the religious and the broadcasting institutions between them, that the mainstream Churches were losing ground. It was a matter of finding the right exponents of belief to make that belief readily understood by the listening – and later, the viewing public.

By the end of the Second World War, the broadcasters had developed two new radio wavelengths defined by class and education, the Light Programme and the Third, later Radio 2 and Radio 3. The Light Programme had come about because of war – it was clear that something special had to be done for the troops who heeded – for want of a better word – 'popular' programmes. The broadcasting executive debated, discussed and wrangled over the term. The audience got light music, light talk and light religion – and liked it. Homilies, storytelling, the tenets of basic Christianity applied to everyday life and, of course, hymns; all done very well indeed. Mostly.

The wealth of religious material on all three programmes was extensive and the quality high. Except when it was egg-head, complex and academic; which is what it had to be if it really intended to introduce the audience to some of the off-stage issues waiting in the wings of theological invention and biblical scholarship for exposure, long overdue. That all belonged to the Third where the literate were most at home. Unfortunately, three-quarters of the population never listened to it![8] Whatever else they might be, religious programmes should not be highbrow. That was the trouble with most religious programmes, said successive directors of religious programmes: something radical had to be done to make them not only more popular but better programmes.

The Bible was naturally the handmaid of the broadcast preacher and the tool of the believer. How it related to modern life was the burden of both, then as now. As broadcasting became more confident, it reached out to wider audiences and found ways to define who they were. One clear captive audience was in the classrooms of our schools. If every other area in the curriculum had a place in Schools Broadcasting, why not religion? Here was an unparalleled opportunity to bring the off-stage issues on to centre-stage. There were great teachers to be trawled from the departments of theology in universities and colleges up and down the country. There were preachers enough and in abundance; what was needed were those who could turn their hand to making biblical scholarship rather than biblical doctrine intelligible to the generality of audiences. This was science not propaganda.

Moreover, there was one grave restriction which gagged the voices of any in the field of religion whose utterance was controversial. Not until 1947 was the ban on so-called 'controversial religious broadcasting' lifted, and the religious advisory bodies confident enough that broadcast religion could stand up to attack by the increasingly mellow voices of the humanists, rationalists and the many other highly vocal groups which demanded that Christian assertion and recital, however sublime or creditable on the air, should also, on the air, be the subject of discussion, debate and, dare one say it, even attack. Back in 1927 when Parliament debated the Revised Prayer Book, the BBC could not discuss it because of the Postmaster General's ban on ALL controversial programmes. This was soon lifted but NOT in religion. The advisers preferred the old protection.

The war had changed everything and especially the BBC's confidence to take initiatives in delicate areas, including religion. It had called many more of the tunes and as the days of peace had come to a close, the Religion Department was thinking of new ways to attract a large audience for its programme output. The Bible was the key: there was already a well-established tradition of broadcast talks and sermons which sought to make the Bible speak relevantly to the changing and indeed very alarming times. There had not been much, however, about the nature of its literary origins; so much was simply taken for granted – the emphasis was upon the 'simply'.

The most notable departure into this vexed scholarly area was undertaken by a famous scholar regarding whom, for many, 'It seemed remarkably odd, that a Cambridge theologian named Dodd, should spell, if you please, his name with three ds, when one seems enough for God.' Charles Harold Dodd gave four seminal talks in 1949: 'About the Gospels' and noticed that the 'apparently artless storytelling has something in it of art that conceals art'.[9]

Dodd, with others like him from the technical world of New Testament Studies, had cut their broadcasting teeth in Schools' programmes and were then asked to address a wider public. The difficulty for many in the Churches' middle management was neatly put by a complaining cleric: 'The foundation I lay down from my pulpit on Sundays is being undermined by the BBC in schools on Mondays.'

Indeed, Schools' programmes had a not insignificant audience and were introducing new ideas to sixth formers which the generality of the public were, of course, not getting in the normal run; religious education for the general public school had yet to encounter the vexed world of biblical criticism. The LCC's new post-war syllabus recognized that there was 'no getting away from the fact that this revolution in the understanding of the Bible carries with it some serious consequences'.[10] Well might it say that this approach had 'undermined once and for all the old easy method of using the Bible as a ready-made reference book'.

It was, as Frederick Iremonger, the BBC's Director of Religion[11] knew so well, a complex affair: the public was not ready for exposure to the complexities of critical biblical scholarship for fear it would undermine their faith, however heavily committed, half-churched or even unchurched they might have been. The clergy had better keep this bundle of trouble to themselves.

Moreover, there was one other huge impediment in the broadcast output: confessionalism. Every denomination produced a clutch of good broadcasters; every denomination had its right to a place in the Sunday output, the Church of England, naturally, having the lion's share. The Christian broadcast utterance, including the Salvation Army and other non-mainstream bodies, in all its confessional diversity, inevitably clawed at the idea of a cohesive unity to which the department was enthusiastically committed. One argument ran: Christianity is diverse and broadcasting should reflect the richness of the broadcast weave with all those aesthetic, liturgical, dogmatic and regional features which comprised the various religious identities in the culture. But, said the other argument, the underlying unity of the Christian message and witness was also crucially important, especially as the Religion Department, then and since, was in the forefront of emerging ecumenical aspirations.

In spite of all that, was there surely not a common thread, a seamless robe, a unifying notion, an agreed agenda to which all would enthusiastically subscribe? They said there was: Jesus the Galilean. Iremonger and many others knew that to get the central biblical message over to the common man, the figure of Jesus was the obvious and simple answer. Bring the historical Jesus to life and the message of Christianity would come alive with it: simplified, undogmatic and convincing. The religious advisory committees around the country in considerable measure saw broadcasting as the 'handmaid of the churches' – it was obvious that the central hero of the Christian story was uniquely amenable to broadcasting. Little did they know!

Enter Dorothy L. Sayers, a writer of detective stories and an unorthodox 'believer' in catholic Christianity. She had strong opinions about the way the Church was failing to reach out to the people in general with the 'real' message of the Galilean. She was outspoken and highly recognizable. No wonder that if the task of broadcasting was to present the Galilean in his time, D. L. S. was worth the asking. Thanks to the initiative of Iremonger and the tact of his successor James Welch, an unsurpassed work of radio drama cascaded from the alpine imagination of this extraordinarily gifted lady and gave the listening public *The Man Born to be King* – being the life of Jesus of Nazareth dramatized in twelve easy stages for *Children's Hour*.

It was a huge success and the BBC had never more letters before or since – almost all in praise. Dorothy L. Sayers had done for the untutored public what German and British biblical scholars were struggling hard not to do for the theological literati – conflate the Gospels of the New Testament as if they were alternative reports from Reuters designed to produce a coherent historical whole from the various literary parts.

Three years before, she had enthused over the greatest drama ever staged, namely the dogma rather than the history of Christian origins.[12] But it was the dogma as publicly perceived that gave the Christian faith, the Bible, the Church and just about everything connected with it the 'bad press' about which, she thought, something dramatic had to be done. By the time she had produced her masterpiece for radio and a headache for biblical scholars, the Schools people had produced another, albeit modest, masterpiece for sixth formers: *The Making and Content of the Bible* was the brain child of a young New Testament scholar, Alan Richardson, devoted to the new science – or so it seemed to many – of biblical criticism. The series was a huge success: for the first time, real questions about the nature of these texts were at last being aired, albeit narrowly. Mainstream broadcasting, said the advisers, had a rather different job to do, among other things, to be popular. These plays achieved that with the flair of nothing less than genius. From now on and as far as getting the Christian message across, 'the old-fashioned ways were done for' – these plays provided the 'finest weapons for the contemporary Church' said James Welch.[13] Broadcasting was 'par excellence, a medium for the telling of stories' and at last someone had shown how it could be done; and moreover, they reached a huge audience – some 12 per cent of the adult population.

The Sayers cycle began a new broadcasting era, by shifting the emphasis of broadcast religion very broadly from dogma and the attempt to make it intelligible, to the Bible and the attempt to make it historical. It was a crucial and unobtrusive change by virtue of Sayers's skill in turning the theologically saturated New Testament episodic narrative into an historically cohesive and assertive narration of events. Inevitably, the storytelling was infused with propositions about cause and effect in the detail of the unfolding drama, all of which encouraged a positive attitude towards the nature of the 'events' which had so skilfully been redrawn. For Sayers and many others since, the dramatist, she hoped, would simply 'trust that the theology would emerge undistorted from the dramatic presentation' since the history and the theology of Christ are one thing . . . 'the drama of his life is dogma shown as dramatic action'.[14] She had not bargained for the epistemological stimulus her plays would provoke. The rank and file were hugely entertained by the drama but not so much by the theology, at least as she and most believers understood it. This consequence was, predictably, quite acceptable to the Churches; it chimed in neatly with the notion that broadcast religion was, in any case, a preparation for profounder things that would develop later.

The upshot was a radically new departure in the public perception of the New Testament picture of the Galilean – the widening fissure between its experience of the liturgically presented narrations of collected biblical text and a positivist dramatization of a specific historical phenomenon which severed factuality from its historical setting. In other words, the first-century historical context which generated the Gospels was totally lost from view and subordinated to the notion of the 'historicity' of the Gospel story itself. This had the effect of reducing incarnational theology to a species of consecutive reportage.

Such an endeavour was bound to raise questions about the how, why and when of the Gospel 'events' once stimulated by the eloquent dramatic proposition. There was a limit to how much the dramatization of, for example, miracle-stories in the New Testament could – as they were designed to do – convey theology if that narrative was rebuilt by the playwright so as to make events intelligible to those outside the circle of the faithful.

The Sayers cycle, for all its brilliance in the emerging art of radio drama, actually put the clock back to the century of liberal theology and had David Friedrich Strauss turning in his grave. The series went out in *Children's Hour* and a vast number of adults, untutored in these technical matters, were naturally totally captivated, especially in light of the huge publicity over Sayers's use of modern language and slang. Those opposing voices about her departure from canonical text upheld the notion that the Gospels were certainly not reportage; they were 'facts' for sure, but not facts like those reported, dramatized and distorted in other modern media, newspapers, novels or the theatre. The words themselves were actually sacred. The opposition believed that the sublime sacred text was history enough; it could be interpreted for sure but not rewritten in a manner designed to debase the story by the mundane language of the street. As much as theology, the discussion was about aesthetics and the place of language in the liturgical arts. The same arguments would come into play when eventually the New English Bible was published in 1961 and later on, as the movement to revise the Book of Common Prayer came to a head in 1979.[15]

Opposition to the Sayers cycle (mostly from high-Churchmen), predictably, was drowned by its popularity, supported in turn by the mainstream Churches which rejoiced in the fact that anything that could get the basic truths of the Gospels over to a wide audience could not do anything but good. Perhaps they were right. Broadcasting, as they were fond of saying, was first the 'handmaid of the

Churches' and perhaps only second a means of educating them! That was the task of the Schools' output where, incidentally, the Sayers cycle had long-term consequences. The Religion Department, rather than using in the general output the initiatives in exploration and the investigative scholarship undertaken by the likes of Alan Richardson, C. H. Dodd & Co. in the Schools arena, deployed the Sayers cycle in the Schools environment on the assumption that the storytelling and dramatic excellence would do wonders for religious programming for the classroom. It did. In a real way, it was a retrograde step; perfectly understandable in the circumstances of the Schools' Religion people being always in search of good material; but retrograde notwithstanding. The exploitation of these plays was, of course, a huge tribute to the team – Valentine Gielgud and Robert Speaight – which turned Sayers's text into a powerful radio drama, slang, sound effects and all! Above all it said that what we have in the New Testament Gospels is historical fact; and if it is history, then let it be dramatized for all and a little fiction never hurt anyone.

The Sayers cycle had been a successful and most impressive liberation of the story of Jesus from the restraints of class and Church as never before. All this thrilled the evangelical sentiments of the Churches' middle management, indeed, beyond their wildest dreams. Rightly. It had got the story 'over' to vast numbers who would never darken a church door; often was it said in suitably biblical tones that 'the common people heard it gladly'. But more than that: it tripped questions about historical facts in which the New Testament Gospels have no interest.

Thus, much to the irritation of the clergy, the advisory committees and religion producers, the 'common people' quickly began to ask common questions – the sort they asked about all sorts of religious assertions and the sort they heard others asking on the radio about political issues, about scientific matters, health, economics, art, things future and things past. The rank and file was gradually being introduced to areas hitherto closed or obscured. By the radio, they were being entertained, comforted and challenged; above all enfranchised in almost every conceivable pursuit and pastime. But not, however, it would seem, in scholarly biblical matters. One opinion said that such things were much too obscure and belonged to Radio 3; others asked why it could be in the Schools' output but not for the majority. Why not indeed? They were all caught on the horns of the old liberal dilemma: if the 'problem' stories in the Gospels had been cut out, feeding the 5,000, the transfiguration, healings, etc., then the Gospel story was 'distorted' and the biography abused. If they stayed in, questions would inevitably be asked which took the discussion to the root issue: the provenance of the New Testament Gospels, their *Sitz im Leben* and the manner of their contrivance, ordering and tradition in the life of the early Church. Keep away from that sort of material; it would only serve to confuse the simple-minded and undermine simple faith. It was not merely a matter of religion. It was politics: the broadcasters of religion had to be seen to do the Churches' bidding as well as to take bold initiatives in the good BBC tradition.

The Sayers cycle thus raised all these issues: the freedom of the Religion Department to strike out in new directions and the need for popular programmes to serve the interests of the Christian estab-lishment and genuinely educate the general audience in matters of faith, belief and ethics. Not to mention debating with humanists, Mormons and all the other fringe groups with enough power to bend the BBC's ear over the monopoly of Christianity on the air. *The Man Born to be King* raised all the theological and exegetical issues in the book and did so in public; and the public called for answers. Dorothy L. Sayers's plays would be used again and again for the general audience and for the schools. The temptation to use them was too great! There were few who could resist.

Enter television in the late 1940s and early 1950s. In the wake of this radio landmark, television crept gradually and inexorably towards the centre of the broadcasting stage. By the mid-1950s, there were two channels. On both, it was soon realized that it could do wonders for the Bible in a way that radio could not: it could show the Holy Land and all the famous places. Not to mention Christianity in action.

As the Children's programmes executive had engineered the Sayers cycle so did it plot a similar scheme for television. Here was a golden opportunity to have some of the historical questions answered and not simply more dogma dressed as drama: the Head of Children's Television emphatically wanted above all a documen-tary, and one which this time would satisfy the likes of Donald Soper, who had complained that *The, Man Born to be King* simply did not convey such realities as the squalor of first-century Pales-tine.[16] Freda Lingstrom did not get her documentary; the project was buried beneath mounds of clerical bureaucracy, as it trundled through committee after delegation, and came to the screen as *Jesus of Nazareth*, this time with Tom Flemming in the part. Complaints naturally rolled in again about the non-authorized-version language but, like the Sayers cycle, the production was smothered by praise from all sections of the audience, including those who saw it as yet another evangelistic opportunity.

The *Children's Hour* executive thought that while it was all quite beyond the comprehension of the young in spite of the beauti-ful filming, intelligent casting and good sets, it was superlative television. Indeed it was. Never mind the educational limitations, it was quite outstanding; but it did raise a great many complex questions which could not be answered – with any sort of simplicity appropriate to the young. Instead of the hoped-for documentary, it was yet another compendium reading of all four Gospels, shaken-down and neatly conflated to provide through the basic Markan chronology an acceptable script for the drama. It was very well done; Joy Harington got a BAFTA award for it! Like the Sayers cycle, however, *Jesus of Nazareth* was not followed up in the broadcast spaces where the increasingly educated general audience – dramatically expanded by the 1953 Coronation – expected it.

Television was gently and deferentially refining the popular taste for drama, documentary and information, all well within rather strict cultural boundaries of good taste and decency, as the broadcasters were obliged to say! The Churches were predictably cautious at first about the use of this medium for liturgical purposes at least. They soon got over it, and on ITV there were plenty of services done well, especially for the housebound. The advisers made sure that television would not deflect the faithful from Evensong, so the screens went blank around half-past six every Sunday evening; it was the 'closed period' later called the 'God-Slot'! In 1956 the period would be filled by religious programmes, and competition between the BBC and ITV for the Sunday-evening audiences began.

During the first year of the 1960s, however, a fuse, lit the year before by Penguin Books, fizzled unstoppably along its path towards a keg of cultural dynamite; before anyone could run for cover, there was one monumental explosion which rocked the ground upon which every major cultural institution in Britain was built, not least the Churches. In 1959, Hugh Greene had taken over the BBC; the Pope had announced the Twenty-first Vatican Council. But on 16 August, Penguin published *Lady Chatterley's Lover*.

That was not all: Richard Burton's Jimmy Porter savaged the nation's silver screens with Osborne's excoriating anger. All sorts of cats were being let out of cultural bags which had been forever closed to the general public. Greene, for one, would not keep them in the dark for a minute longer: television, he decided, was – the sooner the better – to play its part in enfranchising a population which should as Robert Runcie said so forcibly in 1990 be 'thinking for itself' about all those crucial modern issues kept from it for so long by the best intentions of an establishment that thought it knew better and, indeed, what people wanted – in other words poor Lord Reith and his like – for whom Greene was beyond the pale and keen to follow the crowd 'in all the disgusting manifestations of the age'.[17]

In religion too, change was at the gate; a bishop stood ready to open it. Not satisfied, they said, with his outrageous remarks in defence of the infamous Lady Chatterley, it was now time for other cherished beliefs to be abused: 'Our image of God must go!' said the *Observer* one Sunday in 1963 and, the day after, the SCM Press published a little book which would be hailed, burned, ridiculed, venerated but never forgotten – and have the most serious consequences imaginable.

Honest to God was John Robinson's signpost for pilgrims in search of new ways of looking at their traditions. The Bishop of Woolwich rocked the religion of the Western world with a little book designed to reach out: 'The gap between the secular mentality and the Churches seemed greater than ever.'[18]

That was precisely the urge of the broadcasters of religion: Greene's enthusiasm had been felt by the religion producers both in the BBC and ITV. Indeed, ABC had been unearthing new questions in its *About Religion* and the BBC in *Meeting Point* for some while. Both agreed that the image of Jesus in Persil-white had to go. Robinson brought issues in modern theological exploration to a wider 'lay' public, admittedly the one interested in religious matters and not often in the pew; the disenchanted but perceptive, often the new humanist. The BBC had not been idle: in this new atmosphere, it had exposed some of his concerns to the wider public, and not without a furore. Alec Vidler had lamented in public the suppression of 'real deep thought and intellectual integrity in the Church' and had been bitterly attacked for his pains.[19]

Back in 1956, Robinson had talked to sixth formers along with T. W. Manson on questions of history and interpretation; but that was quite a different audience: the 'lay' believer would not be listening and almost certainly not prepared for any scholarly Robinson-styled challenge: 'Asking the historian is a risky business,' he said.[20] All the more risky when the bulk of the religious output – one way and another – was in the 'liturgical' spaces in the schedules, mostly on Sundays with supporting talks, meditations and hymn-sandwiches, admittedly for a wide general audience but still committed to intelligibility. Discussions in scholarly circles about history and hermeneutics were rightly thought by the broadcasting executive to be either above the common mind or insufficient audience-pullers. Religious programmes, it was often thought, were dull enough as it was. There were too many talking heads, even if some of them were exciting, vibrant and modern. Controversy was always interesting, even in religion. Robinson was even trendy and some thought he was better on *That was the Week that was* than in the closed period during which the faithful, anyway, were at their devotions.

Nevertheless, the broadcasters believed an attempt had to be made to enfranchise lay opinion in matters of history and truth as well as provide entertaining or comforting or even challenging programmes in the religious field. One BBC producer, Colin James, thought it was time that Bultmann's contribution to the discussion about the historical Jesus be brought to a wider audience than the clergy. The biblical scholar Dennis Nineham led the Bultmann-form-criticism campaign and in 1962 James took the initiative to get Nineham on the air; he was more or less preaching to the converted; he gently approached the Gospel material in the light of the results of modern scholarship, trying 'to take us back to the days of Jesus's ministry on earth' but did not examine the processes by which he and others made this attempt.[21] Had he done so, there would no doubt have been the usual carp that, yet again, Oxford dons were unnerving the faithful.

The Religious Departments, however, were not going to give in, notwithstanding the emerging Mary Whitehouse and her longing for the return of the imaginary 'Christian Britain' of yesteryear. The huge progress being made in the scientific study of Holy Writ which Robinson had brought before a wider public was their inspiration. The great figures of theological innovation – Rudolf Bultmann, Karl Barth and Bonhoeffer, together with their insights into questions about mythology, historicity, morality and a host of others, should no longer be only the preserve of the clergy, the custodians of Robinson's 'established religious frame'. Dennis Nineham, Joachim Jeremias and others had yet another go at 'The Question of Historicity' and again the advisers were unsure: Donald Soper was sure that it was bad for the faithful to unseat their certainties. Television went to the Holy Land and reiterated the biblical stores. Television dramatized the Jesus event yet again, this time in jeans with the cascading images of the pop world designed to divert, attract and even capture the attentions of the bewildered young.

In 1969 – enter Dennis Potter, playwright and dramatist; like Dorothy Sayers, unconventional and abrasive. Unlike her, quite unconvinced and unsure about everything to do with Christianity in general and the central hero, Jesus of Nazareth, in particular. Potter's play *Son of Man* was broadcast in April 1969 and his Jesus was a reformer, a socialist, above all a human being who 'deserved to be crucified for his sheer cheek'.[22] Christopher Evans of King's College, London rightly concluded that 'Potter's Christ was a figure from whom it was not plausible that Christianity ultimately emerged'.[23] Potter's Jesus was angry, irascible and hated the establishment of his time. It was clear that Potter was – as *The Times* noted – 'uninfluenced by any critical work . . . and his conservatism [was] obvious by his diminution of the civilization and traditional culture of the Jews'.[24]

This was exactly the point: for all its stimulating originality, not the least in the restoration of the Galilean from Renaissance paint-work and stained glass, as so many said very enthusiastically, the fact remained that here again Potter's *Son of Man*, like Sayers's *Man Born to be King*, Harington's *Jesus of Nazareth*, Hugh Bishop's *Christ in Jeans* and Ernest Marvin's *A Man Dies*, was choosy about what could be dramatized and what ought to be left out.

It was precisely the malaise of the nineteenth-century liberals, long since left behind by the post-war theological revolution begun by Albert Schweitzer, which some theologians and historians of the 1960s were trying hard to get over to the rank and file, first of all in the pews, and then to anyone outside who wanted answers to their questions about the nature and reliability of the Gospels as historical documents and the increasing talk about demythologizing. The stronger commitment was to make a popular statement; the more cautious was the commitment to explore in public the histori-cal, methodological and philosophical initiatives being taken by the scholarly establishment, embroiled as it was in all manner of destabi-lizing uncertainty coupled with astonishing excitements. After all, the Dead Sea Scrolls had been discovered in 1947 and before that the Egyptian papyri; all hugely important for our understanding of the biblical manuscripts, let alone for their use. This was not the private property of the arcane company of New Testament scholars and some of them were anxious that the public should know exactly what was going on; and indeed, what had been going on in this area for decades which the clergy had a neat way of keeping to themselves. For good reason no doubt: the untutored would be unnerved by these sorts of questions.

In 1965 however, Kenneth Lamb, the first non-clerical Head of Religion at the BBC, thought otherwise: this might be good for the new BBC2 audience. His initiative produced a series of four outstanding lectures – talking heads from the highest scholarly ech-elons. Like those German theologians suspected of undermining the faithful, these were Anglican scholars concerned not only with scholarly endeavour but with parish life and the provision of a robust intellectual base for Christian belief. *The New Testament Gospels* was designed to bring 'the most recent trends in New Testament scholarship to the informed, the uninformed and the misinformed'.[25]

It was a courageous decision by the producers and their advisers; a small voice which had the audacity to question with open-minded exploration against a background of broadcast religion policy com-mitted by and large to affirmation rather than discussion. The Cen-tral Religious Advisory Committee had come near to complete col-lapse in the early 1960s over this very question: should broadcast religion proclaim or discuss? Could the broadcasters not see what they were doing? They were leading the untutored into the deep waters of scholarly criticism and that would only lead to chaos: had no one noticed, asked the affirmers, that the churches were emptying? Are you surprised, they asked the broadcasters, that common belief is being dismantled by all this sceptical talk? If only there were another Dorothy L. Sayers, they lamented, who could present the simple truth with such power.

In 1972, broadcasting hours were relaxed by government decree and it looked as if the closed period might no longer be protected. Happily, it remained: both authorities agreed to a 'gentlemen's agreement' to keep it intact. A sigh of relief was heard from the advisers. It was clear, however, that the heat was on: the closed period was now not merely a religious ghetto but a space for even better programmes, albeit religious. Religious producers had to look to their mettle. They needed more money if they were to produce programmes comparable to other parts of the output, especially documentaries. None of this was lost on Lew Grade, whose energy and flair produced *Moses, the Lawgiver*, which in turn gave him huge encouragement to tackle the 'really big one', *Jesus of Nazareth*.[26] Meanwhile, *Horizon, Panorama* and other series were enfranchising substantial audiences in political, economic, cultural, technological and medical debates, not to mention the natural sciences. There had been the monumental *Civilisation* series with Sir Kenneth Clarke in 1969 and this had set the tone. Where, they asked, was religion being comparably treated? Why could not the central issues of belief and authority, the tricky historical questions about ancient manuscripts, the moral issues in a secular society, be similarly dismantled, explored and debated in such documentary ways? Such productions needed a great deal of money and only very slowly had the religious producers been given the wherewithal to prove themselves in this highly professional field.

And they did: in 1977, just as Lew Grade and Franco Zeffirelli's affirmatory dramatization *Jesus of Nazareth*, costing $45 million, was going out on ITV, Peter Armstrong and Don Cupitt's monumental but less costly two-hour investigation *Who was Jesus?* was being broadcast on BBC.

'We have become – and not the least through broadcasting,' said Marghanita Laski in her introduction to the series, 'a sophisticated and sceptical people', and moreover, 'what scholarship has discovered in this field isn't sufficiently known to us general public'.[27] Just so! That year, protected time was halved and religious programmes were 'floated' in the general output. Robert Runcie called it a 'bonanza year' – religious documentary had come of age: it was entertaining, professional and courageous.

Suddenly, huge amounts of money were poured into religious

exploration: Bamber Gascoigne's *The Christians* looked back on two thousand years; Magnus Magnusson on *The Archaeology of Bible Lands* and, on an even larger scale, Ronald Eyre's *The Long Search* looked for clues to the religious mentality the world over – with Angela Tilby bringing up the rear with an accompanying series on radio. A bonanza year indeed! Armstrong's *Who was Jesus?* however, was in a class of its own simply because it investigated the foundational Christian documents with the philosophical and scholarly tools which Western Christendom had put at the disposal of scholar, believer and priest alike. Upon these documents so much faith, practice and dogma depended; upon these foundational documents a huge, modern edifice had been built which it was believed would secure the future of belief and Church in a secular age when both seemed so vulnerable. Modern science could be made to affirm their truth.

Not so, said the scholars – as, indeed, they had been saying since the days of David Friedrich Strauss: it is not quite so simple. Such confidence is flawed; such argument is trivial: it assumes that the Man of Nazareth must be universally intelligible and that those who argue otherwise are dismissed as 'academic or elitist'.[28] The clergy knew it, the scholars knew it but the rank and file did not; that is why they asked ludicrous questions about walking on water, turning white up a mountain and disappearing into the sky like a rocket. Some blamed the RE teachers and others the pulpit which had done so much over the years to produce 'an ignorant laity'.[29]

Thus it was television that boldly presented the public with this sensitive programme of 'classified' biblical investigation. Before long, the right wing clamoured for the 'right of reply' to put the alternative case. It was an unseemly disputation which reflected the grim reality that vast numbers of 'the informed, uninformed and misinformed', especially those moving in the orbit of congregant Christianity, should have been so duped by a reading of modern science which eschewed uncertainty and applied a secure solution before the questions had been asked. William Temple in the 1940s had made the same complaint; he too thought that if radio did not enfranchise in this area, no one else would!

Armstrong and Cupitt put the scientific study of the Bible along-side other documentary investigations in the field of religion which in 1977 had crowded the schedules. This was long overdue. Soon enough, there would be more such programmes doing for the wider audience what the clergy should have been doing for the smaller, and long before the 1970s. Television documentary in 1977 had set the agenda for modern religious programmes, and in the early 1980s Channel 4 set out on a similar venture, just as Armstrong and Cupitt were plotting another investigation, this time into the development of dogma and the contingency of faith.

Religious television observers, meanwhile, were beginning to worry about what might come from across the Atlantic. Indeed, the very first *Everyman* in 1977 (outside the closed period and slap in the middle of late prime-time Sunday evening) had looked at Robert Schuller, a 'televangelist' from California who sent a grim shudder here down the spines of producers, advisers and Church leaders alike – or most of them! Others were frantic to raise huge audiences as the televangelists were doing at that time. So was Yorkshire Television's *Stars on Sunday* here: it was, they said, a wonderful use of the Bible today: it was being read aloud and listened to by millions. Cupitt and Armstrong, however, were taking it to pieces. The BBC was at it again.

In 1984, all was ready for two further investigations, both notorious and both courageous. Cupitt and Armstrong's *Sea of Faith* examined doctrine and the philosophical climates in which dogma deriving from Holy Writ is argued, formulated and defended. Channel 4 commissioned *Jesus, the Evidence* from London Weekend Television and a few explosions took place! Yet more clamour for the right to reply from Mary Whitehouse and even an offer of another set of programmes to put the 'orthodox' view. Complaints came thick and fast, not the least because *Evidence* was shown at Easter! Some thought it vulgar, others ludicrous. Either way, it was one more attempt to put people in the picture; against a background of substantial affirmation in religious programmes, why not a modest crack at some of the central issues in biblical scholarship in the light of archaeological discoveries and a good deal more besides? Fortunately, the broadcasters stood their ground. The BBC's Religious Affairs Correspondent put it neatly: 'It can do nothing but harm to the Christian cause if the impression is created that the Church still wants to burn heretics – or at least their books and films – and get everyone back behind gothic arches mumbling the Apostles' Creed in unison.'[30] *Jesus, the Evidence*, said a former Third Programme religious producer, 'was the kind of thing TV should do.'[31]

With the 1980s now well behind us, we may have cause to celebrate a combination of a 'coming of age' with a 'golden age' of the broadcasters' commitment to investigative documentary in the sensitive area of biblical scholarship. As the application of the 1990 Broadcasting Act begins to take effect, there are loud cries of censorship, 'gagging the Church' and demands for more freedom and less regulation. Understanding the nature of biblical witness, its emergence from antiquarian mists and the huge problem of integrating the manuscripts seem far from the evangelical objectives of substantial numbers who see in deregulated broadcasting the opportunity to do what the authorities have not permitted for so long: recruiting – and never mind the doubters. The foundations should not be shaken for any longer than necessary.

The irony of the 1980s was never more striking than when during that same 1984, the present Bishop of Durham made a few controversial remarks on LWT's *Credo* and took the rank and file by surprise; vast numbers bayed for his removal. There was uproar as Gerald Priestland had guessed there would be! What was naturally wanted was something firm, secure, affirmative and evangelical: the simpler story which had been told for centuries. Rather than Cupitt or Jenkins, Lew Grade's *Jesus of Nazareth* along with the dramatized versions of Potter, Harington and Sayers is what majority Christian opinion seems to continue to want from the broadcasters and the film-makers. It needs reassurance in the midst of decline, secularity, doubt and relativism – all the more urgent in the face of the vast swathes of human tragedy which television brings so dreadfully into the place of homely safety.

Television documentary in the field of biblical studies was doing the clergy's job and the Churches complained when it did not go the way they wanted it. The public thus remained ill-informed and untutored in the one area about which they might have developed a more mature understanding after centuries of progress: the use of the Bible today in the world of today with the scientific and philosophical tools of today brought into play by the broadcasters of today to meet the questions of today. None of them will go away. They will take us by surprise again and yet another segment of the cultural coastline will be gently washed into the sea of – dare we say? – unfaith.

Part II

PERSONAL DISCOVERY
AND COMMUNITY

Chapter 8

The Bible and the God of Israel

Don Cupitt

At home we used to have an old biscuit tin filled with miscellaneous pieces of the children's constructional toy, Lego, and there was a game of trying to build something recognizable that would use up as many of the pieces as possible. They couldn't all be used, for there were too many oddments, and they could of course be assembled into a variety of different shapes. Nevertheless, some solutions to the problem were manifestly better than others.

So it is with belief in God. We have inherited and we still use an extraordinary miscellany of idioms, ways of thinking and speaking about God. Nothing guarantees in advance that they will all fit together into one tidy systematic construction. Quite the opposite, for what we have is a jumble of fragments from kits acquired at different times in the past. Many pieces have been lost, and of those that survive some are more useful than others. No single logical thread ties them all together. We have to try to make what we can out of them; but we must remember that the more pieces we incorporate the more ragged and unstable will be the thing we construct, so it may be better to leave a good deal of material unused in the interests of building something stronger, more coherent and recognizable. That any rate is my own preference.

One further application of the analogy: people used to think that the Church or the Bible gave them a ready-made construction, or at least a complete kit of pieces designed to be assembled into just one construction. Today, though, our new sense of history and our closer study of the individual pieces has shown us that the Bible and the Christian tradition present us with something much more like my children's Lego tin, which grew slowly over many years with some substantial additions, and also many small losses that went unnoticed until we started building.

Most users of the Lego tin were quite happy to speak of 'the Lego' as if it were a unity, and had many hours of fun using the pieces as they came to hand to make what they pleased of them. A theologian is rather like a heavy parent who moves in with big systematic ambitions, and then starts complaining that the material is too incomplete for his design to be executed. He spoils the fun, but there it is. There are such people, and I am one of them. At least by now I have learnt to attempt something small. Like this:

When the heathens asked, 'Where is their God?', they were taunting a people in trouble. In the ancient world being a god was all about power, and nothing could be more galling than to be told that you were in such poor shape that your god was obviously absent or impotent. The heathen regarded a god as being a kind of tribal mascot or guardian angel. He embodied the people's identity and their cultural values, and he was supposed to look after them. In fact the god's prestige or glory rose and fell with his people's: when they flourished he was evidently powerful and active on their behalf, but when things were going badly for them it seemed that he must be feeble or negligent. The internationally recognized glory of your god was in those days what the strength of your currency on the foreign-exchange markets is nowadays. National gods rose or fell and were strong or weak according to the prevailing perception of a nation's stability, vigour and prospects, much as today when the dollar is high Americans walk tall, the Churches flourish and the Administration does well in the polls; whereas when the dollar tumbles and people ask maliciously, 'Where is it now?', Americans feel humiliated. So in the Old Testament we often find great concern being expressed about God's international standing. He promises to make his name great among the nations by exalting Israel, for the glory of the god was indeed the chief index of national well-being, just as the strength of the currency is today. Hence the huge effort that went into building great temples and maintaining the cult.

However, although such ways of thinking about God and the function of religion are indeed found in the Old Testament, the Psalmist does not accept them. Staying within the same field of picture-language, he insists that the power and authority of the God of Israel does not decline like the currency when the nation's fortunes decline. As he puts it, God is not just a tribal mascot or an index of national prosperity, for 'he is in heaven and does whatever he wills'. God's sovereignty is absolute and logically independent of how Israel happens at the moment to be faring. Israel's strength may be variable, but God's is not.

How are we to interpret this affirmation? It seems that the faith of Israel is and has to be doggedly and deliberately counter-factual. You cannot infer what God is like from the way things go, because what is true of God is true *a priori*, or independently of the facts. This means that when things are going badly for you, you should not conclude that God has become weak or indifferent, for to make such an inference would be to relapse into the typically heathen notion of god. Admittedly, in bad times human faith may fail, but the failure in that case is a failure of human faith and not a failure of God. Like some other biblical writers, the Psalmist seems to be saying that God functions as a transcendent, supra-factual, *a priori* and necessary reference-point in human life, whose authority is not conditional upon the facts about how things are going, but is unchangeable.

We see this insight emerging in those biblical prayers in which people are wrestling with God and questioning his justice. As they work their way through their own violently conflicting feelings about God they gradually come to see that they are resolving a problem in their own religious psychology, rather than a problem in theology. Their prayer-struggle is resolved when they are at last able to grasp what is meant by the unchangeability of God. He is not an anthropomorphic tutelary deity, a personal protector whose job it is to protect us from harm. On the contrary, he is tough. He changes us the hard way, by being himself unchangeable. So the prayer of one who strives with God ends when he can at last bring himself to say, 'Nevertheless, not my will but thine be done, Amen' – and *that* is the victory of God. For the true God is victorious only when we have purged ourselves of the last remnants of the heathen conception of god.

All this makes clear the meaning of the most important and intense kind of prayer, the trial of faith in the time of affliction. It teaches the believer that God is not like the gods of the heathen. The true God is supernatural and not merely natural. He is a pure guiding spiritual ideal which constrains us. Being truly transcendent, he is not a fact and does not vary with the facts. His authority and power to save reside in his very eternity, immutability and invulnerability, for they mean that however bad things become he remains our refuge in just the same way. He is that which we should cling to whatever happens, because it remains reliable whatever happens.

God is therefore not a personal god in the same sense as the gods of the heathen are personal gods. What made the God of Israel Israel's god and bound them to him was not any special personal pay-off or protection that they could expect to receive, as if a Church were a Mafia family run by an exceptionally efficient Godfather. Rather, Israel was astonished to find that to her alone among ancient peoples had it been given to arrive at this peculiarly exalted, spiritual and consciousness-raising conception of God. Israel, it seemed, possessed the only god who was not his people's possession, because he was truly transcendent. Their tribal god was the only God who is *not* a tribal god.

I am attempting to grasp what really is distinctive and out of the ordinary in the ancient Hebraic idea of God. I do not deny that my account uses only a small selection of the pieces available to us, and

I admit that it is difficult and paradoxical, hard to get hold of and hard to retain. Nevertheless, I think it is what matters most. On it hinges the entire history of belief in God to this day, for the struggle between the heathen and the Israelite conceptions of God goes on perennially within Israel itself and within every one of us who believes in God, of whatever tradition. To be seriously committed to belief in God is to find yourself undergoing a progressive purging. Gradually the cosy objective personal god of the heathen is expelled and replaced by the more spiritual and demanding concept.

The shift is oddly difficult to describe. We can try various vocabularies, and talk about moving from heteronomous to autonomous faith, from a realist to a non-realist conception of God, from a natural to a truly supernatural God, from a metaphysical to an existential faith, from an external God to a God within, from objectivism to voluntarism, and so on. I have tried all these models, and others as well. They are all doubtless unsatisfactory. Never mind: the fact remains that belief in God allows you no rest. There is not any one true dogmatic philosophy of religion, as many people suppose, but instead only a long process of refinement or purification.

I am not talking about the conflict between universal and particularist or sectarian strands in belief. Some people have seen in the Bible a gradual movement from tribal to universal faith. The idea is that God starts like an old-style king, contracted to his people. He unifies them and has absolute sovereignty over them. He leads them in battle, and is glorified when they win and temporarily eclipsed when they lose. He is the fount of their law, and they petition him and are judged by him. Gradually in the Bible, though, this primitive idea is generalized and extended to the whole human race. God comes to be seen as the King of Kings and Lord of all the earth. All peoples stand in the same relation to him, and morality becomes universal – but, as we know too well, universal monotheists go on claiming that their own particular community nevertheless retains a special relationship with God. All the nations worship God, each in its own way, but *we* worship him in *his*.

Certainly there is a conflict of this type between universalism and sectarianism in the teachings of many religions, but it is not what I am here discussing. The deeper conflict is that between the heathens who see god as being somehow factual and varying with the facts, and the Israelites whose God is supernatural. Call him a transcendent and unvarying reference-point for assessing human life whose potency lies precisely in the fact that he is not part of this changing world, and does not change; call him a pure guiding spiritual ideal; or cut out the personal pronouns altogether and speak only of a religious imperative: whatever your preference, it is hard to find the right words for the true God who is not an objective being, not a person, and does not exist as things exist. The great teachers speak of him as indescribable and incomprehensible, and say that since God cannot be talked about directly we must resort to indirect techniques. These techniques may include imaginative stories designed to break people out of their ordinary ways of thinking, expositions of the spiritual life to show how faith in God works practically, and even all-out iconoclastic attacks on the false heathen idea of god. They may all be used, but if they are used well they will hurt and will provoke anger, for true faith in God is what most people think of as atheism. So it always has been, and no doubt always will be.

Yet the clues are there. For God traditionally has two sets of attributes, the metaphysical and the moral. The metaphysical attributes decisively separate him from the world of fact, insisting that he is not in space or time and has no limits, body, parts or feelings. In short, he is like a pure ideal; and his moral attributes also remove him from the world of fact. Thus he is love, period. Not any particular love, neither an object-selecting love nor a selectable love-object, but love simple, universal and objectless – and therefore not himself an object. Indeed, the Christian ideal of love as universal, disinterested and selfless rules out the notion that God can be an objective personal being, because he cannot be thought of as one who is singled out from others as the preferred love-object, nor as one who himself singles out preferred objects of his love. So the ideal of love requires the decentring of God; and so also it is with God's other attributes of justice, wisdom, beauty, goodness and the rest.

It is this decentring both of God and of oneself in religion that makes the phrase 'my God' so paradoxical. To attain a kind of life-love which is subjectless and objectless and no longer egoistically or moralistically selective, I must become decentred and me and my-ness must go. I have to lose my possessions, my relationships, my very life and become nothing suspended in nothingness. I am only fit to use the word 'my' in connection with my God when . . . Nothing is mine. So, a final linguistic tease: God is such that when nothing is mine and I am nothing, then God is mine.

Chapter 9

The Bible and Jungian Depth Psychology

Leon Schlamm

Introduction

To introduce the work of Carl Jung (1875–1961), the founder of the school of analytical psychology, into a collection of essays illustrating how the Bible is relevant in the modern world might at first appear surprising. Jung's criticism of Christianity for its use of the Bible to underscore the significance of faith in, rather than knowledge of, God is well known. Indeed, throughout Jung's life he argued that a new relationship with God was necessary – based on immediate religious experience – which was profoundly antagonistic to that advocated by the biblical Christianity of his father, a pastor of the Basel Reformed Church. He was critical of his father's blind obedience to the Bible and his emphasis on religious belief, which, he argued, led not only to the inhibition of critical thinking about religious issues, but also, more important, to the repression of vital religious experiences disclosed by God in the depths of our unconscious. Jung regarded his father as typical of all too many modern Christians, who tragically do not know the immediate living God who stands omnipotent and free above his Bible and his Church, indeed who put their Church and Bible between themselves and their experiences of holiness located in the unconscious. The Bible, Jung maintains, can and all too often does prevent the occurrence of religious – or numinous[1] – experiences, because it is misused and misunderstood by its readers.

However, Jung's attitude to the Bible was by no means completely negative. In spite of his alienation from the biblical Christianity of his father (Jung never embraced either Protestant or Catholic Christianity), he continued to draw inspiration from the Bible during the course of the development of his ideas on the psychology of religion. Jung regarded the Bible as filled with numinous images which, when correctly understood, provide a reflection of, and a bridge to, the powerful forces of man's unconscious psyche, the archetypes.[2] When the Bible is experienced in a psychologically fruitful way – that is, when the psychological forces of the unconscious are attracted into consciousness by biblical images – it can provide not only profoundly impressive, psychic healing and stability, but also for those who are psychologically well-developed a mirror reflecting the forces of the unconscious. This produces greater self-understanding leading, for those who are ready, to individuation,[3] the goal of psychic development for Jung.

Thus Jung was far from hostile to the Bible. Rather his relationship to the Bible was determined by what he saw as the psychological function of all religious texts, whether Christian or non-Christian. Their function is to establish contact with the forces of man's unconscious, either with a view to maintaining an essentially unconscious, but stable and contented dependence on numinous images which prevent mental illness – and this is the essentially conservative psychological function of most religious materials most of the time – or to make human beings aware of the difficult-to-achieve goal of psychic development, the growth of consciousness leading to individuation. If the Bible fails to provide either of these psychological services to man, then it has ceased to be useful, and clinging to it with faith will only bring unnecessary pain and unhappiness. It is these psychological principles which determine Jung's tactics of interpreting the Bible, and lead him to argue that there are in fact hidden messages in the Bible, which have been waiting for some two millennia to be discovered by those relatively few heroic individuals who are now seeking and approaching individuation. It is to some consideration of these tactics of interpretation and Jung's hidden messages, especially regarding the careers of Job and Christ, that I now turn.

Jung's Tactics of Interpretation

Jung regards the Bible as the product of the interplay of conscious and unconscious psychological forces, and this fundamental assumption determines the direction of his hermeneutical programme. The Bible is to be understood not just from an historical, social or literary point of view (all offering differing *conscious* perspectives on biblical material), but as in part giving expression to the powerful forces of both the personal and the collective unconscious. Jung is particularly concerned with uncovering evidence for the collective unconscious in biblical material which, he argues, will contribute to our understanding of both the biblical author and his community and the biblical interpreter and his community. Neither can be understood except in the light of the interaction of the unconscious psyche with consciousness.

To repeat, Jung is drawn to the study of the Bible only because in it he finds that which is quite extraordinary from a conscious point of view – indeed, to borrow a phrase from Rudolf Otto, 'wholly other' to consciousness. He draws attention to the scriptural images and ideas which stand out against a background of consciously created religious materials as numinous and archetypal, and which challenge every conscious assumption which we possess. What is the value of the Bible today? Jung's answer to this question is clear: to remind the interpreter of the divine forces of the unconscious which are ignored or repressed by consciousness. To put this another way, the purpose of archetypal biblical images and ideas is to provide a form of compensation for the inadequate conscious attitude of human beings. Consciousness, for Jung, typically suffers because it is one-sided and often in a dangerous state of disequilib-rium, and archetypal biblical images and ideas can, like dreams, waking visions and other products of the unconscious, provide in an apparently purposive way the healing that it so desperately needs. Such compensation for the one-sidedness of consciousness, Jung points out, is felt to be a gift from the unconscious or from God and absolutely spontaneous and autonomous – that is not subject to our will or conscious control. Thus Jung can liken the experience of compensation, whether provided by archetypal biblical materials or by dreams and visions, to the experience of those biblical writers who report having been seized by the Word or the Spirit of God.

Clearly Jung's reading of the Bible is determined by the principle that the function of scripture is not primarily to provide information, but spiritual or psychological transformation. Accordingly, he challenges the assumption of many modern biblical scholars about the univocal, unambiguous nature of biblical language. For Jung, a literal interpretation of biblical language can never provide an adequate understanding of the depths of God – or the depths of the collective unconscious which he effectively equates with God. Rather, he argues that there may be several layers of meaning which are con-cealed by the literal meaning of biblical materials. Such hidden meanings, where they exist, simply await discovery by those biblical students who are sufficiently psychologically developed to distrust and be impatient with the literal meaning of scripture.

Of course, this belief that an exclusively literal interpretation of scripture prevents spiritual development is certainly not a novel one. It has a long, if somewhat chequered, history going back to the beginnings of the Patristic and Rabbinic traditions. Many of the Church Fathers as well as Rabbis of the Talmudic and post-Talmudic periods believed that the hermeneutical engagement with the biblical text – with the intention of uncovering a host of esoteric meanings – could be a profoundly spiritual experience; and it is partly out of this experience that there gradually evolved in Patristic and Rabbinic circles an assumption that four ways of interpreting scripture can be justified: the literal, the allegorical or typological, the moral and the anagogical (concerned with the mysteries of heavenly realities), as the Church Fathers defined them. It is these rules of engagement with scripture (largely discredited since the Reformation – at least in the Christian tradition) – and the religious experiences which accompany them – which provide the background to Jung's tactics of interpretation.

What distinguishes Jung's hermeneutical endeavour from the traditional fourfold interpretation of scripture of the Church Fathers and Rabbis are two methodological assumptions which determine the direction of his work. The first is that one does not have to be a confessing Christian to interpret the Bible profitably. Indeed, he suggests that as a non-believer he may be in a better position to reveal hitherto concealed meanings of biblical materials than believers themselves. Such biblical materials, he argues, have been awaiting the scrutiny of analytical psychology for approximately two millennia. Second, Jung does not regard the four rules of interpretation of scripture as equally valuable. He is primarily interested in the allegorical and particularly the anagogical modes of interpretation. Put boldly, the primary focus for Jung's efforts is to uncover what the Rabbis called the mysterious 'secret' (in Hebrew *sod*) of biblical materials.

However, in spite of these differences I want to suggest that if we take Jung's testimony at face value, then there appears to be a striking similarity between Jung's *experience* of interpreting scripture and the experience of many Christian and Jewish writers of Bible commentaries, especially those with a desire to pursue some mystical encounter with God. Just as many Christian and Jewish Bible commentators have in the past sought divine assistance (in the form of encounters with God within the depths of the soul) in their search for the most hidden meanings of scripture, so Jung seeks the assistance of the numinous forces of the collective unconscious in his attempt to interpret the Bible. This psychological process he calls active imagination.

Active imagination is a form of waking fantasy – or dreaming with open eyes – a technique in which one concentrates on an image or event or mood and then allows a chain of further images or events to arise absolutely spontaneously without the interference of consciousness. As a general psychotherapeutic technique for coaxing unconscious contents into consciousness Jung favoured it over the use of dreams, since the ego is stimulated to react more immediately and directly to the contents of the unconscious. Active imagination, which must be contrasted with the conscious invention of daydreaming, leads to a growing awareness that unconscious contents

have a life of their own, and this in turn may lead to greater collaboration between consciousness and the unconscious and eventually to
individuation.

Now Jung suggested that this psychological technique of waking
fantasy could be profitably applied to the interpretation of the Bible.
Through the use of it, the interpreter would be able to uncover a host
of hidden meanings which had remained inaccessible to previous
generations of Bible commentators – indeed which had been fer-
menting for centuries in the unconscious and waiting for the right
moment to break into consciousness. In his essay *Answer to Job*
Jung demonstrated in a particularly vivid way how this process of
engagement of active imagination with the Bible works, and argued
that it led him to discover three profoundly important, hidden meanings of scripture, hitherto buried in the unconscious, which today
demand to be acknowledged by modern consciousness. The first is
that God is not only good, but also evil; the second is that God, like
man, is seeking higher consciousness and in particular individuation, and the third is that God is present in human beings and
we must discover Him in our own inner lives. It is to a detailed
consideration of Jung's *Answer to Job* that I now turn.

Answer to Job: **Putting God on the Couch**

Jung reported that 'if there is anything like the spirit seizing one by
the scruff of the neck it was the way *Answer to Job* came into being'.
He regarded its contents as the product of divine consciousness
coming up from the unconscious, and argued that only by making
conscious this – some would say grotesque, blasphemous and perverse – piece of theology could he maintain his psychological equilib-
rium. Certainly, the active imagination, which, by the psychological
law of compensation, produced this extraordinary, heretical reinterpretation of the careers of Job, Christ, St John, the author of the Book
of Revelation and many other biblical figures, was accompanied by
intense emotion. In no other work on religious issues does Jung
become so personally involved as in his deliberations here on the
fate of Job. However, the presence of such emotion is by no means
incidental to Jung's hermeneutical approach to the Bible. Rather, its
purpose is to stimulate active imagination to greater activity, which
will, it is believed, create more psychological understanding.

Jung begins *Answer to Job* by focusing his attention on the image
of Yahweh as 'a God who knew no moderation in his emotions and
suffered precisely from this lack of moderation . . . Insight existed
along with obtuseness, loving-kindness along with cruelty, creative
power with destructiveness. A condition of this sort can only be

described as amoral.' This observation provides the starting point for Jung's active imagination, the point at which the compensatory forces of the unconscious can begin to respond to the 'darkness of God' which has been denied – or repressed – by the Judaeo-Christian tradition for more than two thousand years. Jung allows himself to be disturbed by 'the shattering emotion which the unvarnished spectacle of divine savagery and ruthlessness produces in us'. He seeks to experience the full effect of the contradictory nature of the God-image at the heart of biblical tradition, even to the point of imitating Yahweh's angry, irrational behaviour, for the purpose of transforming this inner violence into conscious knowledge. Only in this way can Jung discover 'why and to what purpose Job was wounded, and what consequences have grown out of this for Yahweh as well as for man'.

Jung is not prepared to accept that Job deserves his suffering. Neither is he prepared to accept that the injustice patiently suffered by Job at the hands of Yahweh can be justified by the fact that it leads to greater human understanding. Endorsing either of these positions means, for Jung, accepting the authority of past biblical tradition and with it the severely restricted experience of conscious-ness which represses an alien wisdom coming from the unconscious. Rather, this alien wisdom alerts Jung to the need for a new interpre-tation of Job's situation, namely that Yahweh's authority needs to be questioned because although He possesses superior power, he is in fact to a large degree unconscious, certainly less conscious than man! Thus Jung discovers that it is necessary to put God on the couch and to offer a depth psychological account of His inner life in the light of His failure to recognize Job's transparent righteousness.

Jung argues that Yahweh's manifest lack of self-reflection (uncon-sciousness) is demonstrated throughout the Old Testament in His violent and inconsistent dealings with Israel as well as in the New Testament in His cruel demand for the sacrificial death of Christ on the cross, which can hardly be reconciled with the loving-kindness reputed of Him. However, the significance of Job's dealings with Yahweh has been underestimated by all previous generations of Bible commentators. This is because they have failed to comprehend the meaning of Job's confrontation with Yahweh. Job recognizes Yahweh's dark unconsciousness – for example, in His wager with Satan which He cannot win without heaping upon Job unnecessary suffering and more generally in His obviously immoral behaviour – and he stands firm in the knowledge of his own morality rooted in consciousness. Yahweh's encounter with such a man who will not bend in the face of His archaic brutality is traumatic, because it makes Him aware for the first time of His own shadow.[4] Yahweh recognizes that Job, because of his consciousness, is raised morally above Him, and that He must learn to know His inner nature that Job is already familiar with. He can no longer torture Job in order to avoid confronting Himself. Rather He must acknowledge that His confrontation with Job forces upon Him real self-reflection. He must raise Himself above His earlier primitive level of consciousness, and the only way He can do this is to become a man Himself in Christ. This is the meaning of the incarnation for Jung. God must become man for two reasons. The first is to recompense man for the wrong done to Job, and the second is to enable God to catch up with man psychologically, in other words to facilitate His own individuation process.

However, the incarnation for Yahweh is only the first step along the road of divine individuation. This is because the sinless Christ figure of the Gospels, the product of the immaculate conception of the Virgin Mary, is an inadequate and incomplete embodiment of individuation. Clearly, this figure is an image of perfect goodness, but the problem created by it, so far as Yahweh's quest for individuation is concerned, is that instead of integrating the divine shadow (evil), it represses it completely. At this point the divine shadow becomes an autonomous, dissociated personality, projected on another being cast out of heaven – Satan. Whereas in the Book of Job Yahweh and Satan are still on speaking terms, in the New Testament Yahweh and Satan become completely differentiated as Christ and Satan become antagonists, indeed absolute opposites. This antagonism between opposites is in fact one of the distinguishing features of consciousness, and confirms for Jung that Yahweh clearly has taken one important step beyond the stage of unconsciousness which determined the nature of His confrontation with Job. But there is now a further step for Yahweh to take: to integrate the opposites (especially good and evil) discovered during the process of attaining the consciousness of man through the incarnation. This integration of opposites signals that one is approaching the goal of individuation, the self.[5]

Jung finds the first evidence of Yahweh's attempt to integrate the opposites of good and evil in the Revelation of St John. In the Apocalypse, Jung argues, we encounter again the wrathful side of Yahweh, which now functions as an unconscious compensation for the God of love preached by Jesus and consciously accepted by the Christian community. While Jesus Christ seemed in the Gospels to be able to repress the dark side of God, his consciously formulated quest for perfection was undermined by those dark religious images coming up from St John's unconscious. Jung argues that the purpose of such images was to remind Christians of 'the fierce and terrible side of Yahweh'. As Jung put it:

The purpose of the apocalyptic visions is not to tell St John, as an ordinary human being, how much shadow he hides beneath his human nature, but to open the seer's eyes to the immensity of God . . . For this reason he felt his gospel of love to be onesided, and he supplemented it with the gospel of fear: God can be loved but must be feared.

Thus we see here that Yahweh has begun to reclaim and to integrate His shadow, although the process is by no means complete, as is made clear in the Book of Revelation by the continuing hostility between Christ and Antichrist. This is why the incarnation of Yahweh in Christ remains incomplete in the Apocalypse, and why, in Jung's opinion, there is a need for the idea of the continuing incarnation after Christ which is provided by Christ's promise of the Paraclete in St John's Gospel.

Jung's discussion of the role of the continued operation of the holy spirit in Yahweh's search for individuation and in His desire for continuing incarnation in all men after Christ provides, I believe, some of his most challenging ideas in *Answer to Job*. He argues that after Christ Yahweh wants to incarnate Himself in all men and women. Christ is the first-born son of God 'who is succeeded by an ever-increasing number of younger brothers and sisters'. 'God wants to become *wholly* man; in other words, to reproduce Himself in his own dark creature (man not redeemed from original sin).' In this way Yahweh's process of individuation and His integration of opposites, including good and evil, takes place in the psyche of man. This is what incarnation means for *Jung*. God has fallen into the unconscious of man, which now becomes the crucible for divine transformation. Accordingly, God needs man's co-operation for His own individuation and completed incarnation. In particular, He is dependent on man to integrate His opposites – including good and evil – when he becomes aware of them operating within his own psyche. Moreover, God seeks the light of consciousness in man, coming up from or through his unconscious, but this again is only possible when man himself is seeking individuation, that is when man is sensitive to the demands and needs of the numinous forces of the unconscious. Thus we see that divine individuation and incarnation cannot be separated from human individuation. This leads Jung to the conclusion that the redemption of both man and God depend upon divine–human collaboration rather than the traditional religious relationship of man's absolute submission to an omnipotent and omniscient deity.

An Evaluation

There is much fascinating material in *Answer to Job* that, for lack of space, I cannot discuss in this introductory account of the work. But clearly, what has been presented requires some evaluation. The reader will not be surprised to learn that many theologians displayed considerable hostility to the work at the time of its publication in 1952. It was called among other things 'frivolous', 'grotesque, blasphemous and perverse', 'a half-spiritual, half-joking farce', and 'childish and paranoid'. Many of Jung's critics have focused their attention on the emotional tone of the work. They argue that the fact that Jung treats so seriously and with such affect the primitive, anthropomorphic image of God rejected by rational atheism demands explanation. It is difficult to resist the temptation, they argue, to explain the major features of Jung's thesis in *Answer to Job* in terms of his personal life, in particular in terms of his own unresolved father complex. *Answer to Job*, with its agonized response to – and angry attack on – God, the loving father of all humanity, is simply a screen which conceals Jung's far more significant and threatening psychological problems with his own father Paul, and later with another father figure, Sigmund Freud. Jung, in reality, is only analysing God's inner life in order either to release him from his childish dependence on his father Paul or Freud, or even less charitably in order to avoid ever confronting his father complex. Even a more sympathetic reading of Jung here suggests that his theology in *Answer to Job* is hopelessly contaminated by his personal life and individual psychology, and that his real purpose is to transform Christianity into a form of analytical psychology.

There is, however, another influential type of theological criticism of *Answer to Job* which needs to be considered. This one focuses its attack specifically on Jung's theory of archetypes, which lies at the heart of the argument of this work. Is it profitable or sensible, it is asked, to analyse a patient's deity without analysing the patient, in this case Job? Is not psychologically sick and spiritually complacent Job, rather than Yahweh, at fault after all? Is not the God–Satan split a product of Job's own ego–shadow split? Does not Jung in *Answer to Job* give excessive attention to the archetypal in psychology and abandon any interest in personal psychology, with the result that he transfers all personal psychopathologies on to our deity/deities? Our gods or archetypes are blamed for deeds for which in fact the individual should be held responsible. The result of such a psychology and theology is that Christianity is in danger of losing the struggle for liberation from the tyranny of those dark gods (archetypes) who exercised absolute authority over mankind in pre-Christian times, and who have continued to be influential in the lives of a significant number of men and women of the last two millennia.

Some response to these criticisms is clearly needed in order to clarify Jung's position. To begin with, it is impossible to establish whether there is any justification for accusing Jung of using the argument of *Answer to Job* to work through and resolve his own father complex. The kind of concrete evidence which is necessary to give substance to such a charge is simply not available. What is more likely is that Jung was working through a residue of childish dependence on God at the tender age of seventy-seven, with which he had been struggling since his disturbing, flamboyantly heterodox religious experiences of childhood. So much for the personal factor in the creation of Jung's theology in *Answer to Job*.

It is my opinion, however, that much more attention needs to be given to the archetypal factor in *Answer to Job*, which is only marginally affected by Jung's personal religious preoccupations and struggles. This is after all what Jung understands himself to be principally concerned with in this work, and we can only begin to appreciate the nature of his controversial claims about the archetypal factor by drawing attention to the kind of challenge which such claims create for the Bible reader today.

Clearly, there are certain features of Jung's archetypal factor which it is not profitable to consider here. The first is Jung's equation of what Christians call religious experience with what he calls numinous experience of the unconscious psyche. Obviously, the issue between Jung and the Christian concerning the continuing incarnation of God in man (what Jung calls 'the Christification of many') is not likely to be settled in the near future. The second feature of Jung's archetypal factor which it is not profitable to consider here is his claim about God's unconsciousness and His search for individuation, which will understandably be rejected by committed Christians. However, what is profitable to consider here – indeed of profound value for a proper understanding of the archetypal factor – are Jung's claims about the shadow in God, which tend to be rejected by Christians. Jung offers the Christian a serious intellectual and spiritual challenge here which requires of him sustained reflection – and honest introspection. Old Testament literature is filled with images of God's psychopathologies, and Jung is critical of those biblical interpreters who appeal to the authority of the New Testament to justify the repression of such images. The result of such repression, and of clinging to the image of the sinless Christ, is not only that 'a positively cosmic or daemonic grandeur in evil is imputed to man . . . [which] burdens him with the dark side of God', but also that one fails to understand or experience God in all His complexity and ambiguity. In other words, one fails to acknowledge what Rudolf Otto called the elements of 'awfulness' and 'overpoweringness' in the 'tremendum' (terrible) moment of numinous experience. Jung questions the wisdom of seeking to liberate ourselves totally from the tyranny of those dark divine forces of pre-Christian times, and argues rather that we need to integrate our experiences of them with our Christian and post-Christian religious experiences. Then we will become aware of a form of wisdom which, while timeless, has a peculiar relevance to our own times, namely that:

> God has a terrible double aspect: a sea of grace is met by a seething lake of fire, and the light of love glows with a fierce dark heat of which it is said *'ardet non lucet'* – it burns but gives no light. That is the eternal, as distinct from the temporal, gospel: one can love God but must fear him.

Chapter 10

The Bible and Human Suffering

Lord Longford

The Bible

I was about to describe myself as a Bible-Christian. After a moment's reflection I drew back. It is true that I read the Bible every day. My total religious reading, unless I have some special purpose, is half an hour, of which at least a quarter of an hour is devoted to the Bible. But nearly all my Bible reading consists of reading the Gospels. I realize that this is a confession of serious limitation.

When I was received into the Catholic Church, an Anglican defector, fifty years ago, I was asked by more or less well-intentioned friends, 'Will that mean that you stop reading the Bible?' Whatever may have been the case in the past, the accusation against the Church could not be lodged today. At Mass (on Sundays at least) we have readings from the Old Testament apart from the Psalms, the Psalms themselves, the Epistles and the Gospels. So a good Catholic, like any other good Christian, has no excuse for confining himself to the Gospels.

While I was writing this chapter, I encountered a Professor of Christian Ethics (incidentally an Anglican) who argued that if one confined oneself to the Gospels one left out the dimension of social justice which could be found in the Old Testament. I said, 'Heaven forbid that we should adopt Old Testament ideas of how criminals and homosexuals ought to be treated. In the Old Testament stoning is the prescribed remedy.' I may be told, no doubt correctly, that profound conceptions of social justice can be discovered in Isaiah and the other prophets. But even in the Psalms, they seem to me to be mixed up with an attitude to one's enemies that I find quite unacceptable.

Moving on to the Epistles, I find myself thoroughly at home with James and Peter, and of course St Paul was a supreme spiritual genius. Nothing preached in the Gospels is more eloquent than Corinthians 13 about charity. But St Paul's views on women are, if I may say so without irreverence, quite intolerable. I do not know how his devotees explain them away. I am sure that he has had to recant long since when it is pointed out to him that they are totally opposed to the way Jesus Christ treated women.

Someone who has been much involved in politics, like myself, growing up as a Conservative and now for over fifty years Labour, is bound to ask themselves whether Christianity leads to any particular political ideology. My dear friend (the Revd Lord) Donald Soper believes I think that a true Christian should be a socialist and a pacifist. I do not doubt the Christianity of Mrs Thatcher but her views on social policy are to me anathema. I read a very interesting article about her by a Methodist leader who explained that she had carried through her life some, but by no means all, of the tenets of her Methodist upbringing. In the House of Lords, Christians are scattered round the Chamber. Does this lead to the conclusion, hinted at by the Professor of Christian Ethics quoted earlier, that there is no social guidance in the Gospels; that the teaching of Jesus was aimed solely at the individual? To such a question I find myself giving a kind of yes and no answer. Personally, I find it impossible to discover a form of government or society which is dictated to us in the Gospels. I am told by those who read the early chapters of the Acts more carefully than I do that one might find something of the sort there but I am rather sceptical. But I do claim with conviction that each of us, Christian or for that matter non-Christian, has a duty to form political and social judgements to the best of his or her ability. Which is not, of course, to suggest that most people should indulge in active politics.

And so I can imagine two people, men or women, political antagonists, kneeling in Church together and hearing the same passage from the Gospel. I can imagine them reaching, after much thought and prayer, totally opposite conclusions. In Matt. 25, the parable of the sheep and the goats, Jesus Christ says to us, 'I was in prison and you came to me. In so much as you did it to one of these my least brethren, you did it to me.' We can all agree that here is an instruction to visit prisoners or care for those in similar circumstances. Yet tremendous differences can open up when it comes to public policy. I struggle hard with the knowledge that born-again Christians often favour hanging, or indeed that for centuries that was the official line of the Church. I can only assert my own conviction that the more one reads the Gospels, the more one soaks oneself in the life of Jesus, the more such an attitude is repellent.

So, back to the Gospels. With supreme audacity I have written three small books which arise from my Gospel studies. One on humility, one on forgiveness and now, recently, one on suffering. In each case I boldly make the claim that Jesus Christ introduced a distinctive virtue. I feel no doubt about this and in so far as anybody has bothered to discuss my views no one has challenged them in this respect. It is admittedly difficult in, shall we say, Britain today when confronted with what Rosalind Toynbee once called 'a good pagan', to distinguish between what such a person owed to 'humanism' and what he or she derives from 2,000 years of Christian tradition. Clem (Lord) Atlee was once asked, 'Are you a Christian?' and he replied, 'Accept the Christian ethics. Can't stand the mumbo-jumbo.' Humanists could hardly claim him for their own in the light of his subsequent answers ('Are you an agnostic?' 'Don't know.' 'Do you believe in an after-life?' 'Possibly.') In fact his formation was strongly Christian and the supreme influence in his later life seems to have been his brother Tom, a Christian pacifist who went to prison in the First World War for his beliefs.

I personally consider that it would be a plausible argument against Christianity if Christians on average did not behave any better than those who lacked the priceless possession of the Christian faith. I say, on average. Of course I am aware that there are countless doctors and nurses in the Third World, or indeed in Britain, whose lives are much more edifying than mine or than those of many Christians. I retain the belief, however, that, if you know that someone is a practising Christian who says his or her prayers night and morning and, one hopes, goes to Church on Sundays at least, you will expect him or her to behave better than someone who does not possess any particular moral code. And Christians must be forgiven for thinking that their moral code is nobler than that of other religions.

As regards humility and forgiveness, I can honestly say that I have seldom met humanists, however high-minded, who preach those values explicitly, even when they practise them. Suffering is perhaps rather different. As I said in my small book on the subject, 'suffering is universal and all-pervasive, whether in the tortures and murders of Auschwitz or in minor pains'. That is said at the beginning of the book and at the end I write, 'it would be presumptuous and indeed ludicrous to pretend that Christians are the only people who confront suffering and death with courage'. But, as a Christian, I venture to claim from prolonged if circumscribed experience that Christians spring to even the more extreme forms of agony and invincible hope.

What is the specific moral in regard to suffering that one obtains from the New Testament? Suffering, as I point out in my book, figures very prominently in the narrative of the Gospels. But until we reach the Passion, it is the suffering that is healed by Jesus Christ. The great healing stories are equally attentive to physical and mental suffering. But when we reach the Passion and later reflect on the crucifixion and resurrection, we acquire a response to suffering that cannot be equalled elsewhere unless derived from the Christian story.

I shall be told that the idea of redemptive suffering is fore-shadowed in Isaiah, for instance, but it is not until the life and death of Christ and the reflections on them of the Christian Church that the doctrine takes shape in any way that can guide and inspire our lives.

In my book on suffering I ask three questions: 'How do we explain suffering? How do we bear our own suffering? How do we relieve the suffering of others?' Millions and millions of people are faced in practice with these questions and in practice have to provide their own answers or lack of answers. But the Christian is assured that the death of Christ was in some sense necessary for the rescue of humanity and the overcoming of evil.

Sister Frances Makower, helplessly bedridden, hardly able to move her limbs, can still write: 'While on the more superficial level I fight both pain and dependence, deep down I find myself grateful for my situation which draws me ever closer to the pierced heart of Christ, to whom I am consecrated and who continues to be reflected in the lives of the powerless, the suffering and the outcast.'

Margaret Spufford writes from within the physical pain of her own incurable disease and from within the mental pain of the fatal disease of her daughter. Nevertheless she can tell us that if we think of the glorified Lord as the disciples saw him before the Ascension, 'we may start thinking of the beauty of God achieved not in spite of pain but somehow through it'. She assures us with heartfelt conviction, 'In the contemplation of that beauty comes joy, not cheap joy but real joy.'

Mary Craig has had four children. One lived to the age of ten, one, much-loved, has Down's Syndrome, two others are fine, healthy, young men. Suffering, she says, is the key to the discovery of what we are and what we have in us to become if only we can summon the strength. No one has more gloriously summoned the strength or in a single book, *Blessings*, been more helpful in passing it on to others.

Professor Mahony, SJ, tells us that today there is a new stress on the theology of the resurrection. The theology of the resurrection, he tells us, 'Helps to explain and interpret the advancement of human culture where the Theology of the Cross and of suffering would not help to explain it. This does not, however, diminish the value of the theology of suffering where suffering cannot be dispelled. For it is here that Christ's work of healing and integrating is still in process and has not yet broken through to victory.'

I am not sure that my own thoughts keep pace with him here. Perhaps they will if I stick to it. At any rate, Christians possess what should be an overwhelming advantage in the inspiration derived from a total reading of the Passion.

Are Christians more humble than non-Christians, again on average? In my experience, they are; certainly they ought to be. Among my humanist friends, I do not find humility rated highly. Certainly it does not compare in their eyes with courage, or generosity, or dedication to a cause. Certainly Christ set an example of humility, unequalled by any other great leader in the world of thought or action. He washed the disciples' feet before the Last Supper. One does not forget that to wash feet at that time was the work of slaves. Again, 'Though he knew that the Father had given all things into His Hands, and that He came from God and was returning to God, He arose from the supper and laid aside his garments, and taking a towel, girded himself.' His teaching matched his example. He taught us that we must become like little children if we are to enter the Kingdom of God.

The humble Christian has admittedly a difficult task. He must see himself as infinitely unimportant compared with God, at the same time infinitely important in the sight of God. But with the teaching, example and grace of Jesus Christ he continues to struggle towards the ideal.

And forgiveness? Here again the teaching and example go always together. Every day, once or twice at least, Christians say the Lord's Prayer. 'Forgive us our trespasses, as we forgive them that trespass against us.' We are told to forgive someone who wrongs us seventy times seven, in other words indefinitely. And no one ever practised what he preached so sublimely as Jesus Christ on the Cross. He called out in his agony, 'Father, forgive them for they know not what they do.'

In my book on forgiveness, I make the claim that forgiveness, like humility and the Christian approach to suffering, was introduced by Christ. I do not find it claimed by Jewish friends that you can find the Christian idea of forgiveness in the Old Testament, though they claim, in my view not quite convincingly, that you can find it in the Talmud. Here again in Britain today, it is impossible to distinguish the forgiveness that comes from 2,000 years of Christian culture from the forgiveness which springs directly from contemporary Christian belief. But as with humility, so with forgiveness you find little if anything about it in humanist writing.

Finally, there is Charity. Here I make a different sort of claim. Mercifully it is universal for human beings to love someone, perhaps many people, perhaps everyone known to them. But Christ said, 'A new commandment I give to you, love one another *as I have loved you.*' Here again is the teaching example, and, if we make ourselves acceptable, the Grace.

Above are a few reflections of someone who calls himself a Gospel Christian. If they offend anyone, Christian or non-Christian, by assuming to claim a moral superiority which is most unattractive, I can assure him or her that I am not speaking about my own performance. I am claiming, however timidly, that the Christians who read their Gospels regularly have a unique source of strength which it is their overwhelming duty to share with all their fellow human beings.

Chapter 11

The Bible and Ordinary People

Christopher Lewis

Bible and Church

Jews, Christians and Muslims are distinguished by their books: they are 'peoples of the book'. Of course, when actual practice is studied, such generalizations require qualification, but nevertheless a sacred book has its central place in each religion. There it is, its great size often emphasizing its importance – to be treated with respect and read with care, even with veneration. But does it reach its people?

For many Christians, the Bible is in itself the revelation of God, to be given supreme place as an authority far above conclusions reached by any other means such as human reason (and experience) and the teachings of the Church. For others, the Bible is one among other 'authorities' and is therefore given a less prominent place. Nevertheless, as the sole record of the key events on which Christianity depends, it follows that for all Christians the Bible is an essential witness to the truth.

Whichever of the many possible positions is adopted, the importance of the book is not disputed. What then should be done with it? How are people to be made aware of its vital significance? Should it perhaps be advertised? Or should it be given out free at supermarket doors so that it is taken home with other necessities and used by each as he or she chooses?

This last question would be answered positively by those who freely distribute the Bible or parts of it (often one of the Gospels), for they see it as containing words of life which can be seen plainly by anyone who has the chance. All should therefore be given access to the Bible, for otherwise they might miss the crucial encounter with the truth which opens up the opportunity for faith. That is the motive of the Gideons, who take great care to make sure that hotel rooms have a Bible by every bed and who also distribute them through training institutions and schools.

Yet even in the case of the Gideons, the question of mediation rears its head. Is it enough merely to make the book available by placing it by the bed? The implied answer is 'no', for texts are selected by the Gideons, mainly for those in trouble (when 'anxious or worried' or when 'tempted') although also for those who are, for example, 'contemplating marriage' or 'feeling strong'. What amounts to a bible within the Bible is printed at the beginning; a point of entry is thus provided to 'the inspired Word of God'. There are selected readings on a number of different aspects of Christian belief and a telephone number and address for people to contact if they have difficulties in understanding the Bible's meaning or any other questions.

How can the Bible be used and understood by people other than scholars? It is a question to which the Gideons give one contemporary answer, but it was of course a principal Reformation question. And the answer given then was that the scriptures should be translated into a language which people could understand and then publicly read and preached upon. Only in this way could the allegorical and mystical interpretations of the medieval Church be side-stepped and doctrines such as that of justification by faith 'discovered' by ordinary people. The Church may have been responsible for 'forming' the Bible, having chosen what should be included and excluded in the canon of scripture, but once the shape of the Bible had been arrived at, then it had an existence of its own perhaps over against the Church. The Church did not own it, nor – whatever its representatives claimed – did it have a monopoly of interpretation.

So the aim was to narrow, to bridge, or to avoid the perpetual gap between the religion of the lettered and the unlettered. Erasmus had shown the way with his biblical paraphrases which were produced specifically in order to bring the Bible to the ordinary person. He held that the ploughman ought to be able to recite scripture while ploughing and the weaver while humming to the music of his shuttle. His simpler, more biblical, theology was the 'egg' which Luther later hatched.

When Luther translated the New Testament into German it was in order to bring it into the homes of the ordinary people. They were to study it as a complement to regular preaching from the minister. And the aim was at least partially fulfilled both in the churches of the Reformation and in Counter Reformation Catholicism. Whether the Church was seen as the means for understanding the Bible or the Bible was believed to give authority to challenge the Church, the Bible became better known. At the same time printing and increased literacy provided the means. The pocket version is not an invention of the twentieth century but of the seventeenth.

Soon, however, the question was not only the eternal chicken-and-egg matter of which comes first, Bible or Church, for it was joined by an apparent threat to the Bible itself. Once it was in the hands of all and sundry it could be put to other uses than that of devotion, for it could also be studied as a book more or less like any other. Put it in the hands of the people and there is no knowing what they will do with it.

As different disciplines became distinct and developed, so they were applied to the Bible. How, for example (and it is still an example!) did its account of the events of the creation of the world accord with evidence from elsewhere? Whatever the clever answers, doubts were sown. And how had the Bible come to be in its present form? As early as 1678 Richard Simon, a French Oratorian priest, published a book which used careful study of the Old Testament to show that Moses was not the author of the Pentateuch. He had studied the text, and found differences of style and more than one account of some events. He was expelled from his order, but such an action by the Church could not prevent his work from being used, built on and gradually popularized.

The spirit of criticism was beginning to be abroad. The age of innocence concerning the biblical texts was being left behind, at least in certain exalted circles, although it was not until the middle of the nineteenth century that the controversies came fully into the open. Was a critical study of the Bible in some sense a criticism of God or at least of central beliefs of the Christian faith? Even if the answer to this question appeared to be 'yes', should not the truth be pursued fearlessly?

Avoiding the Bible

In the contemporary Church, the debate is usually carried on in terms of biblical fundamentalism. Fundamentalism is the term commonly used for those who treat the Bible as a divinely guaranteed repository of knowledge and will only have it interpreted in a particular way on the grounds that other ways represent a diminution of authority. Without sure ground for authority there is a loss of religious certainty. The attitude to the Bible is then reinforced by preaching and by getting together with other like-minded people. The Bible does not err, although there may be a need for other supportive people to help in seeing where the truth lies.

In the debate, fundamentalists are ranged against those who interpret the Bible in a more liberal manner, conscious both of the way in which the books of the Bible came to be written, their social and religious contexts, and of the twentieth-century context in which the Bible is now read. Here authority is more dispersed, the journey towards the truth being travelled by reference to a number of authorities.

Yet to arrange the debate in this way is misleading. It is too neat and extreme a polarization, but it also misses the way in which many people who are not scholars come to the Bible. They may have learned to say that it is enormously important but may in fact not read it. Such an observation calls to mind the survey figures quoted by Will Herberg,[1] where it was found that over 80 per cent of Americans believed the Bible to be the revealed word of God, but 53 per cent could not name even one of the four Gospels.

People may not read it because they do not read books at all, or because when they try to read the Bible they find it impenetrable, even though they know from school or elsewhere that it is held to be of crucial significance. I once stayed in a house where a child had won three prizes at school, all Bibles and all neatly arranged on the shelf beside each other, bearing no evidence of ever having been opened. Those who point to sales of Bibles as evidence of faith should attend to such examples.

There are many Christians who have always preferred to read about the Bible than to read the book itself. They have found this more informative, with all the hard work of weaving together different strands of meaning already done for them. To pick up an entertaining paperback which gives some insight into the life of the Christian and is full of contemporary illustrations is often a more attractive proposition than tackling the Bible. Or better still, in an age when other media than books predominate, many prefer to watch and listen. After all, faced with a Bible, where do you start?

Also, if the Bible seems to be the property of one particular group and that group is abhorrent for other reasons – for example they are perceived as arrogant – then the Bible will be avoided and other religious experiences sought instead. God, after all, is often believed to reveal himself in other ways as well as through the written word about him, so participating in worship, engaging in work with the poor or discovering God by reflecting on the wonders of his creation may all become alternatives to coming to grips with the Bible.

So there are a number of ways of avoiding the Bible and a variety of reasons for doing so. The main area on which I wish to focus, however, is more collective. I shall use the Church of England as an example as it is the Church which I know best, although in this respect as in others it is not unique. In many parishes of the Church of England there is a kind of conspiracy to avoid discovering how to interpret the Bible, which means that people have a justification for not learning from it. The conspiracy starts with the clergy. They may fear that to read the Bible seriously will lead inevitably into a discussion of biblical criticism and therefore will undermine the faith of people who feel that the Bible (even the Bible unread) is the only sure foundation.

When I worked in a theological college the staff became used to students and other critics who considered the place to be an ivory tower from which students were eager to escape into the real world of parish life. In the theological college, it was said, the concerns were academic in the worst sense, whereas in the parish the true questions were being addressed, for here the Christian faith was experienced and lived in the context of everyday life.

It is worth asking whether this view represents a true picture of parishes. No doubt some of the concerns of theological colleges were esoteric, but there seemed to be a firm intention to engage with the Bible as it is and then to reflect on it in the light of the issues which were really of concern to many people. Whereas in a parish, truth is often not pursued in the same way. The reason given is that of pastoral sensitivity – that actually to read and study the Bible in the light both of contemporary knowledge about it and of contemporary issues, would undermine simple faith.

The result is that clergy discuss the Bible but 'not in front of the servants'. It is reminiscent of the case of Edward Benson, later to be Archbishop of Canterbury, who defended the fact that there was a copy of the controversial book *Essays and Reviews* in Wellington College in the 1860s on the grounds that it was not accessible to the boys. In other words, the masters should be exposed to all kinds of learning and in this case to a book which held that the results of biblical criticism could not be ignored, whereas the faith of the boys should be protected.

An example of such an attitude in the contemporary Church can be found in preaching. For many clergy, preparation of the weekly sermon (or two) will be the main occasion for some reading and for systematic reflection. What most in fact preach is the conclusions of this reflection, with the working not shown. If questioned, this method is justified on the grounds that a sermon is to strengthen faith (often in the devotional context of the eucharist) and that there is not the time nor is this the place to conduct a Bible study. Also that the preacher preaches as a representative of the Church and it follows that he should preach what the Church teaches. Clergy without tenure have said that they fear the loss of their jobs if they were to say how they interpret the Bible.

The consequence is that people hear some reflections on a biblical passage which often amount to the hanging of a theme on a biblical peg, but there is little or no study of what the biblical writer is trying to say or of the various stages of theological reflection which might lead into guidance for Christian life now. Perhaps there are other occasions when the working is shown, but often this is not the case.

If the people listening to the sermon are, in the view of the preacher, being protected from fundamentalists on the one flank and from speculative theologians on the other, then in an age which stresses the importance of an educated and participative laity, they should perhaps be told. Who is protecting whom – and from what?

The fear on the part of the clergy may be that they could not handle the question of biblical interpretation if it were raised. For there could then be profound questions among their 'flock' about central tenets of the faith: the creation, the incarnation, the resurrection. And also profound reflections might arise on the revolutionary nature of the Gospel and its demands. Once exploration is engaged in, there is no knowing where it will end. Beliefs would be re-examined.

Yet the conspirators are not only clergy. Leslie Houlden tells the story[2] of standing around talking before a parish meeting to which he was to speak about the New Testament. 'The Vicar came up to me and said, "Do be careful what you say. I like the kind of thing you say, but my people are easily upset by new ideas about the Bible and their faith." A minute later, a member of the group came up and said, "Do be careful what you say. We like the things you stand for, but the Vicar easily gets upset by new ideas." ' There can be a conspiracy which makes a congregation into more of a closed world than any academic institution. Yet they did ask him!

The way to dispel those fears is to study the Bible, letting it speak for itself. Now that historical knowledge and biblical scholarship have given us some understanding of the context in which different parts of the Bible were written, we can begin to study what the writers of the various books of the Bible were trying to convey. Often the most striking and challenging Bible studies are those which do this and little more, with the next stage completed by the hearers; the attempt is to read the Bible without making too ready a jump to the check-list of questions which we may want answered. Once we have learned as best we can what the writers were saying, then some application to our own situation may be in order.

Bible Study

The crucial question to ask is: can such a process be engaged by putting the Bible in the hands of the people and if so, what help is needed? The most common approach to Bible study is for a group to be formed, studying a theme with a leader, and with prepared material as a guide. The consequence is that the combination of leader and material is so powerful that the writers of the biblical books have little chance to be heard and nor do most of the participants in the group get much of a word in either. Whether in more protestant or more catholic contexts, it is therefore the Church in one form or another which is listened to, and the main consequence of Bible study is to confirm people in beliefs already held. Faith may be deepened, but the pastoral interest is dominant; no risks are taken. The tidy authority of the Church is maintained. A private world, an ivory tower, is created. In these circumstances, a constant reformation is needed (which paradoxically includes the most protestant circles) in order to put the Bible in the hands of the people.

One option is for the individual to study the Bible alone, perhaps with a commentary, and to try to discover what it has to say and then what it has to say to the person concerned. That is what many people do, but it is lonely work and probably not suited to all. The stimulus of other people also searching for truth and wishing to take the Bible seriously is a help in a task which is not simple. Insights concerning the biblical text can be shared, as can experiences of life and as can action in the world. Groups, well led, often show great resilience in handling hard questions.

On the matter of biblical study the methods of 'basic communities' in Latin America are instructive. Insights from a very different culture are not immediately transferable, so the picture painted by Leonardo Boff[3] is not quite ready for Middlesbrough or Potters Bar: 'The group may meet under a huge tree and every week they are found there, reading the sacred texts, sharing their commentaries, praying, talking of life, and making decisions about common projects.' Yet here and elsewhere in the methods of the Latin American Church are important themes. The study takes place as part of the activity of a community, coming together to listen to what the biblical writers say. A theologian (perhaps in the form of a commentary!) may be part of the group, but not in order to dictate what the text means. The professional is part of the community as a servant of the group; it is essential for the group to appreciate that it is not impossible for ordinary people to read the Bible. Where the theological professional is important is to bring another perspective to the meeting, and where he or she is there in person to listen and learn.

Then, perhaps most important of all is the question of what 'study' of the Bible means. The picture we may have is one of people sitting in comfortable chairs in a warm room (or indeed under a tree), reading the text and thereby learning something. Latin American theologians, however, point out that this by itself can be a very academic matter. For the situation of the people participating in the study is itself a part of the study. As they listen to the biblical writers and bring their insights and experiences to the group, so they may discover what it means to act like Jesus. It is in the action that the interpretation of the text is completed. So the Bible may both challenge the assumptions brought to it and also be a stimulus not only to reflection but also to individual and corporate activity.

Lessons may thus be learned from another culture. Ideally, the text is allowed to speak for itself without being drowned by people 'bringing questions' to it or being keen instantly to find something which 'strikes a chord' or illustrates a theme. Some modern British material adopts this kind of approach,[4] but often the final part of what some Latin American theologians call the 'hermeneutic circle' (the ethical consequences) is not included.

Whatever the culture, it is important that the primary source-book for Christians be in the hands of the people. The task of the Church and its representatives is to enable that genuinely to be the case. So here are some guidelines: to enable people to meet and study the Bible; to provide material which helps them to hear what the writers are saying in their own context; not to provide pre-determined answers; not to be afraid of the consequences of Bible study either for the individual or for the Church.

Chapter 12

The Bible and Ethics
Peter Baelz

Biblical Morality and its Claim to Authority

THE BIBLE THEN AND NOW

It is misleading to look to the Bible directly for solutions to the concrete moral problems which confront us today, whether these are personal, as in the sphere of sexuality and family life, or structural, as in the sphere of economic and social policies.

The reasons why it is misleading are several. First, the moral problems which concern us today are rarely identical with the moral problems which concerned the biblical writers. There is doubtless a general likeness between them, human nature being what it is, but the passage of time has brought significant changes to both detail and circumstance.

Second, the Bible is not a single document. It is a series of documents, composed, collected and edited over a period of approximately one thousand years. Careful reading reveals that these documents do not all speak with a single voice. For example, rules of purity and holiness governing daily life, such as are to be found in Leviticus, are either set aside or transformed in the writings of some of the prophets and in the teaching of Jesus.

Third, there is the all-important question of difference of culture. The unspoken assumptions which governed everyday beliefs and expectations then are not the unspoken assumptions governing everyday beliefs and expectations in our technological and largely secular society today. We have, then, to ask ourselves the hard question whether biblical morality is bound and restricted to biblical culture, or whether in some way it can transcend the limits of its own culture and speak to us authoritatively also today. Granted that we ascribe to the Bible a measure of real authority in moral matters, how are we to envisage such authority?

BIBLICAL AUTHORITY AND CULTURAL CONTEXT

Does the biblical text, just as it is, carry timeless, ultimate and unconditional authority? Does it of itself provide the given and unquestioned starting point for our own moral decisions?

Or does the text mark a succession of moments in a living tradition of insight and reflection, arising out of a community's historical experience and embodying that community's own interpretation of its experience? Is the authority of 'revelation' mediated through the culturally conditioned – and consequently limited and limiting – filter of human experience and judgement? If so, then the biblical text is an amalgam of vision and interpretation, and presents us with the task of discriminating between teaching that continues to be valid for us today and teaching that has lost s va idity through the passage of time.

Such a task, necessary as it becomes, once all ideas of an absolute textual authority have been rejected, is by no means as easy as might at first be thought. How, and by what criteria, are we now to judge what does and what does not remain morally valid? Are we thrown back simply on our own native moral convictions? If so, what happens to the 'authority' which we had previously ascribed to the Bible? To put it baldly, why bother with the Bible in the first place?

THE TASK OF INTERPRETATION
At the risk of over-simplification, I want to put forward just two considerations. First, we are right to give an important place to our own moral experience, insight and judgement. We may not evade the moral responsibility of making up our own minds. That is part of what it means to be a moral being and to act conscientiously.

Second, we should at the same time recognize that our own moral convictions are neither timelessly nor necessarily true. On the contrary, they arise out of a continuing process of listening, learning and responding. In this process due attention and weight has to be given to the experience and judgements of others, especially of those, past and present, who have gained our considered personal respect.

As this process of learning and responding develops, our moral experience begins to take shape and our moral insights acquire a distinctive pattern with a centre and focus. This focused pattern we may call, if we wish, a moral 'vision'. Such a vision has both pattern and power, for it directs and shapes our subsequent moral judgements and actions. Vision and response interact.

In short, the moral authority of the Bible does not reside in the bare text and its uncritical appropriation. Rather, it resides in the central and controlling moral vision which the Bible elicits from us when we engage with it in open, responsive and discerning dialogue. To this dialogue we bring our own experience and insights as well as the insights we have learned and appropriated from other sources, not least from the living tradition in which we have been nurtured.

In one sense the moral authority of the Bible remains, as we had originally assumed, a matter of 'given'-ness, acceptance and faith. But in another and equally valid sense it also becomes a matter of discovery, discernment and recognition. Furthermore, in this latter sense it depends in part on the continuing life and reflection of the community to which the Bible has given rise and which it continues to shape.

The Heart of Biblical Morality

GOODNESS AND GODLINESS

'The Lord has told you mortals what is good, and what it is that the Lord requires of you: only to act justly, to love loyalty, to walk humbly with your God' (Mic. 6:8).

Throughout both Old and New Testaments it is assumed that morality has its roots in religion. Right actions flow from right relationships, and right relationships between human beings are established on the basis of a right relationship with God, whether with God as Creator, as in his covenant with Noah (Gen. 9), or with God as Redeemer, as in his covenant with Moses (Exod. 24). So, when Jesus tells his disciples to love their enemies and to pray for their persecutors, he adds: 'Only by so doing can you be children of your heavenly Father, who causes the sun to rise on good and bad alike, and sends the rain on the innocent and wicked' (Matt. 5:45). Similarly, the writer to the Ephesians, summing up his moral teaching, writes: 'In a word, as God's dear children, you must be like him' (Eph. 5:1).

Morality, so understood, reflects the mind and purposes of God. It is grounded, not in any arbitrary human decision, whether individual or corporate, but in the very order of things that God has established. To act morally is to go with the grain of God's universe. To act immorally is to go against that grain. In the Old Testament certain forms of immoral behaviour are described as an 'abomination' (Hebrew: *toebah*). The basic meaning of this word seems to be a 'violation of natural and proper order' (cf. Lev. 18: 22–3).

ORDER AND COVENANT

Within the created order, according to which everything has its own proper nature and place, God has established a 'covenant', or firm relationship, with humankind, and especially with his people Israel.

This covenant is the free expression of God's loving-kindness and grace. At one and the same time it is a promise of fullness of life and a call to obedience:

Today I offer you the choice of life and good, or death and evil. If you obey the commandments of the Lord your God which I give you this day, by loving the Lord your God, conforming to his ways, and keeping his commandments, statutes, and laws, then you will live and increase . . . But if in your heart you turn away and do not listen, and you are led astray to worship other gods and serve them, I tell you here and now that you will perish. (Deut. 30:15f.)

This theme of life and death recurs throughout the Bible. It is found in the teaching of Jesus and Paul as well as in the Law and the Prophets of the Old Testament (cf. Mark 9:43; John 10:10; Rom. 6: 20–3).

COVENANT AND COMMUNITY

God's covenant establishes communities of right relationship. Together these relationships are an expression of love, justice and peace. They embrace relations between between man and man, man and woman, family and family, master and servant, resident and alien, nation and nation. Their character reflects the character of God himself – faithfulness, righteousness, loving-kindness and mercy.

COMMUNITY AND LAW

These relationships are protected and promoted by the 'commandments, statutes and laws' of God. Whatever damages such relationships is forbidden, whatever protects and nourishes them is enjoined. Thus the whole of life, economic, social, sexual and political, is subject to the divine order. If this order is kept, life will flourish, and God's people can look forward to peace and prosperity. If this order is broken, the outcome will be destruction and death. Thus obedience will have its due reward, disobedience its due punishment.

LAW AND LIBERTY

Biblical morality is a morality of 'obedience'. What God has commanded is to be obeyed because God has commanded it. However, the commands of God are not the commands of an arbitrary and inscrutable tyrant. They express a care and loving-kindness which are at the heart of God's covenant with his people. Hence the order that God has established as the norm of human behaviour is also the pattern of human blessedness and fulfilment. The requirements of this order have, not inaptly, been called 'the Maker's instructions'. Their observance leads to life, their infringement to death.

LAW AND WISDOM

The divine order is also the expression of the divine wisdom. In the course of time both Torah (instruction, law) and Wisdom were personified and believed to be present with God at creation. The divine order is reflected, therefore, not only in the various codes of law to be found in the Bible, but also in the many 'sayings' of 'the Wise'. Thus a tradition of wisdom, based on experience and reflection, and finding expression in proverbs and parables, marches hand in hand with a tradition of law, expressed in rules and regulations. Jesus himself, according to the witness of the Gospels and Epistles, stands within this tradition of Wisdom as well as in the tradition of the Law and the Prophets.

Biblical Morality Today

MORALITY AND RELIGION

Today a biblical morality rooted in religion faces the objection that anyone who does not believe in God is thereby excluded from its moral universe. From the viewpoint of a religious morality such a person can possess no ultimate grounds for acting morally.

It is also objected that unquestioning obedience, whether to God or to anyone else, itself needs moral justification if it is to be anything other than prudential. The promise of reward for obedience, and the threat of punishment for disobedience, reduces morality to a matter of calculated self-interest. The only moral reason for acting in one way rather than another, it is argued, is that such an action tends either to increase the amount of shared human happiness or at least to decrease the amount of shared human misery.

MORALITY AND HUMANITY

The main point of these objections need not be disputed, even by those standing in the biblical tradition. It need not be denied, for example, that morality is concerned essentially with human flourishing. We have spoken of the divine law metaphorically as 'the Maker's instructions'. There is nothing arbitrary about a maker's instructions. They are to ensure the good working of the artefact. So the divine law is concerned with the 'good working' of humanity, that is, with human flourishing. Both those who believe in God and those who do not can agree on the point and object of morality, even when they disagree on its ultimate grounding.

Agreement on the point of morality is one thing. Agreement on its grounding is another. But there is still a third area – probably the most important of all – where agreement may or may not occur. This third area concerns the content of morality.

No doubt there will be a large measure of agreement by almost everyone on many of the things that constitute and define human flourishing. But not on everything. Some may regard as acceptably human forms of behaviour that others reject as unacceptably inhuman, such as abortion, or capital punishment. It must be noted, however, that on these and other concrete issues differences of moral judgement occur among believers themselves, and not only between believers and unbelievers.

MORALITY, REWARD AND PUNISHMENT

Since morality is concerned with human flourishing, the biblical themes of reward and punishment may be interpreted in terms of the actual consequences of moral and immoral behaviour. Human well-being is the 'reward', or outcome, of righteousness. Similarly, human diminishment is the 'punishment', or outcome, of unrighteousness. It must be remembered, however, that these 'rewards' and 'punishments' are not external inducements or threats. They are part of the order of things that God has created. And they take into account not the interests of the individual in isolation, since that would make them considerations merely of prudence, but the interests of the community as a whole.

MORALITY, OBEDIENCE AND MORAL RESPONSIBILITY

The obedience called for by God from his people need not be understood as an unreasoned or unquestioning obedience. It is true that God's commands are to be obeyed because they are God's commands. But the underlying and unspoken assumption is that God is a God of loving-kindness and mercy, and that his commands are therefore for his people's good. Furthermore, since human error can never be completely ruled out, it is always necessary to ask if what has been perceived as God's command really is God's command. To answer this question, tried and tested moral convictions concerning the character of God and his purposes for human well-being become an important touchstone. (The objection to the apparently divine origin of the law that a woman taken in adultery should be stoned to death [Deut. 22:23–4; cf. John 9:2–11] is the moral objection that such a law contradicts the known character of God's loving-kindness and mercy.)

Obedience to God is best interpreted as a kind of responsiveness. Such obedience is not incompatible with a sense of responsibility, moral reflection and freedom of choice. But it is only when individuals and societies act in accordance with the divinely established moral order that they are truly free. Disobedience leads to disorder. Disorder leads to ruin. An arbitrary and wilful freedom is no freedom at all. True freedom is the freedom of an appropriate, thoughtful and 'obedient' response. 'If you stand by my teaching, you are truly my disciples; you will know the truth, and the truth will set you free' (John 8:31–2).

The Bible as Moral Resource

A COMMUNITY OF VISION

Part of what it means to be a human being is to have some vision of what it is to be a human being. Human beings have to reach out to become what they truly are.

The books of the Bible, taken together, are a record of a people's vision of the human community it is called to become, and of its interpretation of and response to that vision. The vision is expressed in the story of God's dealings with a world of his own creating and a people of his own calling.

For Jews the story is centred and focused on Moses and the liberation of the people of Israel from Egypt. For Christians the story is centred and focused on Jesus and his death and resurrection.

The vision determines the essential character of the community, its basic beliefs, attitudes and values, and plays a fundamental and continuing role in the community's formation. First and foremost it determines the sort of person a member of the community is to be, rather than the sort of deed that person is to do or to refrain from doing. In this way it gives rise to a morality of being rather than of doing, and it is sustained and nurtured by the use of the Bible for prayer and worship as well as, more specifically, for moral guidance.

PRINCIPLES AND PERSPECTIVES

What one is, however, cannot be divorced from how one acts. Character and action go together. Consequently the vision generates principles and perspectives which shape the way in which the community is to order its life and relationships. For example, common to both Jewish and Christian traditions is the centrality of the command to love one's neighbour as oneself (cf. Lev. 19:18; Mark 12:31). Care for the poor and outcast is another principle common to both Old and New Testaments. Non-violence is a principle which some Christians – though not the majority – believe to be essential to Christian self-understanding and obedience.

RULES AND REGULATIONS

Principles and perspectives need to be embodied in practical rules of action. Who is my neighbour? What does care for the poor and outcast involve? Is non-violence a desirable ideal that has in certain circumstances to give way to other principles, such as the principles of order and justice, or is it an unexceptionable obligation?

At this level of moral deliberation two things need to be noted. First, in any concrete situation it may not be possible to reconcile all the moral principles which one holds. Priorities need to be established and difficult decisions made. Sometimes compromise is necessary. What in normal circumstances is accepted as a binding moral rule may in certain abnormal circumstances no longer be judged to be morally binding. On the other hand there may be some fundamental moral rules, such as that which forbids the deliberate killing of innocent human beings, which are judged to admit of no exceptions. On this basis infanticide would not in any circumstances be morally permissible. (Whether direct abortion would ever be permissible would largely depend on the moral and human status of the embryo or foetus.)

Second, principles are more fundamental than rules. Rules may not adequately embody relevant principles. What is more, changing circumstances, or changing knowledge, may render existing rules inadequate or inappropriate.

It follows that the various moral rules which we find in different parts of the Bible need to be assessed in terms of the vision and principles to which the Bible bears witness and to which those who live in the biblical tradition are committed. For example, it is nowadays generally agreed that some social institutions, such as slavery, which were acceptable in biblical times, can in terms of the underlying biblical principles no longer be accepted. Similarly, it is still a debated question whether biblical attitudes to relations between the sexes reflect fundamental theological and moral principles or only antiquated cultural assumptions. Those who hold to the second view argue that in the light of fundamental biblical principles culture-based biblical androcentrism ought today to be rejected. Those who share the same vision and principles do not necessarily come to the same practical conclusions.

USING THE BIBLE FOR MORAL GUIDANCE

The Bible is not a textbook of moral dilemmas. It is a mistake to look for isolated texts to provide authoritative solutions to our present moral dilemmas, even if they are believed to express the teaching of Moses, or Paul, or Jesus. Texts belong to their contexts and need to be read and understood in their contexts. They may not simply be transferred from one context to another. At best, they are a useful reminder of a larger vision and a possible interpretation.

On particular moral issues, where the Bible may be thought to offer relevant guidance, it is wise to remember that different parts of it, addressed to different situations, may express different points of view. For example, on questions of sexual love Genesis, Proverbs, the Song of Songs, 1 Corinthians and 1 Timothy take very different approaches and have very different things to say. To respond faithfully to the biblical vision it is not necessary to accept everything that is said in the Bible, nor to try somehow or other to harmonize it all, but to listen to what is said and to assess it in the light of the biblical vision and the best insights and actual circumstances of today.

Two last points. First, we should not hesitate to recognize that some important moral insights consonant with the biblical vision of true humanity have originated from individuals and communities outside the biblical tradition. This is not surprising. If, as the biblical tradition maintains, human beings are the creatures of God, then it is not to be expected that all insight into what makes and keeps human life human will be restricted to any one tradition.

Second, the biblical emphasis on holiness, which could so easily lead to a kind of moral separatism linked to a code of moral 'purity', can also be interpreted as a reminder that the springs of morality lie deeper than morality itself. Conformity to moral rules falls short of that truly human response of heart and mind to which those who have been created in the image of God and who are destined for eternity are called. 'When you have carried out all you have been ordered to do, you should say, "We are servants and deserve no credit; we have only done our duty" ' (Luke 17:10). Humanity finds its origin and goal in the love with which God loves his whole creation.

Chapter 13

The Bible and Killing for Food

Andrew Linzey

> And God said, 'Behold, I have given you every plant yielding seed which
> is upon the face of all the earth, and every tree with seed in its fruit;
> you shall have them for food. And to every beast of the earth, and to
> every bird of the air, and to everything that creeps on the earth, every-
> thing that has the breath of life, I have given every green plant for food.'
> (Gen. 1:29–30; RSV).

> And God blessed Noah and his sons, and said to them '. . . Every
> moving thing that lives shall be food for you; as I gave you the green
> plants, I give you everything.' (Gen. 9:1–4; RSV).

At first glance, these two passages may be taken as epitomizing the
difficulty of appealing to scripture in the contemporary debate about
animal rights. The sheer contradictoriness of these statements
presses itself upon us. Genesis 1 clearly depicts vegetarianism as
divine command. Indeed 'everything' that has the breath of life in
it, is given 'green plant for food'. Genesis 9, however, reverses this
command quite specifically. '(A)s I gave you the green plants, I give
you everything' (9:3). In the light of this, the question might not
unreasonably be posed: cannot both vegetarians and carnivores
appeal to scripture for justification and both with *equal* support?

Food of Paradise

In order to unravel this conundrum we have first of all to appreciate
that those who made up the community whose spokesperson wrote
Genesis 1 were not themselves vegetarians. Few appreciate that
Genesis 1 and 2 are themselves the products of much later reflection
by the biblical writers themselves. How is it then that the very
people who were not themselves vegetarian imagined a beginning
of time when all who lived were vegetarian (herbivore to be precise)
by divine command?

To appreciate this perspective we need to recall the major elements
of the first creation saga. God creates a world of great diversity and
fertility. Every living creature is given life and space (Gen. 1:9–10;
24–5). Earth to live on and blessing to enable life itself (1:22). Living

creatures are pronounced good (1:25). Humans are made in God's image (1:27) given dominion (1:26–9), and then prescribed a vegetarian diet (1:29–30). God then pronounces that everything was 'very good' (1:31). Together the whole creation rests on the sabbath with God (2:2–3). When examined in this way, we should see immediately that Genesis 1 describes a state of paradisal existence. There is no hint of violence between or among different species. Dominion, so often interpreted as justifying killing, actually precedes the command to be vegetarian. Herb-eating dominion is hardly a licence for tyranny. The answer seems to be then that even though the early Hebrews were neither pacifists nor vegetarians, they were deeply convinced of the view that violence between humans and animals, and indeed between animal species themselves, was not God's original will for creation.

But if this is true, how are we to reconcile Genesis 1 with Genesis 9, the vision of original peacefulness with the apparent legitimacy of killing for food? The answer seems to be that as the Hebrews began to construct the story of early human beginnings, they were struck by the prevalence and enormity of human wickedness. The stories of Adam and Eve, Cain and Abel, Noah and his descendants are testimonies to the inability of humankind to fulfil the providential purposes of God in creation. The issue is made explicit in the story of Noah:

> Now the earth was corrupt in God's sight, and the earth was filled with violence. And God saw the earth, and behold, it was corrupt; for all flesh had corrupted their way upon the earth. And God said to Noah, 'I have determined to make an end of all flesh; for the earth is filled with violence through them.' (Gen. 6:11–14; RSV).

The radical message of the Noah story (so often overlooked by commentators) is that God would rather not have us be at all if we must be violent. It is violence itself within every part of creation that is the pre-eminent mark of corruption and sinfulness. It is not for nothing that God concludes: 'I am sorry that I have made them' (Gen. 6:7).

Ambiguous Permission

It is in *this* context – subsequent to the Fall and the Flood – that we need to understand the permission to kill for food in Genesis 9. It reflects entirely the situation of the biblical writers at the time they were writing. Killing – of both humans as well as animals – was simply inevitable given the world as it is and human nature as it is. Corruption and wickedness had made a mess of God's highest hopes for creation. There just had to be some accommodation to human sinfulness. 'Every moving thing shall be food for you; and as I gave you the green plants, I give you everything' (Gen. 9:3). For many students of the Bible this seems to have settled the matter of whether humans can be justified in killing animals for food. In the end, it has been thought, God allows it. And there can be no doubt that throughout the centuries this view has prevailed. Meat eating has become the norm. Vegetarians, especially Christian vegetarians, have survived from century to century to find themselves a rather beleaguered minority. The majority view can be summed up in this beautifully prosaic line of Calvin:

> For it is an insupportable tyranny, when God, the Creator of all things, has laid open to us the earth and the air, in order that we may thence take food as from his storehouse, for these to be shut up from us by mortal man, who is not able to create even a snail or a fly.[1]

What Calvin appears to overlook, however, as has most of the Christian tradition, is that the permission to kill for food in Genesis 9 is far from unconditional or absolute:

> Only you shall not eat flesh with its life, that is, its blood. For your lifeblood I will surely require a reckoning; of every beast I will require it and of man . . . (Gen. 1:4–5; RSV).

Understanding these lines is far from straightforward. At first sight these qualificatory lines might be seen as obliterating the permission itself. After all, who can take animal life without the shedding of blood? Who can kill without the taking of blood, that is, the life itself? In asking these questions we move to the heart of the problem. For the early Hebrews life was symbolized by, even constituted by, blood itself. To kill *was* to take blood. And yet it is precisely *this* permission which is denied.

It is not surprising then that commentators have simply passed over these verses, suggesting that some ritual, symbolic significance was here entertained but one which in no way substantially affected the divine allowance to kill. But this, I suggest, is to minimize the significance of these verses. Rereading these verses in the light of their original context should go rather like this: The world in which you live has been corrupted. And yet God has not given up on you. God has signified a new relationship – a covenant with you – despite all your violence and unworthiness. Part of this covenant involves a new regulation concerning diet. What was previously forbidden can now – in the present circumstances – be allowed. You may kill for food. But you may kill only on the understanding that you remember that the life you kill is not your own – it belongs to God. You must not misappropriate what is not your own. As you kill what is not your own – either animal or human life – so you need to remember that for every life you kill you are personally accountable to God.[2]

If this reading is correct, and I believe few scholars would now dissent from this interpretation, it will be seen immediately that Genesis 9 does not grant humankind some absolute right to kill animals for food. Indeed, properly speaking, there is no *right* to kill. God allows it only under the conditions of necessity. A recent statement by the Union of Liberal and Progressive Synagogues expresses it this way: 'Only after the Flood (contends Genesis 9:3) was human consumption of animals permitted and that was later understood as a concession, both to human weakness and to the supposed scarcity of edible vegetation.'[3]

To give a more complete account of biblical themes requires us to move on from Genesis 1 and 2, to Isaiah 11. We need to appreciate that while killing was sometimes thought to be justifiable in the present time, biblical writers were also insistent that there would come another time when such killing was unnecessary. This is the time variously known as the 'future hope of Israel' or the 'Messianic Age'. Isaiah speaks of the one who will establish justice and equity and universal peace. One of the characteristics of this future age is the return to the existence envisaged by Genesis 1 before the Fall and the Flood:

> The wolf shall dwell with the lamb, and the leopard shall lie down with the kid, and the calf and the lion and the fatling together, and a little child shall lead them. The cow and the bear shall feed; their young shall lie down together; and the lion shall eat straw like the ox. The sucking child shall play over the hole of the asp, and the weaned child shall put his hand on the adder's den. They shall not hurt or destroy in all my holy mountain; for the earth shall be full of the knowledge of the Lord as the waters cover the sea. (Isa. 11:6–9; RSV).

It seems therefore that while the early Hebrews were neither vegetarians nor pacifists, the ideal of the peaceable kingdom was never lost sight of. In the end, it was believed, the world would one day be restored according to God's original will for all creation. Note, for example, how the vision of peaceable living also extends to relations between animals themselves. Not only, it seems, are humans to live peaceably with animals, but also formerly aggressive animals are to live peaceably with other animals.

We may sum up the main elements of the biblical approach as follows: killing for food appears essential in the world as we now know it, influenced as it is by corruption and wickedness. But such a state of affairs is not as God originally willed it. Even when we kill under situations of necessity we have to remember that the lives we kill do not belong to us and that we are accountable to God. Moreover, God's ultimate will for creation shall prevail. Whatever the present circumstances, one day all creation, human and animal, shall live in peace.

Living without Violence

It should now be seen that far from being confused and contradictory, the biblical perspectives on killing for food have not only internal integrity but also enormous relevance to the contemporary debate about animal rights and vegetarianism. There are three ethical challenges in particular that we should grapple with.

The first thing that should be noted is that the Bible does not minimize the gravity of the act of killing animals. So often in our heavily industrialized societies we think of animals, especially farm animals, as merely food machines or commodities that are to be bought or sold for human consumption. This can never be the biblical view. Genesis 1 specifically speaks of animal life as that which 'has the breath of life' (1:30). This life is a gift from God. It does not belong to human beings. It may be used only with the greatest reserve and in remembrance of the One from whose creative hands it comes. Those who wish to use animals frivolously or with no regard for their God-given worth cannot claim the Bible for their support.

Karl Barth is instructive on this point and deserves to be read in full:

> If there is a freedom of man to kill animals, this signifies in any case the adoption of a qualified and in some sense enhanced responsibility. If that of his lordship over the living beast is serious enough, it takes on a new gravity when he sees himself compelled to express his lordship by depriving it of its life. He obviously cannot do this except under the pressure of necessity. Far less than all the other things which he dares to do in relation to animals, may this be ventured unthinkingly and as though it were self-evident. He must never treat this need for defensive and offensive action against the animal world as a natural one, nor include it as a normal element in his thinking or conduct. He must always shrink from this possibility even when he makes use of it. It always contains the sharp counter-question: who are you, man, to claim that you must venture this to maintain, support, enrich and beautify your own life? What is there in your life that you feel compelled to take this aggressive step in its favour? We cannot but be reminded of the perversion from which the whole historical existence of the creature suffers and the guilt which does not really reside in the beast but ultimately in man himself.[4]

The second challenge is that we have no biblical warrant for claiming killing as God's will. God's will is for peace. We need to remember that even though Genesis 9 gives permission to kill for food it does so only on the basis that we do not misappropriate God-given life. Genesis 9 posits divine reckoning for the life of every beast taken even under this new dispensation (9:5). The question may not unnaturally be asked: how long can this divine permission last? Karl Barth writes that 'it is not only understandable but necessary that the affirmation of this whole possibility [of killing for food] should always have been accompanied by a radical protest against it'. And yet he concludes: 'It may well be objected against a vegetarianism which presses in this direction that it represents a wanton anticipation of what is described by Is. 11 and Rom. 8 as existence in the new aeon for which we hope.'[5] Whatever may be the merits of Barth's arguments here, it should be clear that Barth cannot and does not claim that killing is God's will. On the contrary it stands in direct contrast to the 'new aeon for which we hope' or, as he puts it elsewhere, 'under a caveat'.[6] In short: even though killing may be sometimes permissible, God will not tolerate it for ever.

In this respect it is interesting that one highly regarded Talmudic scholar, Abraham Isaac Kook, maintains that the most spiritually satisfying way of reading the practical biblical injunctions concerning killing is in terms of preparation for a new dawn of justice for animals. 'The free movement of the moral impulse to establish justice for animals generally and the claim for their rights from mankind,' he argues, 'are hidden in a natural psychic sensibility in the deeper layers of the Torah.' Given the corruption of humankind, it was natural and inevitable that moral attention had first to be paid to the regulation of human conduct towards other humans. But in Kook's view the various injunctions concerning the selection and preparation of meat (in, for example, Lev. 17:13; Ezek. 16:63; Lev. 22:28 and Deut. 22: 26–7) were commandments 'to regulate the eating of meat, in steps that will take us to the higher purpose'. And what is this higher purpose? None other it seems than universal peace and justice. Kook maintains that just as the embracing of democratic ideals came late within religious thinking 'so will the hidden yearning to act justly towards animals emerge at the proper time'.[7]

The third challenge to be grasped is that those who wish now to adopt a vegetarian or vegan lifestyle have solid biblical support. Biblical vegetarians will not say, 'It has *never been* justifiable to kill animals,' rather they should say, 'It is *not now* necessary to kill for food as it was once thought necessary.' The biblical case for vegetarianism does not rest on the view that killing may never be allowable in the eyes of God, rather on the view that killing is always a grave matter. When we have to kill to live we may do so, but when we do not, we should live otherwise. It is vital to appreciate the force of this argument. In past ages many – including undoubtedly the biblical writers themselves – have thought that killing for food was essential in order to live. We now know that – at least for those now living in the rich West – it is perfectly possible to sustain a healthy diet without any recourse to flesh products. This may not have always been true in the past. Conventional wisdom was always that meat was essential to live and to live well. Only during the past 200 years has vegetarianism become a publicly known and acceptable option.

Those individuals who opt for vegetarianism can do so in the knowledge that they are living closer to the biblical ideal of peaceableness than their carnivorous contemporaries. The point should not be minimized. In many ways it is difficult to know how we can live more peaceably in a world driven by violence and greed and consumerism. Individuals often feel powerless in the face of great social forces beyond even democratic control. To opt for a vegetarian lifestyle is to take one practical step towards living in peace with the rest of creation. It has been estimated that over 500 million animals are slaughtered for food in the UK every year. In the US the numbers are 6–9 billion annually. To become vegetarian is to take a practical step to reduce the rate of institutionalized killing in the world today. One fewer chicken eaten is one fewer chicken killed.

Nevertheless, we do well to appreciate the biblical perspective that we do not live in an ideal world. The truth is that even if we adopt a vegetarian or vegan lifestyle, we are still not free of killing either directly or indirectly. Even if we eat only beans and nuts and lentils, we have to reckon with the fact that competing animals are killed because of the crops we want to eat. Even if we decide not to wear dead animal skins, we have to face the fact that alternative substances have been tested for their toxicity on laboratory animals. Even if we eat only soya beans we do well to remember that these have been force fed to animals in painful experiments. As I have written elsewhere, there is no pure land.[8] If we embark on vegetarianism, as I think we should, we must do so on the understanding that for all its compelling logic, it is only *one* small step towards the vision of a peaceful world.

Prince of Peace

Before I conclude, there is one major – and some would say conclusive – objection to my pro-vegetarian thesis that should be considered. It is this: Jesus was no vegan and possibly no vegetarian.

There are no recorded examples of Jesus eating meat in the Gospels. The only possible exception is the Passover itself, but it is not clear, to say the least, that Jesus ate the traditional Passover meal. Jesus did, however, eat fish if the Gospel narratives are to be believed. How are we to reconcile this to the established Christian view of Jesus as the Prince of Peace? There are four possible answers to this question.

The first is that the canonical Gospels are mistaken and Jesus was actually a vegetarian. However implausible this view may appear, among those who are pro-animals there have always been a significant number who have never believed that Jesus ate the flesh of other living creatures.[9] Those who take this view argue that 'fish' in the New Testament did not actually mean fish as we know it today. Moreover it is sometimes argued that Jesus was really a member of the Essene sect who were, it seems, strict vegetarians. Indeed there are various 'Essene gospels' in which Jesus is depicted as a committed vegetarian.[10] On the face of it, it does seem highly unlikely that such a convenient view is true and the Essene gospels strike me as of rather doubtful antiquity. Nevertheless, I would like to keep an open mind. It is just conceivable that some of these gospels do somehow contain genuine historical reminiscences (we know so little about the historical Jesus in any case) but I think it is a rather remote possibility.

The second possible answer is that Jesus was not perfect in every conceivable way. Jews and Muslims would, of course, have no difficulty with this proposition but orthodox Christians would surely find this idea difficult. After all traditional Christian belief has always been that Jesus Christ was truly God and truly man. Most Christians would hold that being sinless was an essential part of being God incarnate. Those who argue that Jesus was not wholly perfect, however, are not, of course, wholly without biblical support. The question of Jesus: 'Why do you call me good?' And his answer: 'No one is good but God alone,' is recorded in all three synoptic Gospels (Luke 18:19; Matthew 19:17; Mark 10:18). Moreover, it is not inconceivable that Jesus could have been *both* God incarnate and less than morally perfect in every way. Some scholars, such as John Robinson, have maintained this.[11] Perhaps it could be argued that while Jesus committed no sin of commission (deliberate wrongdoing), it could be argued that of necessity every human being commits some sin of omission (things left undone). However, such a view certainly falls short of traditional Christian doctrine and biblical texts such as Hebrews 4:15 which argues that Jesus 'was tempted as we are, yet without sin'.

The third answer is that the killing of fish is not a morally significant matter or, at least, not as significant as the killing of mammals.

There is something to be said for this view. Even those who argue rigorously for animal rights sometimes do so on the basis that animals as God's creatures are 'subjects of a life' – that is they have sensitivity and consciousness and the ability to suffer – but it is not clear that all fish do actually possess all these characteristics. In many cases we simply do not know. This must mean, I think, that their moral status is somewhat different from those animals where self-consciousness and sentience can reasonably be taken for granted. Nevertheless, do not fish merit some benefit of the doubt? Are they not also fellow creatures with some God-given life and individuality which means that wherever possible their lives should be respected?

The fourth answer is that sometimes it can be justifiable to kill fish for food in situations of necessity. Such a situation, we may assume, was present in first-century Palestine where geographical factors alone seem to have suggested a scarcity of protein. Such a view would on the whole be more consistent with the biblical perspective that we may kill but only in circumstances of real need. Hence we may have to face the possibility that Jesus did indeed participate in the killing of some life forms in order to live. Indeed we may say that part of his being a human being at a particular stage and time in history necessitated that response in order to have lived at all.

Of all the four possible responses, I find this last one the most convincing. As I have indicated before, the biblical view is not that killing can never be justified and ought to be avoided at all costs. There are times, for example, when euthanasia may well be the most compassionate response to an individual undergoing unrelievable suffering. But even if we accept that killing for food may be justified in those situations of real necessity for human survival, such as may be argued in the case of Jesus himself, this is no way exonerates us from the burden of justifying what we now do to animals in circumstances substantially different. This last point is centrally important and must not be obscured. There may have been times in the past, or even now in the present, where we have difficulty imagining a life without killing for food. But *where we do have the moral freedom* to live without killing, without recourse to violence, there is a *prima facie* case that we should do so. To kill without the strict conditions of necessity is to live a life with insufficient generosity.

It would be wrong, however, to give the impression that the life and teaching of Jesus is a disappointment as far as the enlightened treatment of animals is concerned. While it is true that there is a great deal we do not know about Jesus's precise attitudes to animals, there is a powerful strand in his ethical teaching about the primacy of mercy to the weak, the powerless and the oppressed. Without misappropriation, it is legitimate to ask: who is more deserving of this special compassion than the animals commonly exploited in our world today? Moreover, it is often overlooked that in the canonical Gospels Jesus is frequently presented as identifying himself with the world of animals. As I have written elsewhere:

> His birth, if tradition is to be believed, takes place in the home of sheep and oxen. His ministry begins, according to Mark, in the wilderness 'with the wild beasts' (1:13). His triumphal entry into Jerusalem involves riding on a 'humble ass' (see Matthew 21:4–5). According to Jesus it is lawful to 'do good' on the Sabbath, which includes the rescuing of an animal fallen into a pit (see Matthew 12:10–12). Even the sparrows, literally sold for a few pennies in his day, are not 'forgotten before God' (Luke 12:6). God's providence extends to the entire created order, and the glory of Solomon and all his works cannot be compared to that of the lilies of the field (Luke 12:27). God so cares for his creation that even 'foxes have holes, and birds of the air have nests; but the Son of Man has nowhere to lay his head' (Luke 9:58).[12]

The significance of these and other verses may be much more than had previously been thought. One small example must suffice. Mark describes Jesus's ministry as taking place first within the context of wild animals (1:13). Richard Bauckham has recently argued that the context in which this verse should be understood is messianic in orientation. Jesus is shown to be in continuity with the Isaianic tradition in seeing the messianic age as bringing about a reconciliation between nature and humanity.[13] If this is true, it may be that Mark is seeking to demonstrate how the Gospel of Jesus has implications for the whole of the created world, and for harmony within the animal world in particular. Those who follow Jesus might argue that in seeking to realize what can now be realized in our own time and space of the messianic age is to live now in conformity with the Spirit of Jesus itself.

In conclusion, reference has already been made to how vegetarians have formed a rather beleaguered minority in times past. But it is worth recalling that not a few of the great figures in Christendom have adopted a vegetarian diet. Among these should not go unnoticed the countless saints who have expressed a particular regard for animals and opposed their destruction. 'Poor innocent little creatures,' exclaimed St Richard of Chichester when confronted with animals bound for slaughter. 'If you were reasoning beings and could speak you would curse us. For we are the cause of your death, and what have you done to deserve it?'[14] There has always been an ascetical strand within Christianity which has insisted that humans should live gently on the earth and avoid luxury food. The rule of life penned by St Benedict for his religious community, for example, expressly forbade the eating of meat. 'Except the sick who are very weak, let all abstain entirely from the flesh of four-footed animals.'[15] Moreover, it often comes as a surprise for Christians to realize that the modern vegetarian movement was strongly biblical in origin. Inspired by the original command in Genesis 1, an Anglican priest, William Cowherd, founded the Bible Christian Church in 1809 and made vegetarianism compulsory among its members. The founding of this Church in the United Kingdom and its sister Church in the United States by William Metcalfe, effectively heralded the beginning of the modern vegetarian movement.[16]

The subsequent, if rather slow, growth of vegetarianism from 1809 to 1970, and its rapid and astonishing growth from 1970 to the present day is testimony that Cowherd may have been right in his view that mainstream biblical theology had overlooked something of importance in Genesis 1. It may be that when the history of twentieth-century cuisine is finally written, the radical changes in diet which we are currently experiencing will be found to be due more to the rediscovery of two biblical verses (Gen. 1:29–30) than anything else. These two verses, we may recall, came into existence by people imagining possibilities in the light of their belief in God the Creator. By rekindling the same vision in our own time, we may be enabled to realize – at least in part – those possibilities which our forebears could only imagine. Forwards, we may say, not backwards to Genesis.

Chapter 14

An Inner City Bible

John J. Vincent

Using the Bible in the Inner City

A volume of essays on *Using the Bible Today* inevitably makes one ask some searching questions. For a start, it would be good to know who uses the Bible. What people? Where? We might, for example, get the hunch that the Bible is used by certain people rather than by certain other people. So then our curiosity – if not our suspicions! – would be raised, and we would ask: for what do they use the Bible? And then, as we might get many answers to those questions, we might have to press a more particular one: what bits of the Bible are used by which people for what purposes? Finally, our awkward questions might end with one like this: do some uses to which people put the biblical bits cohere with the original purposes of the Bible better than other uses? Especially, then, how do you extricate the uses of the Bible from one context so that they can be used in another, particularly if the uses of some contexts seem to be fundamentally out of sympathy with the original contexts?

These reflections and questions come to me because I live a dual existence – or rather one existence with two foci to it – as biblical student and theologian, and as Christian disciple and minister in an inner city. I can hardly avoid the question: where is the biblical story most at home? With the biblical student or with the inner city disciple?

The Bible is certainly 'used' by biblical scholars. It is used as a means of searching for the truth, or searching for the context and meaning of biblical happenings; or as the way of discovering the historical origins or theological springs of contemporary Judaism or Christianity.

Since 1960 I have been a member of the International Society for New Testament Studies (Studiorum Novi Testamenti Societas). From time to time I attend the society's conferences, when they are near enough or I can stay with friends (the conferences are expensive). I attend especially the papers and seminars about the Gospels, and about the Gospel of Mark in particular, and about Discipleship in Mark especially. Geoffrey Fisher was right that a scholar is someone who knows more and more about less and less, until he knows practically everything about practically nothing! Discipleship in Mark is my 'practically nothing'. But there is endless delight in it, and pleasure in knowing that there is at least one area in which one is competent!

However, biblical scholarship is very much the victim of passing fads and fashions. A study of Discipleship in Mark written (as mine was) in 1960 looked very strange beside studies of the 1940s and 1950s. And every decade since has seen new studies, written within the then current methods – redaction criticism, then source criticism, then theological criticism, then socio-historical criticism, now audience criticism. One would have to say: the text has remained the same, but the scholarly *context* has changed rather frequently. And certain parts of the text get a better airing in some scholarly contexts than in others. And certain truths of the Gospel, or aspects of the story, are more easily expressed, or more adequately heard, in one decade than in another.

The stages by which the study of the synoptic Gospels has proceeded in recent decades in fact correspond to the stages by which I land myself as a biblical student into the lap of myself as an inner city disciple.

The stages of the argument go as follows:

1   The heart of the Bible for would-be Christian disciples is the story of Jesus Christ.
2   The story of Jesus Christ is best understood by means of the earliest Gospel, that of Mark.
3   The Markan tradition works best for those who can in some ways feel at one with the situation and events of Jesus and the first disciples.
4   The story of Jesus and the first disciples is best understood as a small-town artisan-based movement for human wholeness and liberation directed against the powers of the day.
5   The situation and events of Jesus and the first disciples have natural resonances with those of inner city disciples today.

I have argued this in some detail in a small volume called *Radical Jesus*.[1] Others have found themselves making similar identifications.[2]

It amounts to a claim that inner city disciples today feel at home with the disciples of Jesus in first-century Galilee. This is not to say that other people in other situations might not similarly feel a oneness with them. It is simply to say that the kind of people we get in the inner city today seem like, or feel themselves to be like the kind of people Jesus got in the Gospel story. This is not to exclude others. Perhaps others elsewhere have other New Testament people with whom they empathize. It is just to say that some people, just because of who they are, and where they are, and what they do, and what they are regarded as by others, have instinctive empathy with a particular group in the New Testament. They have what the liberation theologians of South America call a 'hermeneutical privilege'.[3] Their 'use' of the Bible is the use of a book that seems in places to be 'about us'.

The Bible thus gets taken over by one context, the inner city. Any context anywhere could take it over, and use it for its own purposes. The only question would be whether the purposes to which the group in its context today used the biblical passages cohered with the purposes of the first readers or disciples in their contexts.

Since 1970, my contexts have been those of the Sheffield Inner City Ecumenical Mission and the Urban Theology Unit. Both contexts exist for the same purpose – to encourage Discipleship and Mission in the Inner City.

In the Urban Theology Unit, this has led to a number of experiences and a few discoveries, on which I reflect elsewhere.[4] In the Inner City Mission, it has led to a conviction that the stories of Jesus and his disciples seem to achieve a new life among us.

Or, to return to the point made at the outset, the 'use' we make of the Bible is that of reflecting on our experiences as inner city disciples, into the stories, and then receiving back from the stories an enlargement, an affirmation and occasionally a revelation about our own experiences now. In the end, the Bible comes back at us, and we are as much 'used' by it as we 'use' it – or so it seems. I shall share several stories about this, and then offer a few conclusions about the 'uses' of the Bible which they indicate.

Jesus among Publicans and Sinners

The story of Jesus with publicans and sinners is a familiar one:

> One day, Jesus went into a house – the house of Levi, a publican who decided to follow Jesus. And in after him went a whole crowd of other tax-collectors and evil people. Jesus welcomed them and sat down to eat with them. The religious people saw it, and said, 'Look at him – nothing but a cavorter with quislings and prostitutes. A man is known by the company he keeps.' The disciples had no answer, but Jesus had. Said he: 'The healthy do not need a doctor – only the sick. I am not come to call righteous people, but evil people, so that their ways will change.' (Mark 2:15–17)

We do not know if the tax-collectors or evil people (prostitutes, says the tradition) actually did change their ways. We may guess that most of them did not. But in a sense it did not matter, as the purpose of eating and drinking with Jesus was so that God's New Order, the Kingdom of God, might be manifested and proclaimed. And, since they were the people, good or bad, in whose presence the Kingdom had been acted out, they got admitted to it before 'the healthy' who had not even recognized it at all. The Kingdom action is created by the arbitrary act of Jesus, not by whether or not other people repent and live differently because of it. The brunt of the story is that the religious people are missing the only thing that really matters – the Kingdom, God's New Order, happening in their midst.

Of course, people could easily be forgiven for missing it. Religious people were not trained, then as now, to be those who 'smelt out' the divine action in a situation so thoroughly questionable and frankly unsavoury. Quislings are quite rightly excluded from normal, good society, whenever they appear; and the tax-collectors, as collaborators with the alien Roman occupation forces, were quislings. In any case, they made their money unjustly, by extorting from travellers far above what they had to pay to the Romans (this was how they earned their living). And evil people, typically prostitutes, are rightly ostracized. So, why does the Kingdom have to be acted out among such people?

A few years ago, my father-in-law, an Irish Methodist minister, and I took a bus up the Springfield Road, in Belfast. We were looking for Moyard Parade, New Barnsley, where a young volunteer community worker was living. The Ashram Community had decided to give its Day's Pay discipline for 1973 to support the work, and I wanted to discuss how best to help. The day before, we had found the place, but not the young man. We had spent a half-hour with two local women paid by the Save the Children Fund, who run the play centre in the community hall in the 98 per cent Roman Catholic estate. At the top of Moyard Parade, there was a big block of sixteen maisonettes. Only three of them had windows intact, and they keep the lights on to make sure no harm comes to them. All the other thirteen were completely wrecked and vandalized. In one of the three lived Stephen.

'Hi there, Steve,' I shout. 'Come on in,' he replies. 'The place is a bit of wreck. I was away for three weeks. My youngsters broke in and stole everything of value. But they've been to say they're sorry, and we're still friends. Sit down, sit down.'

'How do you get on here?' we ask.

He laughs. He laughed constantly over the next six hours together – not the nervous laugh of an uncertain man, but the honest laugh of a man who can laugh at himself and at everything around him. 'It's tricky,' he confessed. 'The soldiers put all the men up against the wall there – twenty of us – and the paratroopers' officer came up and said to us each in turn, "Call me Sir." I replied that I did not know him, and that I could not do so as I did not know in virtue of what he was demanding to be called Sir. So he threw me over to his men, and they took me off and beat me up. I've been beaten up by the army five times. But then, later, a few of the paratroopers used to come and talk to me. I invited them in, but had to ask them to stop coming, as the local people would start thinking I was a member of the Special Branch. There are IRA people in most parts of the Parade, and they naturally watch me carefully. But all my friends are in the community, and my friends watch my house to see that no harm comes to me.

'The army and the IRA both find it odd that I am, as I tell them, a conscientious objector. So when I discuss it now with them, I say I'm not a conscientious objector, but *a conscientious affirmer*. I tell them I do not object to anything. I *affirm* them, and all humanity. They don't quite know what to make of me!'

Who would? What did this strange phenomenon mean? This social worker (with a degree in it) helping Catholic communities of 49 per cent unemployed to get their community working, caring for their delinquent youth whom they cannot control, even though they ravage his home? The Quakers in South Belfast kept asking him, 'What is there you need?' and he kept replying, 'Well, there isn't anything I need, really.' We in Ashram Community tried to send out a colleague for him, and he welcomed that, 'if he's open and friendly and cheerful'. That is, I suppose, if he could *affirm* the people outlawed by society, *affirm* their neglected children, *affirm* the army and the IRA, both in their good work and in their repression.

On the way back, my father-in-law and I talked excitedly. The whole thing had the whiff of Jesus about it. The laughing Galahad, with long hair, doing good to those who persecuted him, and binding up wounds, whosoever they were, and inviting in army and 'enemy' alike – this was a kind of Jesus man. And there was more of the 'smell' of Jesus there than there was in the Church, which still talked about justice, equality and right solutions.

Why did we say so? Why did it have the whiff of Jesus about it? Why was it a 'Snap' situation for us? Back home in Bangor, I raced through the Gospel of Mark. Then I found the story of Jesus eating with the publicans and sinners. 'This is it,' I said. 'It's Jesus with the publicans and sinners. It's the celebration of the Kingdom among those who probably do not change, but yet have the Kingdom in their midst.'

This incident started me thinking: how can we encourage ourselves and others to see Gospel stories happening now? How can we learn to play 'Snap' with the Gospel?

We still call this the method of 'Snap'. It is the simple method of asking: 'When have I seen something like this? What *Snap* have I to this Gospel story?' And within the congregations and the mission, we build up our own ever-growing volume of 'snaps', which record our experiences of Gospel stories at work among us, and lead us into 'Studies' of pieces of the Gospel story.

Our experience is that this 'use' of the Bible in interpreting practical stories opens up endless possibilities. There is plenty on the cards, plenty in the Gospel story to evoke our response.

Week after week, year after year, moment after moment, we sit with the Gospel story, the story of Jesus happening, then and now. And at times, parts of it hit us – what John calls 'the Spirit taking of the things of Jesus and showing them to disciples' (John 15:14).[5]

The Affluent Givers and the Poor Woman

One morning at Upper Wincobank Chapel, we were reading the story of the widow's mite. We had read it over together.

> Jesus sat down opposite the Treasury, and watched the people putting money into the offertory. Many wealthy people put in large amounts of money. A poor widow came up and put in two small copper coins, worth a penny.
>
> He called his disciples to him and said to them: 'I'm telling you. This poor widow has put in more money than all the rest who are giving to the Treasury. For all of them made contributions out of their affluence. But she has contributed out of her poverty. And what she put in was everything she had, all she had to live on.' (Mark 12:41–4)

So the story was before us.

Then, I had begun my 'explanation'. The incident took place in the temple, in which offerings were made, of all kinds. There were large receptacles into which gifts of money could be placed. Monetary gifts were often over and above the regular gift offerings, which marked certain stages in life, or certain needs for forgiveness.

So, givers of money were, in a special way, giving of themselves. Not surprisingly, it was good that people should notice who gave in this way.

But the important thing is not the amount of money you give (I said). The important thing is what the money represents. The giving of the rich was obviously great. But then so was the wealth out of which they gave. The giving of the poor woman was obviously minuscule. But so was the wealth out of which she gave. And what she gave was all she had. So, proportionately, she gave an enormous gift, whereas the wealthy people had only given minuscule ones.

Suddenly the service erupted.

'I can't see your problem,' said Margaret. 'We saw this happen last night.'

'Oh?' said the rest of us. 'How?'

'Well,' she replied. 'It was the Annual Festival of Queens at the City Hall. All the May Queens from the different churches were all up there, sitting on the platform. And our chapel's little Louise was there.

'They'd put all the May Queens from the west of Sheffield – where the rich churches are – on one side of the platform. And all the Queens from the east and north were on the other side. Our little Louise looked a bit pathetic, I must say. You all remember how we'd had to scrape around for her costume. And she looked so small beside the big girls from the west.

'And I felt: well, I'm glad we're here. But it's the same old thing – the west has the money, and we haven't.

'But then, at the end of the evening, they started reading out the totals of money that the different churches had raised. They read out the totals for the west of the city – and they were really quite good. But then they read out the totals for the churches in the east, and they were bigger. And the people from the east all started cheering, because we'd done better.

'Isn't that like the widow's mite?'

'Yes,' we all said. 'That's exactly it. The poor churches are still looked down on, because they are poor. But they often give money better than the richer churches. And better not just proportionate to their incomes, but better in real terms.'

So, the poor widow's story is alive and well in Wincobank.

We have others, too. We are busy collecting them. Maybe a sort of *Gospel in Solentiname*[6] in Wincobank.

Jesus and his Contemporaries

So, what does the whole Gospel sound like, heard through the inner city, or at least through the experience of inner city Christians?

My conviction is that the Good News for all of us today can only be a rediscovery of the primary Good News of Jesus.

> The Kingdom of God is here.
> Change yourselves completely
> And commit your life to the Good News. (Mark 1:14)

And if we ask more precisely what that Good News is, then we would have to say first of all who we are.

The Gospel of Mark differentiates rather sharply between different groups of people who use the Good News in very different ways. I think there are at least five such groups.

1 *Those in need*. Jesus is the bringer of total reversal of fortunes for

people in need. The classic statement of Mark's story is in fact in Luke's Gospel:

> The Spirit of the Lord is upon me
> Because he has anointed me
> To proclaim Good News to the poor
> Release to the captives
> Recovery of sight to the blind
> And to let the oppressed go free,
> To proclaim the year that the Lord can love. (Luke 4:18–19)

Most of the ministry of Jesus is taken up with being used by the procession of unfortunates who receive their liberation through him. They receive a little bit – what they then need of healing, exorcism, freedom from oppression, internal or external, and they receive a little of the wholeness that belongs to all things and all people in God's Kingdom.

We know this group well in the inner city. They are the procession of people on the dole, or on 'benefits', or on 'training programmes', who exist, in a land of luxury, in bad schools, bad housing, with bad medical facilities, and with little hope.

2   Then for another group, there is another Good News. They are the group of *people who are called*.

> If you want to be my disciple,
> Deny yourself,
> Take up your cross,
> And follow me. (Mark 8:34)

For those who give up life in this way will gain it (v. 35). They are the people, the twelve and the women, who form an alternative society based on commitment to Jesus. Sharing possessions as well as ministry, they have all things in common, and become a sort of miniature of the future Kingdom.

We have this group in the inner city. They are the faithful in the tiny churches, joined by a few middle-class incomers. They are into survival, but also radical modesty and prophecy. They even represent, I think, a new way to change things in society.[7]

3   There is another group of people who are *sympathetic fellow-travellers*. Sometimes they can show their sympathy – like Nicodemus, or Joseph of Arimathea, or Jairus, or the Canaanite woman. But they remain outside the disciple group, perhaps reluctantly. They ask questions. But one at least gets told:

> Only one thing you lack.
> Go, sell what you have
> And give the money to the poor.
> Then come and follow me. (Mark 10:21)

We do not have many fellow-travellers in the inner city. There are many Church people and middle-class people, professionals and politicians, who would like to be fellow-travellers. Sometimes they make it. More often, they remain an embarrassment to themselves.

The Gospel story is that Jesus is continually fishing among this third group – the sympathetic fellow-travellers, to try to get them to join the second group – the committed disciples, in order to help him minister to the vast needs of the first group – the poor and the sick.

4 *The nice people*. There are, of course, other groups of people who do not get into it at all. One group are, quite frankly, *too nice* for it. They have already got themselves sorted out. They take a dim view of the whole business. Jesus cannot do anything with them.

> Those who are whole
> Don't need a physician.
> I didn't come to call the insiders
> But the outsiders, to bring them in. (Mark 2:17)

It remains unclear how far Jesus did really approve of the 'righteous', and how far he is 'tongue-in-cheek' about them.

Happily, for good or ill, we still have the nice people in the inner city. Sometimes they are the locals who hold on to life and decency with amazing tenacity. Sometimes they are the professional day-visitors from the suburbs, the teachers, doctors, health visitors and social workers. They do their bit, even if we would like them to move to being fellow-travellers and disciples.

5 *The enemies*. There are more sinister people around – people who see that what Jesus is doing is going to undermine their power, and destroy their station. They send questioners to trick them. And they produce the unbeatable combination of religious and political power, plus the occupying army, which crucifies him.

There is always a lot to be said for this group. A postcard from 'the Economic League' describes Jesus's activity thus:

> Christ, J. . . . Palestinian nationalist of doubtful parentage. Known for hostility to market forces, e.g. overturning workstations of independent financial consultants in the Temple area. Unorthodox distribution of bread and fish products may have effect of depressing prices.

The movement knows the power of the powerful: as we do in the inner city.

It is my conviction that much the same is happening in Britain today. There is the Kingdom, breaking in with revolutionary implications, representing a total, radical, upside-down reality that challenges everything. There is Good News for the poor, which we are supposed to declare and represent, but hardly dare to. There are the little groups of disciples, seeking ways to represent the alternative lifestyle, finding out how much they can have in common. There are the sympathetic fellow-travellers, keen to talk about this and that, up to the point where they might have to do something radical, and then they disappear.

And there are the rest. There are the nice people, who are presumably the righteous, or self-righteous, anyway, and who regard the whole thing as ridiculous, immature, unnecessary, or just bad taste. And there are the people in power, who from the establishments of education, politics, society, and even at times the Church, seek to annul the revolutionary effects of what is threatened. They are the enemies.

The inner city merely points up an analysis of society and people that is valid for the whole of society. But it also contains the elements that made up the first responses to the Gospel.

Jesus as Paradigm for Lifestyle and Ministry

The New Testament writers presume to do more than set occasional, recurring unexpected traps for us – Snaps, and even dramatic reductions of all of us to characters in the divine drama – disciples, fellow-travellers and the rest. They also presume to give us a total framework within which to operate. In the New Testament, every writer hunts around for ways to say 'in their own tongue' that Jesus is not only the judgemental and determinative 'Word of the Lord' at decisive points in existence, but also the 'whole shooting-match', the start and the finish, the one who holds it all together, and holds people together in it.

So that every piece of the New Testament must be looked at as a whole. There is also a Johannine, a Pauline, a Matthean and Lukan view of how all things fit in with Jesus at the apex. There are very different ones in the epistles of James and John, or Hebrews, or Colossians. Each offers us a special challenge and invitation. You can create a total style of life, a total orientation, a whole view of existence, out of the Jesus story, and use any one of the New Testament views as a model.

The one which helps us most in the inner city, in my experience, is the view of existence which I think Mark had. I think that Mark meant us to take the uncomprehending disciples seriously, and to see them as types of irrelevant followers (perhaps Church members), who cannot prevent the Jesus thing happening, and who even, against their better judgement, get caught up from time to time in it. I think Mark is picturing an action, a set of deeds, a dynamic, a happening, which Jesus embodies and represents, which he talks about in his teaching and parables in terms of a Kingdom, and which he sets out before the disciples as a Cross and a joy.

There are many elements to Mark's picture of 'the Jesus Thing'. The whole creates a sort of lifestyle model, which embodies a way which we seek and see in the inner city today:[8]

1 *Incarnation*. Mark's Jesus is already a grown man, when he appears; and he is 'anointed' to be God's special agent. He is a man from among men, accredited to get on with a divine vocation and mission. He begins where people are.

2 *Healing*. Mark tells more healing stories than straight miracles. Jesus is 'available' for people. He is 'used' by outsiders. He heals friend and foe alike.

3 *Parables*. Mark has Jesus teaching in parables, and discusses why they are incomprehensible. At all events, the parables are about how the Kingdom is already happening, unnoticed, in the midst of secular existence. They show how people deal with the ultimate in the secular.

4 *Acted parables*. Mark has Jesus and the disciples performing symbolic acts, doing things 'as a testimony to others'. Disciples must take heed of what they say and do, for words and deeds make the Kingdom present.

5 *Discipleship*. Mark has the disciples invariably acting foolishly, but yet being called to be with Jesus, to go out and mission, and to be those who repeat his own life and death.

6 *Suffering*. Mark's story is one-third Passion story, but not because the death is of prime importance, but because the death is a prime problem. Jesus is rejected. Men kill him, the Master!

7 *Resurrection*. Mark has an empty tomb, and that is about all. I think he means us to go back to the beginning again. The reappearing Jesus 'has gone before you into Galilee', that is, he had gone back to chapter one, and repeats ever and again the story of incarnation, healing, parables and discipleship, in the midst of his disciples, and in the person of his disciples.

8 *Parousia*. Mark has a future 'Coming'. It is all a bit unclear, as Mark 13 demonstrates. But it is the final affirmation of what the whole story asserts.

Such then, as I see it, is Mark's view of Jesus, and of discipleship, and of the Church, and of reality, and of salvation – his view of life.

My experience is that this paradigm of Jesus is reflected in the lifestyle and ministry of disciples in the inner city. I first saw this in the work of our Ashram Community House in Sheffield. A group of us reflected on it thus:

1 *Incarnation*, or *Empathizing*. Incarnation, in our time, means

inundation: it has to do with *place and station*. So, the House stands in the place of need, and starts with people prepared to come and live here for a few years, 'to live the life of Christ in the midst of the poor' (Kenneth Kaunda).

2   *Healing*, or *Being used*. Just to be there, as people who 'needn't', is affirmation and thus healing. To be there when you are needed is even more – as when the members put up a large notice, 'Warm House: please come inside', during the power cuts of a cold winter.

3   *Parables*, or *Pointing*. 'A voice for the neighbourhood' is often greatly needed. It sometimes has to be a vicarious voice, as many who need to speak cannot. But it has to be a voice from within the neighbourhood. We have learnt that class matters less than presence and commitment in this.

4   *Acted parables*, or *Mission*. The House debated long that it seemed to do little 'together' – though that was largely because the residents were already engaged whole time and spare time in all kinds of local clubs, organizations, street groups, etc. Later, an Advice Centre was run from the surgery.

5   *Discipleship*, or *Clustering*. The inner city does not lack leaders, but lacks those to get things together. So the House helped form the Nottingham Street Neighbourhood Group which fought successfully for the area to become a General Improvement Area. And the House acted as a 'roof' for local people and groups, including Sheffield radicals at a monthly Agape.

6   *Suffering*, or *Committing*. Any community commitment has to be serious, and demanding. In the House, we spoke of a dual commitment to 'creating a para-church' and 'to serving the neighbourhood'.

7   *Resurrection*, or *Realizing*. From the style of the House, individuals said they got a whiff of what a true Church should be; the social workers said they saw how social work must be from within the community; the local residents got hope (and painted their houses bright like ours). All, of course, momentarily, and fragmentarily, like a 'new coming'.

8   *Parousia*, or *Finality*. The Ashram House closed after a decade. In Kingdom-style enterprises, nothing lasts for ever. But now there is another project – the Ashram Shop Centre, with the same ultimate aims of looking towards a new future.

Thus, the Christ-centred pattern of incarnation to parousia becomes a model for lifestyle and ministry, not just as a series of 'Snaps', but rather as a whole pattern, and sequence.

Such, then, are a few examples of the use of the Bible in Christian mission in the inner city. It amounts to a contemporary appropriation of part of the biblical story by part of our contemporary world. Is it legitimate? That could be answered only by someone not committed to either rich or poor, educated or uneducated, suburban or inner city. And such a person does not exist. We all take our contexts with us. And ultimately the conflict of biblical interpretations is also a conflict of contexts.

Whether readers like the result probably depends on their contexts, with all the commitments they imply. Perhaps even our context will be a call whereby some will pursue their impulsion towards the Gospel sagas. At least in the inner city we do not have the old problem of not having any use for the Gospel stories!

Part III

THE BIBLE AND THE WORLD

Chapter 15

The Bible and Scientific Discovery

John Habgood

The Bible is pre-scientific. The same is true of the thinking of many people today who, though living in a culture strongly fashioned by the fruits of scientific discovery, remain largely unaffected by its intellectual basis. Thus difficulties which might have arisen from the impact of scientific ways of thinking on the Bible are often not felt as acutely as perhaps they should be. There is a widespread assumption that, give or take a few much-discussed problems, the Bible can be read as if it came out of the same kind of world as our own.

Others fall into the opposite error, and assume that a pre-scientific book has nothing to teach the twentieth century. To equate scientific knowledge with the totality of knowledge is as foolish as imagining that the Bible has some kind of quasi-scientific purpose.

There is an expectation in some quarters, for example, that the Bible can somehow give direct answers to twentieth-century questions, despite the fact that these questions could not possibly have been in the minds of those who wrote it. Psalm 139 was extensively used in recent debates on embryo research. It was assumed almost without question by many people that verses 13–16, which describe the secret fashioning of a human being in the womb, could give authoritative guidance about precisely when, in the complex and gradual process of human generation, it is possible to identify human personhood. The Psalm makes profound and important points about God's loving care for all human life from its beginning to its end, but it cannot adjudicate in scientific and philosophical disputes about the nature and stages of that beginning, because the questions which need to be answered could not even be formulated until a few decades ago.

This is not to say that the Bible cannot often deepen our insight into scientific issues. The example merely cautions against attempts to use it in a direct fashion as a source of scientific understanding. To read the Bible with integrity means coming to terms with the fact that in the last 300 years the world has undergone a major intellectual revolution. Despite current criticisms of the Enlightenment and its aftermath, there is no going back on the main features of that revolution. Nor can the claim that the Bible offers an alternative world-view to science, on science's own ground, be convincingly maintained.

One consequence of these changes has been a certain distancing between most people's experience of the natural world and perceptions of God's activity. Thus the description of a thunderstorm in Psalm 29 vividly portrays it in terms of God shouting through the trees, whirling the desert sands and inducing the cattle to calve. The fact that twentieth-century readers know a great deal more than the psalmist about weather patterns and electrical discharges need not diminish the feelings of awe which thunder and lightning can generate. Nor is it impossible to respond to them as images of God's glory and power. But it is more difficult nowadays than in biblical times to ascribe them to God's direct intervention unless, as happened with the lightning strike at York Minster, there is a prior wish to make theological capital out of an otherwise natural event. On average about a hundred churches in England are damaged by lightning every year.

It is more usual to speak of God as ultimately responsible for the majesty of a storm in the same sense in which he is ultimately responsible for everything, and to see him as ultimately revealed through such events in the same sense in which he can ultimately be revealed through other phenomena. But the relationship thus described is a good deal more distant than that envisaged by the psalmist. Science has focused attention on immediate and intermediate causes, and it is preoccupation with such causes which chiefly distinguishes our own world from that of biblical times. In the biblical drama God is the main actor. In the context of scientific rationality he is more likely to be identified as the producer of the play, and its author or, more distantly still, as the owner of the theatre.

There is no easy way to overcome this sense of distance. It is partly, as I have hinted, a matter of expectations. To treat the Bible as a source of information on all sorts of subjects which lay outside the ken of its authors is to invite disappointment. To treat its contents as documents of their time which, within the particular constraints of their time, can reveal God's presence in history and in the world of nature, is to find it still speaking, albeit in a different mode. The God thus revealed may not be a God who directly causes thunderstorms, but he remains the God whose glory shines through such phenomena, and whose awesomeness is reflected in their power.

Creation

This contrast between direct and detailed intervention, and divine activity made effective through intermediate causes, comes to sharp focus in different interpretations of the act or process of creation.

'By the Word of the Lord were the heavens made.' Psalm 33:6 echoes the theology of such passages as Isaiah 45:18 and the formal account of creation in Genesis 1. Creation is by God's direct command, by fiat. God speaks and it is done. All things come directly from God, and the implication is that most natural things are what they are because God designed them that way. Genesis 1 not only describes the ordered universe as expressing God's intention for his creation, but sets out the stages by which he actually brought it into being. Such was the view almost universally held by biblical interpreters until scientists began to disclose something of the size, age, complexity and interrelatedness of the natural world, and the causal connections within it.

An alternative account of creation, taking seriously the story as told by scientists, sees the role of God as at one remove from this direct kind of interventionism. God works through natural laws. In the words of one theologian, 'He makes creation make itself.' The biblical story sets out the inner meaning of the scientific story by revealing the dependence of all existence on God, and the ultimate meaning of it as finding its fulfilment in God. But it does not provide detailed information about how and why things come to be. Answers to such questions have to be found by study of the things themselves, not by looking for shortcuts in Scripture.

Thus crudely stated, the contrast can help to reinforce the point already made about the distancing between God and everyday experience of the world. Nevertheless it is only half the story. Biblical statements about creation did not arise out of philosophical reflection or from the kind of concerns which motivate scientists. The great passages in Isaiah 40–55, which historically mark the first clear and unequivocal statements about the oneness of God and his creative power, were written to a people in exile who needed to rediscover themselves as a nation, and to summon up the immense effort required to return and rebuild their country. They were reminded in glowing language of God's deliverance in the past and his supreme authority over world history in the present. And they were called to allow themselves to be re-created, to allow God to do 'a new thing' (Isa. 43:19) with them. The concept of God as universal creator, in other words, grew out of the lived experience of being rescued from exile.

Genesis 1 was almost certainly written at about the same time and represents essentially the same theology, developed and expanded and set in a different context, but rooted in the same lived experience. The God who separated light from darkness and ordered the world of nature, and showed man his role within it, is the same God who creates a nation out of runaway slaves from Egypt, and re-creates it after its death in Babylon. And he is the same God whose Word is made flesh in Jesus Christ for the salvation, not just of a single people, but of the world.

Read against this human and historical background the Genesis creation narrative can speak just as directly of God as it did before Darwin wrote *The Origin of Species*. Perhaps even more directly, because it no longer has to do Darwin's work for him.

There is a further twist to the story in that the origin of modern science itself is nowadays increasingly seen to have depended on philosophical assumptions in medieval Europe derived from this very same biblical doctrine of creation. For science, as we now know it, to be a worthwhile enterprise, there has to be a prior belief that the universe is intelligible, but that its intelligibility is of a kind which cannot be deduced from first principles – in the way that Aristotle deduced that the orbits of the planets must be circular because this is the perfect shape in a perfect heaven. Without the belief that the world is intelligible there is no point in trying to understand otherwise puzzling phenomena. Without the recognition that deduction from first principles will not yield true knowledge of it there is no point in experimenting to find out how nature actually works. Only belief in an orderly creation made to be what it is by the sovereign will of God (and hence not deducible from anything prior to that) was able to provide for those first scientists the philosophical framework they needed. This is why the modern world was born in a Christian culture. It was the Bible's gift to science.

Miracles

Worries about the miraculous element in the Bible are not peculiar to a scientific age. Some alleged miracles have always caused difficulties, and one of the devices used by the earliest biblical interpreters was to allegorize stories which seemed too outrageous when taken literally. Another favourite device has been to put forward naturalistic explanations of events interpreted as miraculous at the time only because they then seemed inexplicable. Many healings, for instance, may not seem so surprising in the light of growing knowledge of the complex interactions between body and mind. Weathermen have been busy explaining the Israelites' crossing of the Red Sea. And there have been more tortuous attempts to come to terms with the miraculous, such as the various unconvincing explanations of the feeding of the 5,000, based on the idea of the members of the crowd being induced to share their picnics.

Science may have changed some perceptions of what is or is not likely, but there is no clear scientific warrant for ruling out miracles as such. In fact the world as disclosed by science grows daily more strange and mysterious, and is far from the totally predictable, self-contained, machine-like entity which once had seemed to be implied by the early successes in physics. There was always an anomaly in the apparent existence of human creativity and free will in the midst of such a closed world, but nowadays physics itself has led the revolution towards an understanding of the world which is much more hospitable to novelty, freedom and indeterminacy. Most scientists very properly still retain a high degree of scepticism about the possibility of miracles because, as allegedly unique events, they cannot be brought within the scope of scientific investigation. But that is by no means the same as denying that they ever occur.

That said, the role of science in helping to distinguish between genuine mystery and absurdity remains vital. Twice in the Old Testament, for example, there are accounts of the sun being stopped, or reversed, in its tracks (2 Kgs 20:11, Josh. 10:13). This would be a stupendous miracle by any standard, but less stupendous in a pre-Copernican universe. If the sun moves round the earth on a crystal sphere propelled by God, and if the inhabited earth itself is believed to be small and centred on Palestine, it is not totally unreasonable to suppose that God might for good reason temporarily stop his propulsion. But if stopping the sun means in effect stopping the rotation of the earth, with the result that everything on it would tend to fly off at huge velocity, and if Palestine is only one small corner of a large and populous world, the 'miraculous effort' involved in assuring Hezekiah that he was going to recover from his sickness, or in allowing Joshua time to smite a few more Amorites, would seem to be disproportionate. It is not enough to plead that with God all things are possible. Possible maybe, but not plausible. The stories either have to be dismissed, or interpreted some other way, if the concept of God they presuppose is not to be discredited. And that is so for theological, not scientific reasons, though science in this instance helps to sharpen the theological questions.

The stories are admittedly marginal to the main biblical themes. However they provide a useful illustration of the notion of 'miraculous effort' which may possibly serve as a criterion in the interpretation of other miracle stories. 'Miraculous effort' is not a crude measure of the extra work God might be supposed to have done in performing a particular miracle, but of the appropriateness of the match between a striking event and the lessons to be learnt from it. A miracle has to be perceived as revelatory, as an event which discloses something of the power and presence of God. Its strangeness invites attention to what God is saying or doing through it. But if God does not seem to be saying very much it becomes a mere wonder, a source of amazement rather than faith. And if the message is trivial in comparison with the disruption of natural forces which might have been entailed, there is every reason for scepticism.

Jesus clearly rejected the description of himself as a wonderworker, and this is why biblical scholars have generally looked with suspicion at alleged miracles, like the coin in the fish's mouth (Matt. 17:27), which seem to fall into the category of wonders, and are probably best interpreted as parables or folk tales. Genuine miracles, by contrast, are best interpreted as signs, and what they signify is more important than the oddity of their occurrence. If changes in understanding make them seem less odd, or throw doubt on the way the story is told, this may not diminish their value as signs whose meaning lies in what they tell us of God. In St John's Gospel the theological superstructure built around the seven great signs which form the core of the Gospel far outweighs the 'miraculous effort' in the signs themselves.

This is even more true in the case of the resurrection. As an event it seems inexplicable by any standards, and attempts to explain it in psychological and quasi-physical terms seem to evacuate it of its primary significance, that death itself has in some way been robbed of its finality. It is at this point supremely that faith has to make its claims in the face of normal scientific expectations. But it is at this point also that the 'miraculous effort' entailed entirely matches the enormous implications. No miracle could be more appropriate, nor more fully vindicated in the subsequent experience of believers.

Science as an Aid to Biblical Study

Though the Bible is not a source of scientific understanding, it records events which may or may not be illuminated, or even directly verified, by scientific study. High hopes have at times been vested in archaeology, but attempts to match archaeological discoveries with particular biblical events have proved frustratingly inconclusive. There is still no agreement, for instance, about the chronology of the exodus. Clear signs of cultural change in ancient village sites can provide evidence of migrations and conquests. But the pattern which has emerged over many years of archaeological investigation in Palestine is a great deal more complex than the Old Testament version of events. The study of the site of Jericho, for instance, has led to intense debates over many years, some striking claims and counter-claims, and no agreement.

Some of the most interesting discoveries have been on the sites of former royal palaces. Solomon's wealth and reputation as a builder can in part be documented, and much attention was devoted some years ago to the excavation of the so-called royal stables at Megiddo. It now appears that these were probably not stables after all, nor were they built by Solomon, and that a later dynasty may actually have exceeded him in material power. Such reversals of opinion are typical of the inherent uncertainties in this kind of study.

Archaeology's main value in biblical interpretation has been to illuminate the culture of biblical times by the study of places and artefacts, and in this role it can help to verify how frequently the biblical narratives ring true. Other sciences can sometimes perform a similar function, though not with much conviction. Medical insights in Luke and Acts have been much discussed, and have persuaded some people of Luke's authorship, while failing to convince others. The famous description of the plague in 1 Samuel 5:6–6:6 with its reference to rats and death-dealing tumours suggests an early and accurate insight into the relationship between them. Some of the plagues of Eygpt in Exodus 7–10 form a more or less credible sequence on the assumption that they were triggered off by a red muddy silt in the River Nile ('blood'), though the fact that the reddening of the Nile tended to be a fairly frequent occurrence obviously weakens the case for regarding the plagues as especially disastrous.

Such meagre gleanings from science in aid of biblical interpretation stand in sharp contrast to the claims made by much contemporary popular fundamentalist literature. This abounds with misconceived efforts to 'prove' the flood by the study of sediments, to 'discover' Noah's ark still mysteriously lodged on Mount Ararat, and to vindicate the scientific accuracy of incidental statements in Scripture as evidence of its verbal inspiration. Such efforts are usually tendentious and futile, and distract attention from the character of revelation to which the central tenets of the Christian faith bear witness.

God, so Christians claim, was incarnate in a human life at a particular place and time, and in being so subjected himself to the limitations of that place and time. In his incarnate life he had no privileged access to knowledge which belongs to the twentieth century, nor did those who in earlier ages wrote out of the lived experience of God's presence among them. The cultural distancing described at the beginning of this chapter means that this age, like other ages before it, has to learn how to read the story of God's dealings with his world in the light of its own best knowledge. It also has to let the story challenge this knowledge and its own presuppositions, and to learn how to integrate both perspectives through reflection (especially on its own past), through worship, and through actually living the Christian life. Signs embedded in the story which enable us to relate it to discoveries in our own era, can help to increase confidence in it. But science itself can neither establish nor disprove its tremendous message.

Chapter 16

The Bible and Peace and War

Ursula King

I am neither a biblical scholar nor someone who works on the exegesis of biblical texts, but I would like to reflect on a subject of great contemporary importance with wide-ranging implications for our social and political life.[1] If we consider the authority, importance and central position of the Bible in the Judaeo-Christian tradition and in Western culture in general, it is appropriate, in fact essential, to examine biblical thinking about the possibilities of peace and the elimination of violence, especially in its most virulent form as organized war between nations. Others have written and spoken at length on this theme with far more competence than I possess. What follows is only a modest attempt to share some ideas which have nourished and sustained my own thought.

General Reflections

The Bible is a great classical text open to ever new interpretations. Each successive generation has to appropriate it anew and discover it as an authoritative source of meaning, a meaning which is not unequivocal or self-evident at a literal level. Much has been said on the metaphorical character of biblical language, on the cultural context and 'Sitz im Leben' of its ideas; generations of scholars have built up a truly impressive biblical science with most elaborate and learned theories of interpretation. For the Bible to become alive and enlivening, and not merely be a book of textual scholarship, we have to engage creatively with it from within our own situation and its demands. Past and present members of the Christian faith community are in on-going conversation with this foundational text of revelation formulated long ago, and it is only through such continuing conversation that the biblical word becomes truly dynamic, alive, revelatory and living now. One may agree on the unique authority of the Bible, yet at the same time one must be aware that the Bible is a book full of contradictions, a book of dialogue and discussion whose words at times are a record of a desperate struggle for hope and humanity.

As Christians we approach this text with both reverence and critical distance. The Bible and its life- and thought-world have sustained the faith of countless generations – as Hebrew Bible it is God's law (*Torah*) for Jews, and as Old and New Testament it is God's living word from which millions of Christians have drawn moral and spiritual sustenance and guidance in many a practical matter. Moreover, the Bible is a foundational text for Western civilization; it has brought its view on God, the world and humanity into all the leading Western languages and literatures. Millions of contemporary secular people who do not see themselves as religious at all none the less live with many basic presuppositions which are originally enshrined in biblical texts. Thus the Bible has shaped many aspects of Western civilization, whether in science, philosophy, theology, law or the arts – we only need to think of painting, sculpture, music, poetry, drama or fiction where even today many biblical themes and allusions can be found.

Over the centuries of Christian history biblical texts have been put to many different uses. I want to look in particular at the use of the Bible in reflecting on peace and war. Many biblical stories bear vivid witness to the human inclination to aggression, violence and depravity, but they also tell us of immense potential and promise: human beings, as God's creatures and with God's help, are called to raise up to the height of the spirit and to new transformative powers. It is written in Ecclesiastes (3:1, 7–8)

> For everything there is a season
> and a time for every matter under heaven . . .
> a time to keep silence, and a time to speak;
> a time to love, and a time to hate;
> a time for war, and a time for peace.

These words make us reflective – we certainly live in a time which is in great need of peace, but is there also still a time for war? Given our socio-political conditions around the globe, it is imperative to seek all possible ways for making peace in East and West. We need all the resources we can find to sustain us in the endeavour of creating peace on earth. Each year we celebrate in the Christian Churches a week of prayer for peace and Peace Sunday. It is therefore certainly appropriate to ask how we can find inspiration and guidance from the Bible to learn about the meaning and practice of peace.

Like all texts – and sacred texts in particular – the Bible is full of contradictions and profound ambiguities. God's will and purpose are not always as clearly enunciated as we might wish and hope for. This conflicting evidence is well illustrated when in the Hebrew Bible, in Exodus 15:3, God is characterized as 'warrior', whereas

Judges 6:24 proclaims that 'the Lord is peace'. Similarly, we come across such opposing injunctions as Isaiah's: 'They shall beat their swords into ploughshares, and their spears into pruning hooks' (Isa. 2:4), while the prophet Joel (3:10) says: 'Beat your ploughshares into swords, and your pruning hooks into spears.' How to reconcile such opposite appeals?

Again, how are we to explain that Jesus, the founder of Christianity, is often called 'the Prince of Peace' and yet Western civilization, so deeply shaped by the Christian story which is clearly pacifist in origin and essence, has become so militaristic from an early stage in its history? The Christian pacifist John Ferguson, who quite some time ago produced a small, insightful study on *War and Peace in the World's Religions* (1977), has said:

> The historic association of the Christian faith with nations of commercial enterprise, imperialistic expansion and technological advancement has meant that Christian peoples, although their faith is one of the most pacific in its origins, have a record of military activity second to none. (p. 122)

Throughout Jewish and Christian history many ordinary believers and learned theologians have wrestled with this ambiguity of biblical texts and pondered in their hearts on how to respond in their belief and actions, individually and communally, to divine disclosure and injunctions in human history – and the variety of their responses accounts for the diversity and pluralism of different groups within both Judaism and Christianity.

We live at a decisive – some believe apocalyptic – moment of world history where peace is imperative for human survival. Before we explore how the Bible can be used as a dynamic and inspiring resource for peace-making, it will help our understanding if we look first at biblical literature in relation to ideas about violence and war. We must also ask ourselves how formative and influential biblical ideas have been in shaping and legitimizing the organized violence of war in ancient and modern times.

Violence, War and the Bible

The roots of violence, internecine strife and war in human history are many, and many are the explanations put forward why war occurs at all and whether it is and will remain an inevitable fact of human life. Socio-economic, political, historical and psychological factors all contribute to the occurrence of wars, but it would be a formidable, if not to say impossible, task to analyse them all. It has been poignantly said that 'Wars are first born in the minds of men.'

It is thus appropriate to ask ourselves critically and honestly how far our different religious traditions and sacred scriptures have helped people first to conceive the idea of war, then to undertake, bless and sanctify it even though such warring acts are in radical contradiction to a universalist ethic which preaches the sisterhood and brotherhood of all human beings created, sustained and guided by the love of God.

How far have the biblical ideas and texts helped to support and sanctify war? Here we have to go back to the Hebrew Bible which became the Old Testament for Christians. In it we can find numerous references which declare the Lord's might in battle as well as his vengeful nature. A multitude of passages speak of the reliance on arms with sometimes the total destruction of the enemy, as is vividly expressed in the books of Judges, Samuel and Kings. What has been called the essentially tribal God of the early section of the Pentateuch is transformed into the national God of the so-called historical books, with a concomitant increase in the degree and extent of the deity's use of force to defend an expanded and well-defined territory. Here seems a people and its God embroiled in an apparently endless series of wars.

Many are the stories of the Old Testament in which the works of a warrior God and his holy war against the enemies of his people are described – stories which proclaim God's kingship and sovereignty over the whole world. For the ancient Hebrews the reality of war was experienced in and attested by history, and then reflected upon theologically. God the warrior leads his people into the promised land and undertakes warfare against the enemies of his people. The idea of the holy war appears in both the narratives of the Old Testament and in laws governing it, as articulated in Deuteronomy 20. It has been said that this idea of the Israelite holy war has no parallel in the ancient world. Gerhard von Rad's study on the holy war in ancient Israel[2] gives us a description of holy war behaviour which is widely accepted by scholars. The first action was the consultation of the deity and if the answer was favourable, war was proclaimed by a blast of trumpets and the war cry, assuming that Yahweh granted victory. The response to this proclamation was voluntary and the volunteers willing to wage war were consecrated – thus the war became a cultic act. The leader of the holy war was chosen as someone seized by the spirit of Yahweh; this enabled him to perform heroic feats during the holy war which was undertaken to acquire and defend the land of promise.

Such wars are described in 1 Samuel, chapters 7, 13–14, and 15; other examples are found in the book of Joshua. However, after King David the wars were no longer 'holy wars' of this kind; his successors fought secular wars of conquest and defence, including the war of the Maccabees. Thus the holy war is not the only kind of war found in the Old Testament; there are other wars of defence, especially against the powers of Assyria and Babylonia. Yet the prophets – Amos, Hosea, Isaiah, Micah and Jeremiah – judged this military resistance as morally wrong, as an offence against Yahweh. There are many counter-references to those celebrating violence and many moving passages setting forth a vision of peace. In fact, from the earliest Chronicles onwards we find evidence of troubled attitudes towards the frequently depicted violence. The world of the Old Testament was a world where history is a struggle and where the coming of peace is promised for messianic times, an eschatological hope to be realized in the future. It has been said that:

> An attentive reading of the Old Testament reveals that . . . no other activity or condition occurs more often than violence. More than six hundred passages deal explicitly with peoples, kings or other individuals attacking and killing others; about one thousand texts speak of God's wrath which often punishes people with death and annihilation; and there are over a hundred instances in which God is said to order the killing of people.[3]

The outpouring of God's wrath is an affirmation of God's power and sovereignty, but it is also seen as God's deliberate action to call people to repentance. Many Hebrew words imply violence but the most important one, *hamas*, can refer to three different aspects, physical violence, exploitation through robbery or commerce, and verbal abuse. But these forms of oppression refer always to acts committed by the stronger against the weaker, whereas the efforts of the weaker to throw off the yoke of the stronger, of the oppressor, are never called violence. The victims of violence in the Hebrew Bible are Israel, the people, the stranger, the widow, the orphan and the poor, whereas the agents of violence are the different nations, kings and officials, persecutors, false witnesses, the rich, the priests and judges.

Yet our contemporary experience and acts of violence are quite different in character from the violent actions of ancient Near Eastern peoples described in the Bible. Biblical texts, as well as those from the scriptures of other religions, have to be interpreted within their specific historical and cultural contexts, so different from our own. Religious institutions have often constrained tendencies to violence through the emergence of the ideal of social justice and through preaching universal values. While a value such as the idea of human brotherhood or a family of humankind 'cannot erase conflict, any more than pleasure can erase pain . . . it may support a consensus that removes occasions for conflict'.[4]

Throughout Christian history, too, biblical texts and ecclesiastical sanctions have been used to justify certain kinds of violence and war. It is important, though, to distinguish three different historical responses which developed. In the early Church pacifism was the dominant position up to the reign of Constantine, when Christianity became a state religion. Until then no Christian author approved of Christian participation in battle, whereas in AD 314 the Council of Arles decreed that Christians who gave up their arms in time of peace should be excommunicated. The second, widely influential response was the formulation of the just-war theory, taken over from Cicero and articulated by St Ambrose and St Augustine. This theory states that Christians can legitimately participate in war provided that it is declared by a properly constituted authority and certain ethical conditions are maintained in the conduct of war. A third and further development was the idea of the crusade which emerged during the Middle Ages and was much influenced by the Old Testament concept of a holy war. The New Testament, so obviously more orientated towards peace than war, has been used as a justification for all three Christian responses to war – pacifism, just-war and crusade. Examining these responses Robin Gill has written:

> The situation of the pre-Constantinian church appears all the more remarkable when it is realised that no major Christian Church or denomination has been consistently pacifist since Constantine. Indeed, Christian pacifism has been largely confined to a small group of sects, such as the Quakers, Anabaptists, Mennonites, Brethren and Jehovah's Witnesses. Further, pacifists within the churches, as distinct from sects, have in times of war been barely tolerated by their fellow Christians.[5]

Conscientious objection or the refusal to give military service is treated by the larger contemporary Churches today as a matter of individual conscience, rather than as a fundamental issue of the Christian community which requires a firm commitment regarding the Churches' stance on violence and war. It comes as a surprise to many people that Christians were pacifist up to the reign of Constantine. Yet nothing could be further apart than the ethic of holy war and Jesus's teaching on non-violence. The spirit of Jesus is a spirit of peace and at no time did Jesus encourage people to use violence nor did he ever use violence to fulfil his mission.

A question we must also consider is why people commit violence and how they are motivated towards its use. It is well known that traditionally the participation in certain religious rites has helped individuals to develop not only courage in general, but also the kind of courage needed to commit violent acts. From this point of view the religious blessings bestowed on warriors and armies through the ages, often taken from biblical texts, have been of the greatest significance in fostering the psychological acceptance of what appears as the legitimate use of violent force in war. Equally important is the perception of the enemy as the 'demonic other' – the 'alien' outside the boundaries of one's own social and religious group, the enemy of God, the representative of a false doctrine, the agent of most hideous crimes. Littleton (1987) speaks of the 'lethal redefinition' of the victim, by the killer and the community that passes judgement upon the killing, as something less than human – a monster, beast, animal, even rotting matter such as 'garbage' and 'trash', for verbal abuse regularly accompanies such redefinition, which establishes that effecting the death of such an individual (or of whole groups of people) is a permissible, even worthy act. But the same author also perceptively points to the final paradox of this pattern of violence: while one must dehumanize one's enemies in order to employ violence against them, one must at the same time dehumanize oneself to become an instrument of slaughter, eradicating such tendencies as guilt, fear and compassion.

Such perceptions of the 'demonic other' had fewer implications when armed conflicts could be contained locally or nationally. Tendencies towards conflict and aggression have been seen as part of human nature,[6] as part of the mysterious and inexplicable existence of evil within and without, and thus the use of organized force and violence in war has been reckoned to be almost inevitable. People have long been pessimistic about eliminating war, but since we have passed the atomic threshold and entered the nuclear age, the shadow of universal death lingers close on the horizon in a way never experienced before. It is not the abolition of differences, disagreement and conflict that matters most, but the decisive question is really whether we as a species can learn to resolve our existing conflicts without recourse to violence and war.

Different religious traditions have provided a great store of mythical and metaphysical explanations to account for the origin and existence of evil in its different forms, for the violent conflicts and struggles that beset human beings and societies. For Jews and Christians these explanations are deeply rooted in the Bible. Many scriptural passages have been used to justify war. Religious institutions have been implicated in aggression and conflicts through legitimizing state violence and wars, especially in societies where the religious and political elites are drawn from the same class and share identical interests. While many other ideological, political and economic factors are important in modern warfare, political leaders of many countries still continue to appeal to religious beliefs, images and sacred scriptures to rally support and create a consensus among people for accepting and participating in organized state violence. The close association of religion with war in past and present is one of the strongest proofs of the fact that religion buttresses the existing social order. Yet there has always existed a tension in religion between giving this support and providing a prophetic critique which challenges the existing order with a vision of a higher morality, a greater unity and universal values which transcend the boundaries of one's group.

A re-examination of the Bible's message on peace challenges the often maintained assumption that questions of faith are in principle separate from questions of politics, and that politics follows its own laws and morality. Peace is to do with the world without and within, with the well-being of the entire community. We do not live in a peaceful world at all, but is peace only a vision of the last days to come when the final battle against all the forces of evil will be won, or can we learn to make peace now, to create a new and better world?

It is important to realize that we are at a new historical threshold which requires a new consciousness and new models of thinking. Due to the existence of modern nuclear technology for militaristic uses, especially the availability of fission and fusion bombs, there exists a sharp discontinuity in the history of warfare, and an entirely new and qualitatively different, unprecedented capacity for violence has come into being. This discontinuity in the outer world of history and warfare needs now to be paralleled by a discontinuity in the religious attitudes and thinking which justified violence and war in the past. This urgent need for new thinking is realized by many people in different political camps and religious groups today. The many peace groups and movements which have sprung up all over the globe are too numerous to list, but for many people who seek alternative patterns for a different, more just and peaceful social order, the authentic biblical teaching on peace has gained a renewed hearing in our time. What, then, can the Bible teach us about peace?

The Bible as Teacher of Peace

Today the striving for peace is strongly associated with the notion of non-violence, a term which came into common English usage only in the early twentieth century through its association with Gandhi and his particular approach to resolving conflict. Like non-violence, pacifism too is a modern word,[7] but the idea of peace can be documented from ancient times. The Hebrew Bible contains many stories of wars, yet some of the great deliverances, such as that of the Israelites from Egypt, were achieved without violence, and the idea of peace runs throughout the Hebrew scriptures where the word *shalom* is found 249 times. But what is this idea of peace – of *shalom* – proclaimed in the face of so much war? It is above all the prophets who proclaim the Lord's vision of universal peace: 'I will abolish the bow, and the sword, and war from the land' (Hosea 2:18), and the psalmist admonishes people to 'seek peace and pursue it' (46:9). *Shalom* comes from a root meaning 'wholeness'; thus it is richer in meaning than our word 'peace'. *Shalom* is also very prominent in the rabbinic tradition where it stands for truth, justice and peace. It is said that the *Torah* was given to make peace in the world, and one of God's names is peace. *Shalom* refers to both spiritual and material conditions. Famous is the passage from Isaiah 2:2–4 which describes how the Lord will gather all nations together in peace:

> Come, let us go up to the mountain of the Lord,
> to the Temple of the Lord of Jacob
> that he may teach us his ways
> so that we may walk in his paths
>
> . . .
>
> He will wield authority over the nations
> and adjudicate between many peoples;
> these will hammer their swords into ploughshares,
> their spears into sickles.
> Nation will not lift sword against nation,
> there will be no more training for war.

The images used by Isaiah in other passages for describing peace were later interpreted as being of three kinds: the peace of the river, the peace of the bird and that of the cauldron. The fullest image is that of the river (referring to Isa. 66:12), a state of being and dynamic movement which carries with it the prosperity and love between peoples and with the Lord. The image of peace as a flying bird (Isa. 31:5) is the peace which is obtained by preparing for war, by maintaining an armed force to keep off, intimidate and destroy the enemy in order to protect and save the people. The Lord watches over his people like the bird spreading its wings to protect its young. One has to be vigilant because evil is near – this is a diminished *shalom* indeed. An even more desperate and diminished kind of peace is that associated with the image of the cauldron (Isa. 26:11–12), a fragile peace full of anguish where divine power is poured out to the detriment of the enemy like a boiling cauldron, and where one has to save one's skin and possessions. Discussing these three kinds of peace, Armand Abecassis has commented:

> There is the peace that comes when violence, injustice and trouble are happening to someone else; there is the peace that comes from the power to intimidate and prevent others from harming us; finally there is *Shalom* imaged in the river that unites, enriches and fulfils the whole human race. Peace that is just the absence of war, or the peace that exists in a cemetery are not the *Shalom* that comes into being when men and women

strive to love each other and to see in every human person a reflection of the infinitely loving and life-giving God.[8]

In the rabbinic tradition peace is described as the cornerstone of God's creation. Peace is given primacy over war and dissension, and peace is to the earth as yeast is to the dough. This vision of universal peace became the horizon of the rabbinic tradition, and many earlier biblical ideas and concepts referring to power and military might underwent a long process of reinterpretation among generations of rabbis so that in the ethics of Rabbi Nathan the greatest hero is one who successfully transforms a foe into a friend.

Peace for the ancient Hebrews was a social concept, for it applied to harmonious relationships within the family, in local society and between nations. The greeting '*shalom*', in use since the time of the Judges and King David, expressed the positive aim of encouraging co-operation, and later this greeting was used by both Jews and Christians. If we enquire about the peace traditions in Christianity, we remember that the Christian story begins with the angels singing to the shepherds in the field 'Glory to God in the highest and peace upon earth' (Luke 2:14): from its inception Christianity carried a universalizing thrust and concern for world peace. Jesus distinguished his way of peace from that prevailing at his time: 'Peace is my parting gift to you, my own peace such as the world cannot give' (John 14:27). The peace of Jesus Christ, the *Pax Christi*, stood in contrast to the *Pax Romana* of the ancient world where peace was maintained by coercion and subjugation.[9] Jesus's peace – the peace which the world cannot give – is a rejection of the politics of violence – for in his teaching the enemy becomes the privileged object of love.

Just as the Hebrew *shalom* means so much more than the absence of conflict and refers to both material and spiritual conditions together, so also the New Testament notions of peace – *eirene* – and reconciliation – *katallage* – go far beyond the idea of freedom from war and unrest, or the notion of passive non-violence. Understood negatively, peace must imply such absence from violence and war, but positively understood peace means well-being and fulfilment as goals of our religious and social life. In the New Testament all Christians are called to the 'ministry of reconciliation'. Such reconciliation has personal, social and cosmic dimensions and is synonymous with salvation and redemption – the breaking into the world of a new reality aimed at ultimate and universal peace. The call to reconciliation therefore implies an active engagement in the process of peace-making.

Glen Stassen has described Jesus's call to active peace-making as consisting of four practical steps: '(1) affirm your enemies' valid interest and pray for them; (2) talk to your adversary and seek agreement; (3) associate with the powerless, who need justice; (4) do not seek to return evil for evil.'[10] These steps can be applied to interpersonal and family relationships, but also to social conflicts of war, violence and other situations requiring peace-making. Jesus's saying in the Sermon on the Mount, 'Blessed are the peace-makers, for they shall be called sons of God' (Matt. 5:44), is now repeatedly cited in discussions of European peace movements. Yet it is noteworthy, and we must not forget that this saying of Jesus has not characterized past attitudes of the Churches regarding questions of war and peace. Can the seemingly powerless authority of the Bible become now more effective in public debate? Can we learn peace-making from the Bible by loving our enemies?

Given Jesus's model and teaching of non-violent love, one is struck by the prevalence of military images in early Christian literature. 'Take up God's armour,' admonishes St Paul, and Christ is 'the captain of salvation' (Heb. 2:10). Early Christian writings contain much military language borrowed from the Roman legion. Even the word 'sacrament', so important in the Church, is derived from the Latin 'sacramentum', the word for the military oath of allegiance which bound the Roman soldier to the 'divine' emperor. 'Let us be armed for peace . . . to fight the Evil One,' wrote Clement of Alexandria, but the *militia Christi* of the early Church was a bloodless host of peace who often shed their own blood in martyrdom.

Our own world is very different from the world of the early Church and the Bible. Yet what can we learn for our own situation if we are attentive to the Bible's teaching on peace? If Jesus's command 'Love your enemies' (Matt. 5:44; Luke 6:27) is not taken to be a Utopian demand, but an instruction for action in the realm of politics, it develops its own dynamics by mobilizing the imagination to seek new ways of peace-making, of more human politics away from the rhetoric of hostility and aggression so often used. Several Church conferences and publications have come to the conclusion that the system of deterrence by the threat of mutual annihilation contradicts the spirit of Christ and his teaching, and that we must overcome the spirit and logic of deterrence by imaginative initiatives of a new kind.[11]

The love of which the Bible speaks is not a matter of feeling but of *praxis* – of practical action whereby love will transform political reality. It will also teach us to see through the eyes of the other and thus perceive the conflict from the other side. As Jesus said: 'Treat others as you would like them to treat you' (Luke 6:31; Matt. 7:12). However, a very difficult question arises when acting in this spirit: namely, how to confront the enemies of peace? The Bible knows that those who tread the way of loving their enemies will thereby create new enemies, for the task of overcoming hostility can ignite new hostility. As Jesus said: 'Do not suppose that I have come to bring peace to the earth: it is not peace I have come to bring, but a sword' (Matt. 11:34). Jesus's person and teaching can become the cause of dissension. Jesus's preaching about the Kingdom brings together love, justice and peace. These may still be small, like a mustard seed, 'the smallest of all the seeds on earth; yet once it is sown it grows into the biggest shrub of them all and puts out big branches . . .' (Mark 4:31–2).

There is a dynamic of hope and a realism in Jesus's teaching which is very different from the teachings of the apocalyptic visionaries of Jesus's own time. The apocalyptic literature of the inter-testamental period was full of visions of violent destruction of the world and prone to rejoice in the destruction of one's enemies. The visionary nature of this apocalyptic literature draws heavily on dualistic language and imagery and has influenced such books as Jude and Revelation. There is a great danger in using these texts uncritically and outside the context of their own times, as happens among certain groups in the USA and UK who believe in the battle of Armageddon and the 'Rapture' – the apocalyptic destruction of our present world. We must recognize the dangerous misunderstandings to which biblical apocalyptic passages are prone and ask ourselves whether those Christians who today discuss the battle of Armageddon are not themselves responsible for preparing our annihilation? There certainly exists a sharp ethical dissonance between Jesus's teaching of loving one's enemies and the sentiments expressed in apocalyptic literature.

Christians, in spite of their violent history and theory of just-war, have a strong tradition of peace grounded in the Sermon on the Mount and in Jesus's parting message to John, 'Peace I leave with you, my peace I give you, not as the world gives it' (John 14:27). Contemporary Christian pacifists have been inspired by Jesus's own example and what one might call the bias to peace in the Christian Gospel. The Church applied the title of 'Prince of Peace', first used for the Davidic king in the Old Testament, to Jesus, and the Christian liturgy often repeats the words, 'The peace of the Lord be always with you.' It also makes much use of the prayer, 'The peace of God, which passeth all understanding, keep your hearts and minds in the knowledge and love of God and of his Son, Jesus Christ our Lord.' In modern times there has been a revival of the 'giving of peace' at the end of celebrating the eucharist, often accompanied by the shaking of hands and kissing in peace. The contemporary Christian peace movement uses the Bible as a teacher of peace, drawing particularly on Jesus's saying 'love your enemies' (Matt. 5:44; Luke 6:27) and the Beatitudes described in the Sermon on the Mount.

Its insights have been directly applied to practical matters in the discussion of contemporary military politics by German peace campaigners, whose call for peace based on a new politics of the Sermon on the Mount has raised widespread debate.[12]

More recently, in Germany at least, much attention has been directed to Carl Friedrich von Weizsäcker's publication *Die Zeit drängt* – 'Time is Short', unfortunately not translated into English. It calls for a 'World Council for Justice, Peace and Preservation of Creation' – a Peace Council of the Christian denominations taking place during 1990. Ultimately, it aims at bringing together members of different religions in order to unite them to work together for peace. Inspired by the biblical teaching on peace, and aware of the urgency for our global political and ecological situation, von Weizsäcker first called for such a 'Peace Council' at the Kirchentag, the national gathering of German Protestant Churches, in 1985. He then said: 'Today peace is the condition for humanity's survival. And peace has not been secured yet. At an ecumenical council, convened for the sake of peace, the Christian Churches, in their joint responsibility should speak a word which cannot be ignored by humanity.' Von Wiezsäcker's book states more explicitly: 'In these three areas (justice, peace and the preservation of creation) it is possible and indeed necessary to unify Christians and to reach harmony among the world religions. We should demand a worldwide politically effective legal order.'[13] Von Weizsäcker's appeal carries on the tradition of several earlier initiatives of peace-making, whether one thinks of the 'Fellowship of Reconciliation', a Christian pacifist movement founded as long ago as 1914, or of the 'World Conference on Religion and Peace', or the relatively recent meeting of world religious leaders at Assisi, on 27 October 1986, to confront the 'transcendental challenge of peace'.

Peace is a political and ethical imperative today. What can we do, then, at a practical level if we take the biblical teaching on peace seriously?

What Can We Do at the Practical Level?

Someone put it very simply and succinctly: 'Dare peace!'[14] – dare to believe in it! Imagine it as a real alternative to our current situation! Work for it! This implies risk and endeavour, renunciation and suffering. Such daring is grounded in faith and hope, but in realism too – a realism which takes the prevailing realities seriously, but dares to dream, to think and work for new realities and structures free from violence. So often in the past Christians have justified their conduct by taking as their model the 'holy war' of the Old

Testament or their own theory of the 'just war' as if Christ had never preached the Beatitudes or as if Christian precepts were only to be followed in personal spirituality and not in social and political realities.

To dare peace and dare it realistically! As John Riches has perceptively commented in his essay on 'The Use of the Bible in the Nuclear Debate': '. . . such attempts at the social embodiment of Christian precepts are marked . . . by a realism which takes seriously both the realities of human aggression and depravity *and* the sense in which, as creatures of God, men and women have it in themselves to rise above such powers'.[15]

To return to the Hebrew Bible where we began, I would like to quote again Micah's prophecy (4:3): 'And they shall beat their swords into ploughshares, and their spears into pruning hooks; nation shall not lift up sword against nation, neither shall they learn war any more.' These prophetic words stand cast in bronze in front of the UN building in New York. With the tremendous political changes all over Eastern Europe, it is interesting to know that this prophetic monument was presented as a gift by the USSR and also, that this verse has had a very special meaning for the work of the Church peace groups which were active for so many years in former East Germany.

The Christian witness for peace carries an evangelical mandate, an imperative to love our enemies. St Paul expressed it like this in his second letter to the Corinthians:

> The love of Christ (*caritas Christi*) leaves us no choice . . . With us therefore worldly standards have ceased to count in our estimate of any person. When anyone is united to Christ, there is a new world; the old order has gone, and a new order has already begun . . . we come therefore as Christ's ambassadors. It is as if God were appealing to you through us: in Christ's name, we implore you: be reconciled. (2 Cor. 5:14, 17, 20)

Jesus's radical love-imperative embraces two actions: saying no to war, violence and lethal resistance; and saying yes to the redemptive possibilities inherent in Jesus's own life and teachings.

But by and large traditional Christianity, throughout much of its past history, has rejected the radical peace witness as utterly impractical, Utopian and other-worldly. Christians have often cultivated personal, inward spirituality while accepting and condoning the most inhuman and most violent political realities. Until now Christian pacifists and peace groups have been marginal in the Christian tradition. During this century the theologian Reinhold Niebuhr was still a most trenchant critic of Christian pacifism, and yet he had to concede that pacifists express 'a genuine impulse in the heart of Christianity, the impulse to take the law of Christ seriously and not to allow political strategies, which the sinful character of man make necessary, to become final norms'.[16]

Timothy George, in his article 'A Radically Christian Witness for Peace'[17] has argued that we have compelling reasons today to re-examine the role of Christian peace dissenters throughout the history of the Church because of our radically new situation. We need a radically different approach from those traditionally offered, for the following three reasons:

1   The massive stalemate of violence and enmity in which the nuclear superpowers find themselves locked. The supposedly 'Christian' theory of a just war is manifestly bankrupt in a world where categories of proportionality and noncombatant immunity have become meaningless. As Martin Luther King succinctly put it, the choice is *either* non-violence *or* non-existence.
2   The second reason is the pluralist context in which the Christian churches must function today. The Christian minority situation in the contemporary world is not unlike that of the pre-Constantinian Church.

   Christians may need to redefine their mission in terms of its faithfulness to the model of Jesus and the early Church rather than its conformity to a culture based on coercion.
3   In the global crisis that threatens to engulf all humanity world peace is not an isolated issue, but one factor in a complex of problems which include mass starvation, political oppression, ecological destruction, terrorism, racism, sexism and much more. Jesus's gospel of love implies a holistic ethic of life which affirms the sanctity of every living being and the whole of the cosmos.

Perhaps we can hear the urgent appeal of the biblical call to love and peace more clearly today when we realize that we live in *one* world as *one* humanity with *one* shared destiny. As the Christian thinker and mystic Pierre Teilhard de Chardin, who was deeply inspired by the biblical vision of one creation, has said, life now has to be raised to a new stage. He wrote: '*The age of nations has passed. Now, unless we wish to perish we must shake off our old prejudices and build the earth* . . . The more scientifically I regard the world, *the less can I see any possible biological future for it except the active consciousness of its unity*'[18] and this unity could for him be achieved only through love and not through outward coercion.

To shake off our prejudices and work for the unification of humankind through love means breaking down age-old barriers outside and psychological barriers inside ourselves so that there remains no demonic 'other', no stranger, no enemy against whom we wish to wage violence and holy wars. If the ideas of conflict and war were eradicated, life would indeed be raised to a new stage, but instead we mostly continue to nourish the roots of violence in our minds. This is even reflected at the level of language. How often do we not use confrontational language and similes drawn from military battle! I was shocked to hear a television news-reader describe an East German proposal for a reduction of tactical weapons as a 'peace offensive'. Why this association between peace and offensive?

We have spent far more resources, time and thought on developing the language and arts of war than we have ever given to peace, which is now *the* decisive issue for human survival. Some perceptive contemporaries are wondering whether humans as a species can really evolve the capacity for true peace-making – not the kind of peace achieved at the end of a war or as an intermittent period between wars, but peace as a new form of life. Not negative peace, but what John Macquarrie calls an affirmative concept of peace,[19] the peace of *shalom* as an all-embracing river. That would be a new wholeness whereby peace would become an imperative which would make all war immoral and free us from nuclear addiction which, as Brian Wicker has commented, is like a cancerous global disease damaging our collective health and threatening us with death. It has also been said by Robert Müller, former Assistant Secretary General of the United Nations and now Rector of the Peace University in Costa Rica, that

> there is even more reason to eradicate armaments from this planet than there was to eradicate smallpox. All conceivable files and proposals for disarmament are ready. They have been painstakingly worked out over the last three decades. All depends on the will of peoples and nations, especially the big nations who bear the main responsibility in this matter.[20]

While most of us feel completely impotent with regard to international power politics, there is much we all can do to bring about a change of heart. A greater consciousness of human sisterhood and brotherhood will strengthen the bonds in the human community. The peace and ecological movement, the women's movement, with its deep commitment towards acting and educating for peace,[21] the many liberation movements to bring about social justice and eradicate debilitating poverty from our globe – all have a spiritual dimension and immense transformative potential for the future of the human community. It is encouraging to know that Christian women practise 'peace preaching' in churches, that the Archbishop of Canterbury and Cardinal Hume published *Prayers for Peace* (1987), that religious leaders from the major world faiths met in 1986 to pray for peace. There are now schools and universities devoted to peace; we have the annual Week of Prayer for World Peace supported by people from different faiths and we have selected testimonies from members of different faiths on *Education for Peace*,[22] a truly inspiring book.

So much can be done, and yet much more remains to be accomplished to eradicate violent conflict from this earth. Peace remains no longer simply an option or a quest, but the nuclear threat impels us to transcend collective violence and war to create peace among societies, cultures and states out of necessity. However, the many professional associations, policy-makers, administrators and scientists concerned with issues of peace often unfortunately do not take into account the important religious resources, teachings, images and spiritual ideals which can inspire and help people to learn how to make peace.

For Jews and Christians this means to return to their roots in the Bible and ask how we can learn new truths about ourselves from our sacred scriptures. To tread the path of peace the Bible does not give us a path ready made. We have to build a new path now, but for this we can draw on the vision of peace in the Bible. It is much less important for us today to know how the Bible has been used and appealed to in times of war than it is imperative to embrace and make come true its message of peace for all human beings.

If we have the real strength of faith and the will to unite in love as one human family, then we can hope to find all the spiritual power, creativity and support needed to respond to the greatest challenge the human mind has ever met: to create peace on earth. Such peace will be both the work of our own hands *and* the gracious gift of God.

Chapter 17

The Bible and Mission

Geoffrey Parrinder

The Logic of Monotheism

In biblical times, as in most ages and lands, religion was the expression of the lives of individuals and societies. In general, it was understood to apply to the conditions of the people and their history, and the notion of a mission to another tribe was slow in appearing.

A classic example of tribal limitation appears in the story of the judge Jephthah, who is said to have told the Ammonites, 'Will you not possess what Chemosh your god gives you to possess? And we will possess all that the Lord our God has dispossessed before us.' (Judg. 11:24). The existence of this Ammonite god is not denied and his right over his people is recognized.

At a later date the narrative of Naaman the Syrian illustrates both belief in the association of God with the land, and also God's effect upon a man of another race. After he had been healed by bathing seven times in the river Jordan, Naaman took two mules' burden of earth from Israel and vowed that he would not sacrifice to any god but the Lord, though he would also have to bow in the temple of the Syrian god Rimmon with his royal master (2 Kgs 5).

The implications of developing belief in monotheism, that there is only one God, appear in many places. First of all, there is only one God for Israel, as expressed in the Decalogue: 'I am the Lord your God . . . You shall have no other gods before me' (Exod. 20:2–3). Then it followed that there was only one real God, who created all things, so 'All the gods of the peoples are idols, but the Lord made the heavens' (Ps 96:5).

The prophets extended this perception to speak of God not only as ruling all people but as teaching them his law. Then there came the visions of Isaiah (2:2–3) and Micah (4:1–2) in depicting 'all nations' going to the Lord's house at Jerusalem to learn his law and walk in his paths. And later Zechariah (8:23) envisaged men from nations of every language taking hold of the robe of a Jew and saying, 'Let us go with you, for we have heard that God is with you.'

That there is one God implied that he is concerned with all peoples, and though Israel was chosen to serve the Lord yet others were chosen also, or had their part in the divine scheme of things. So Isaiah (19:24) saw a time coming, 'on that day', when Israel will join with Egypt and Assyria to be a blessing in the earth. The Lord declares, 'Blessed be Egypt my people, and Assyria the work of my hands, and Israel my heritage.'

That earlier there had been narrow nationalism, which persisted later even alongside universalistic statements, does not detract from the noblest prophetic visions and the logic of monotheism.

In the New Testament also there appear both restrictive and wider attitudes. A much debated example is in the story of the Syrophoenician woman (Mark 7:24f.). Here Jesus had left Galilee and sought for quiet, 'but he could not be hid'. When the woman, who was a Greek, asked for her daughter to be healed, Jesus said that the children should first be fed. But when she persisted by saying that she could have crumbs from the table at least, her clever reply brought relaxation and a cure. But the parallel passage in Matthew (15:24) has Jesus saying, 'I was only sent to the lost sheep of the house of Israel'. Here the modern critical study of the Bible is important, for it enables comparisons to be made between the texts, establishes the priority of Mark, and reveals the attitudes of particular evangelists.

Again it is Matthew alone (10:5–6) who says that the disciples were sent out on a healing mission and told not to go among the Gentiles or the Samaritans, but only to 'the lost sheep of the house of Israel'. Mark says nothing of such a restriction in his parallel passage (6:7), nor does Luke mention it in his account of the missions of the twelve or the seventy (9:1; 10:1).

Matthew seems to have been particularly concerned with a Jewish mission, but he does record words and actions of Jesus that look beyond that. To the centurion, a Roman or at least a Gentile, Jesus is reported to have said, 'I have not found such faith, even in Israel' (Matt. 8:10), and he continued by saying that many would come 'from east and west' and sit down with Abraham, Isaac and Jacob in the kingdom of heaven. Luke also records these words, but in a different context (7:9 and also 13:28–9).

Knowledge of Other Religions

There is little trace in the Bible of interest in or knowledge of the beliefs and practices of other races and religions. Second Isaiah mocks the images of foreign gods being carted away into captivity and shaking as they go: 'Bel bows down, Nebo stoops, they bow down together, they themselves go into captivity' (46:1–2). What the Babylonians would have said of their gods and their imagery is not known, and the symbolism is not examined.

The Bible has a constant aversion to 'graven images', from the Decalogue onwards: 'you shall not make yourself a graven image, or any likeness of anything' (Exod. 20:4). There was a proper conviction that God could not be depicted or compared to anything. Second Isaiah descriptions (40:19f.; 44:9f.) of men making images out of wood, and then with the residue making a fire to cook food, are amusing pictures but they show no understanding of religious symbolism. Yet there was not a complete abandonment of religious art, as decorations in synagogues have shown, in excavations at Doura-Europos and elsewhere.

There is little knowledge of other religions shown by speakers and writers in the New Testament either. Paul criticized vain 'philosophy' (Col. 2:8), and he declared that the world did not know God through wisdom (1 Cor. 1:21). But it is doubtful if he knew anything of the philosophy of Plato or Aristotle who did claim a knowledge of God. Yet in his reported sermon at Athens Paul made one of the few attempts to find points of contact with the beliefs of his hearers, by quoting from well-known Stoic poets who had said that 'we are God's offspring' (Acts 17:28). Elsewhere he quoted a Cretan 'prophet' (Titus 1:12).

Following many passages in the Bible there persisted down the ages criticism of the 'heathen' and their 'idols'. So nearly 200 years ago Bishop Heber wrote the hymn, for long very popular, which declared that,

> The heathen in his blindness
> Bows down to wood and stone.

In the first draft of this hymn Heber referred it to the people of Java, but somebody must have told him that the Javanese were Muslims who would have been horrified at such accusations of idolatry. So the reference was changed to 'Ceylon's isle' (which did not scan), but the Singhalese Buddhists also might have objected that while they did indeed have statues of the Buddha they did not worship them, or the Buddha himself, but the Law which he had preached.

In modern times there has developed a great deal of knowledge of the many religions of the world. Countless texts and scriptures have been translated into many European and other languages, and there have been innumerable descriptions and pictures of religious buildings, rituals and beliefs. Much of this knowledge has come through the work of missionaries, from Matteo Ricci in China, William Carey in India, and very many others. To know what other religions teach is now regarded as essential for mission, at least among the older and more established organizations, although some of the fundamentalist sects and televangelists seem prepared to ignore what others hold dear and to utter blanket condemnations of pagans and idolaters.

Exclusive or Inclusive?

Attempts have been made in recent years to define the proper attitudes to be taken towards other religions than one's own. An Exclusivist attitude rules out any other way of salvation or any other practice of devotion; all are wrong, all have fallen short, all are out of step except us. But an Inclusivist attitude seeks to bring all peoples into one fold, regarding them as having variant understandings of the one truth. So people in other religions have been called 'anonymous Christians', or followers of 'the unknown Christ of Hinduism', or other religions. A further attitude seeks to demonstrate Pluralism, noting that religions have their own validity and should exist alongside each other.

Exponents of these attitudes have sought justification from the Bible, since it is an anthology that expresses different points of view, though as a prophetic book it makes definite statements, such as 'I am the first and I am the last, and beside me there is no god' (Isa. 44:6). The many assertions in the Bible about the abominations of the 'heathen', the nations, whether in worship or in morality, display strongly Exclusivist attitudes, both in safeguarding Israel's religion and in rejecting foreign cults and customs. But the context of such statements needs to be taken into account, and their relevance to the special circumstances of that time, and whether they have an abiding significance.

Students of the New Testament are well aware of texts that also have prophetic dogmatism, expressing Exclusivist views, not only in affirming one true way but also appearing to rule out others. John 14:6 is often quoted: 'No one comes to the Father but by me.' But a careful study of the context shows that these words were addressed to a particular disciple, Thomas, who sought to know the way. Similarly John 10:8 says that 'all who came before me are thieves and robbers'. Who were these? All other teachers, or false prophets and hireling shepherds? Yet at the end of this parable it is affirmed that there are other sheep, not of this fold, who must be brought in (10:16).

These discourses in John's Gospel are recognized by modern commentators as often providing the reflections of the evangelist and the later Church, making comments on statements or matters of faith, adapted to the continuing life and needs of the community.

In the first chapter of this Gospel it is declared that the Logos is 'the true light that enlightens every man' (John 1:9). Archbishop William Temple in his devotional commentary on John applied these words to leaders of other religions, such as Zoroaster, Buddha and Confucius, since whatever light they had must have come from the one Logos. This was a truly Inclusivist interpretation.

Another popular Exclusivist verse is attributed to Peter in Acts (4:12), 'there is salvation in no one else, for there is no other name under heaven given among men by which we must be saved'. It is a statement of faith, after the crucifixion and resurrection, in the context of questioning by religious rulers, and it claims divine authority for a work of healing. Yet in a different setting, the same book also attributes to Peter another attitude when he was faced with the clear faith of the righteous Gentile Cornelius, who had received an angelic visit during his prayers. Peter is said to have responded to this evidence by declaring that 'in every nation any one who fears God and does what is right is acceptable to him' (Acts 10:35). This is clearly Inclusivist, recognizing the validity of faith in the one God and acknowledging righteous living, even if they appeared in another race and religion. The statement expresses the sentiment of the Church when it was working among Gentiles.

A similar recognition of good life among different peoples was shown by Paul, when he wrote of 'the Gentiles who have not the law, yet do by nature what the law requires' (Rom. 2:14). He applies the logic of monotheism, in that God is not the God of the Jews only, he is 'the God of Gentiles also', and so these also are justified 'because of their faith' (Rom. 3:29–30).

Rarely, if ever, is there a suggestion of a Pluralist position, that we have our religion and they have theirs and that differences will persist. Such an attitude would be more appropriate to Jephthah, since the logic of monotheism seems to demand a mission, though the manner and condition of missions will vary from time and place.

Mission

The first biblical missionary was Jonah, sent to cry against Nineveh, in the north of modern Iraq. It is a pity that popular notions of Jonah and the whale, literally a great fish, have obscured the parabolic nature of the story. The parable represents the Exile and the Restoration, and it shows that Israel had a vocation and message to the Gentiles, and was sent to proclaim the judgment and the knowledge of God.

The story is Inclusivist. The people of Nineveh are called to repent of their sins, and it is assumed both that they know of the one God and that they accept his authority, since they do repent, to Jonah's disgust. Then God takes pity on the oppressing Ninevites, as well as on the gourd in a sub-parable, and he spares the thousands of ignorant people, 'and also much cattle'. There is an added ecological concern, that could be applied to modern Iraq.

Jonah is exceptional, in going out as a missionary. As we have suggested earlier, the general trend is towards coming in, the Gentiles coming to learn the law of the Lord in Jerusalem. The vocation of Israel is to be 'a light to the nations' (Isa. 42:6), and while darkness covers the earth 'nations shall come to your light, and kings to the brightness of your rising' (Isa. 60:3). Perhaps the nearest parallels to the message of Jonah are the words addressed to the Persian emperor Cyrus, who is called the 'anointed' of the Lord, and it is 'the God of Israel who calls you by your name' (Isa. 45:1–4).

In the New Testament it seems that Jesus, while praising the faith of Gentiles, did not preach to them, and he passed through Samaria quickly, though John suggests a great harvest there (John 4:35). But his eating with the outcast 'publicans and sinners' naturally led on to and justified the commensalism of Jews and Gentiles which Paul and the expanding Church practised. The struggle between Paul and Peter, and behind him the more orthodox James of Jerusalem, is revealed vividly in Galatians 1–2.

'All Christians were called Nazarenes once,' wrote the Church father Epiphanius, and recent studies have shed more light on the Jewish Church which retained the title of Nazarene. James, the younger brother of Jesus, became head of the Church in Jerusalem, and his other brothers and relatives travelled to Galilee and beyond. Law-abiding and humanistic Jewish-Christian communities endured for centuries.

The Gentile mission was particularly the work of Paul and his companions, and Acts gives a sketch of the division of labour. James claimed thousands of believing Jews (Acts 21:20), but in the so-called Council of Jerusalem Paul and Barnabas were sent to Antioch and beyond. In the speech put in his mouth, James spoke of the rebuilding of 'the dwelling of David', and the seeking for 'the Gentiles who are called by my name', but the Gentile converts were exempted from most of the requirements of the law (Acts 15:16f.). Paul and Barnabas went off to Antioch and Syria and Cilicia, and it was indeed at Antioch that these mixed congregations were first called Christians (Acts 11:26).

With the fall of Jerusalem to the Romans, and the scattering of followers of both orthodox Judaism and of Christian Jews, the Gentile Churches became by far the most numerous. The Gospels and later books of the New Testament were written in the light of this great expansion. Christianity became a missionary faith, going out beyond land and place, like Buddhism before it.

Most, if not all, religions welcome converts from other faiths or none, and some seek them out as part of their own vocation. Buddhism was the first great international and missionary religion, spreading from India into south-east Asia, and then to the north to Tibet, China and Japan, and in our times it has come to Europe and America. Christianity followed such expansion, and Islam arrived later, as international and inter-racial faiths. The New Testament was written for the purposes of this mission and some of its most used verses express its conviction.

At the end of Matthew's Gospel we read, 'Go and make disciples of all nations, baptizing them in the name of the Father and of the Son and of the Holy Spirit.' To critical eyes this looks anachronistic, reading back later convictions into the early period, since the doctrine of the Trinity only developed slowly, but the verse expressed the faith of the growing Church. Similarly the injunction to 'make disciples of all nations' also fits the attitude of the later Church, when Peter had received Cornelius and Paul had evangelized Asia Minor and Greece, and was planning to go to Rome and Spain. But it has always been claimed that the Gospel is available for all people, without distinction of race, class or sex.

There are other missionary verses, such as 'As the Father has sent me, even so I send you' (John 20:21), and more specifically, 'you shall be my witnesses in Jerusalem, and in all Judea, and Samaria, and to the end of the earth' (Acts 1:8). In old translations of Mark 16:15 it is written, 'Go into all the world and preach the Gospel to the whole creation.' This was a later addition to the text of Mark, not in the oldest manuscripts , but even so it expresses the faith and practice of the growing Church.

In recent times there have been many searching examinations of the meaning, purpose, justification and limitation of missions. There was a great surge of missionary activity in the nineteenth century, following the evangelical revival but also in Roman Catholicism, and there was much success in some areas, especially Africa and Latin America. Now there are independent and self-governing Churches in those continents and it is hardly appropriate still to speak of missions. One thing is clear, that is the changing nature and task of mission in time and place. Today specialized works in education, social service and famine relief, are particularly prominent.

In theological concerns, it has been noted earlier that one great contribution made by missionaries in recent centuries has been the study of the teachings of different religions, with translations made of innumerable scriptures and sacred texts. This has implied comparison with the Bible, and has given opportunities for dialogue with followers of other religions. In the continuing existence of different religions, the pluralism of our times, dialogue and mutual understanding and respect are important ways forward.

Dialogue can be justified from the Bible, from Jonah to Cornelius, but it can be greatly extended since nowadays we know far more about the varied religions of humanity than our forefathers or fore-mothers ever knew. John Wesley, in preaching on 'Catholic spirit', adapted the words of Jehu to Jehonadab, 'Is your heart right? Give me your hand' (2 Kgs 10:15).

Chapter 18

The Bible and Christian Witness

Michael Nazir-Ali

But Peter, standing with the eleven, lifted up his voice and addressed them, 'Men of Judea and all who dwell in Jerusalem, let this be known to you, and give ear to my words. For these men are not drunk, as you suppose, since it is only the third hour of the day; but this is what was spoken by the prophet Joel:

' "And in the last days it shall be, God declares,
that I will pour out my Spirit upon all flesh,
and your sons and your daughters shall prophesy,
and your young men shall see visions,
and your old men shall dream dreams;
yea, and on my menservants and my maidservants in those days
I will pour out my Spirit; and they shall prophesy.
And I will show wonders in the heaven above
and signs on the earth beneath,
blood, and fire, and vapour of smoke;
the sun shall be turned into darkness
and the moon into blood,
before the day of the Lord comes,
the great and manifest day.
And it shall be that whoever calls on the name of the Lord shall
be saved."

'Men of Israel, hear these words: Jesus of Nazareth, a man attested to you by God with mighty works and wonders and signs which God did through him in your midst, as you yourselves know – this Jesus, delivered up according to the definite plan and foreknowledge of God, you crucified and killed by the hands of lawless men. But God raised him up, having loosed the pangs of death, because it was not possible for him to be held by it.

'For David says concerning him,
' "I saw the Lord always before me,
for he is at my right hand that I may not be shaken;
therefore my heart was glad, and my tongue rejoiced;
moreover my flesh will dwell in hope.
For thou wilt not abandon my soul to Hades,
nor let thy Holy One see corruption.
Thou hast made known to me the ways of life;
thou wilt make me full of gladness with thy presence."

'Brethren, I may say to you confidently of the patriarch David that he

both died and was buried, and his tomb is with us to this day. Being
therefore a prophet, and knowing that God had sworn with an oath to
him that he would set one of his descendants upon his throne, he
foresaw and spoke of the resurrection of the Christ, that he was not
abandoned to Hades, nor did his flesh see corruption. This Jesus God
raised up, and of that we all are witnesses. Being therefore exalted at
the right hand of God, and having received from the Father the promise
of the Holy Spirit, he has poured out this which you see and hear. For
David did not ascend into the heavens; but he himself says,
  ' "The Lord said to my Lord, Sit at my right hand,
  till I make thy enemies a stool for thy feet."
'Let all the house of Israel therefore know assuredly that God has
made him both Lord and Christ, this Jesus whom you crucified.'
  Now when they heard this they were cut to the heart, and said to
Peter and the rest of the apostles, 'Brethren, what shall we do?' And
Peter said to them, 'Repent, and be baptized every one of you in the
name of Jesus Christ for the forgiveness of your sins; and you shall
receive the gift of the Holy Spirit. For the promise is to you and to your
children and to all that are far off, every one whom the Lord our God
calls to him.' And he testified with many other words and exhorted
them, saying, 'Save yourselves from this crooked generation.' So those
who received his word were baptized, and here were added that
day about three thousand souls. And they devoted themselves to the
apostles' teaching and fellowship, to the breaking of bread and the
prayers.
  And fear came upon every soul; and many wonders and signs were
done through the apostles. And all who believed were together and had
all things in common; and they sold their possessions and goods and
distributed them to all, as any had need. And day by day, attending the
temple together and breaking bread in their homes, they partook of food
with glad and generous hearts, praising God and having favour with all
the people. And the Lord added to their number day by day those who
were being saved. (Acts 2:14–47)

Peter's speech in Acts 2 is one of several in the book which sum up
for their hearers the Christian faith and the invitation to live a
Christian life. Peter, in fact, in this first speech has the world for his
audience. Just before he begins, there is a list of all sorts of people
who were present at Jerusalem at that time of pilgrimage. It is
interesting to read the list because it begins from the east and goes
towards the west and there are just two categories that do not fit
into that scheme. It begins outside the Roman Empire with the
people living in the Persian Empire and gradually moves westwards,
and so you have the Parthians and Medes and Elamites, you then
have residents of Iraq, then Judea, Cappadocia, Pontus and Asia.
Asia, of course, in the New Testament never means the continent
of Asia but the Roman Province which is more or less the modern
country of Turkey. The list then moves on to Egypt, Libya and so

on to Rome. Those odd categories there, Cretans and Arabians, nobody knows why they are put right at the end like that.

Of course, these people to whom Peter spoke were not only Jews but also converts to Judaism and perhaps also God-fearers, people who were not formally converts but who, nevertheless, worshipped only the God of Israel.[1] The whole world is there in microcosm, and this happens a great deal in the New Testament. In St Matthew's Gospel it is seen perhaps in the coming of the wise men to the infant Jesus, people coming from the east, people coming from another cultic religious tradition to worship the incarnate Lord (Matt. 2:1–12). It is seen in the genealogy of Luke which begins not with Abraham but with Adam (Luke 3: 23–38) and it is seen, of course, in the Great Commission that in one way or another is found in all the four Gospels, Jesus commissioning the Church to be universal, and it is found here in Acts 2.

This concern for the *world*, in fact, permeates the whole of the Bible. Israel's recognition from the very first that their God was not simply a tribal god like the other gods of peoples round about them, but that he was the God who had made the universe. This realization raises questions immediately about the relationship of this God then to all the other people who have been created by him. He cannot simply be the God of Israel, he must also be the God of the Egyptians, the God of the Assyrians and of all the people surrounding Israel. At first, perhaps, Israel thought that the way in which their God would show his universality was by giving them conquest, by giving them victory – and this again is very deeply rooted in our own psyche, the need for victory; it was also to be found in ancient Israel.

During the conquest of Canaan, we find that Israel treats different people differently, some are assimilated, some are pressed into their service and some, indeed, are eliminated (cf. the books of Joshua and Judges). Even before the entry into Canaan, when Israel leaves Eygpt at the exodus, it says that a whole rabble joined them (Exod. 12:38). All the other oppressed peoples of Egypt who trusted that the God of Israel was liberating the Hebrew people, joined in with them.

But later on Israel began to consider systematically how their God related to other people and they began to think that perhaps the way was for all people in the world to become Zionists, for everyone to have the same vision of God that Israel had. And so you have those great passages in Isaiah and Micah where all the nations are seen as streaming to Mount Zion (Isa. 2:2–4, Mic. 4:1–4). Well that is one way of thinking about the universality of Israel's God.

But already there are signs that the prophets, at least, have begun to think in other ways. In Isaiah 19, for example, it is clear that

God is working already among the Egyptians and Assyrians, the traditional enemies of the people of Israel. A day will come when Yahweh, the God of Israel, will say, 'blessed be Egypt my people and Assyria the work of my hands and Israel my heritage' (Isa. 19:25). In the book of Amos God reminds Israel of his great work at the exodus when he brought them out of Egypt and he says, 'Are you not like the Ethiopians to me, O people of Israel? Did I not bring up Israel from the land of Egypt, and the Philistines from Caphtor and the Syrians from Kir?' (Amos 9:7), emphasizing the universality of Israel's God. Indeed, when Israel is seen to be faithless, in the book of Malachi, we find that the sincerity of seekers after God in other nations becomes an example for Israel to emulate (Mal. 1:11).[2]

This consciousness of the universality of God is an aspect of the mission of Jesus himself. There is a growing realization, it seems, during the earthly ministry of our Lord, that his mission, his coming, had to do with all the peoples in the world and this is why it is right that the Great Commission should come at the end of the Gospels and not at the beginning.

The world is present in microcosm for Peter and he *welcomes* those who come to hear him, he welcomes them by calling them brothers. He welcomes them, and then he speaks to them in language which they understand. He refers them to the prophecies found in the book of Joel (2:28, 29) and in the Psalms. We have known, since the discovery of the Qumran scrolls, that these prophecies were often quoted by all sorts of sects expecting the Messiah at that time and, indeed, they are quoted in other parts of the New Testament.[3] Peter speaks their language, his understanding of the Psalms, his interpretation of particular Psalms in a messianic way, is something that his hearers would easily have understood, though it is perhaps difficult for us to understand.

This welcome for people when they come to hear the Gospel is basic for mission, it is often taken for granted, but I believe it needs to be drawn to our attention. Peter, of course, could speak their language because he was one of them, he knew how they thought, what their hopes and fears were, and he addressed them directly.

We find in the history of Christian mission that it is very often people who belong to a particular group who are able to communicate the Gospel to that group. Even in the history of CMS, there are people like the Evangelist Baba Muboni in Nigeria and Abdul Masih in India, people who received the Gospel and who then took the Gospel to their own people. As the Church becomes stronger in every part of the world, this aspect of mission becomes even more important: to enable people to take the Gospel to their own people.[4] Cross-cultural mission, of course, has a place and the apostles later went on to become great cross-cultural missionaries, but here Peter, and indeed the other apostles, in their own ways, begin with their own.

Then Peter *witnesses*; he has the world before him, he welcomes them and now he witnesses to them. It is often said that there is a particular kind of preaching by the apostles, which is a little different from the preaching of Jesus himself, the *kerygma* of the apostles and the *kerygma* of Jesus, if you want theological language. The *kerygma* of Jesus in the first three Gospels, certainly, is about the Kingdom of God. Jesus does not preach about himself but he preaches the Kingdom (this is a commonplace way of putting it). The *kerygma* of the apostles – and St John in his theological commentaries which he attaches to incidents in the life of Jesus is already moving to this – is the preaching of Jesus, the preaching about Jesus, and they did it because they had come to appreciate in their being with him the important truth that the Kingdom of God was present in Jesus.[5]

This is found already, in fact, in the teaching of Jesus himself and not only in St John's Gospel, it is also found in the first three Gospels: 'All things have been delivered to me by my Father' (Matt. 11:27) and when the high priest asked Jesus at the beginning of the Passion, 'I ask you solemnly, tell me, are you the Son of God?' Jesus said, 'I am' (Mark 14:62). The 'I' sayings are not only to be found in St John's Gospel, they are scattered throughout the New Testament record. Peter, then, witnesses to the world of what God has done in their lives, in the lives of the apostles.

It is one thing to witness to what God has done in my life or in your life, and that must always be important. Without that there is no witness. If God has not done anything in our lives we really cannot begin to testify. But we can legitimately go on to witness to what God has done in the lives of others and a great deal of the educational work of Christian Mission has to be about that. It is testimony about what God is doing in the lives of others. It is bringing that testimony to bear on the life of the Church in this country, it is enabling Churches worldwide to exchange their testimonies. Whatever else we may say about international organizations such as the World Council of Churches or indeed the Anglican Consultative Council, in this century there is an unprecedented opportunity for Churches worldwide, for Christians worldwide, to share their testimony with each other for mutual enrichment and renewal, and we should be grateful to God for this opportunity denied to past ages.

Whether the testimony is personal or whether it is about God's work in other people or in another Church, it must be based squarely on the death and resurrection of Jesus Christ. All the great speeches in Acts addressing different kinds of audiences – Jews, Jewish leaders, Gentiles, kings, all sorts of people – all have a particular form. When Paul is speaking to the Gentiles in Lystra or in Athens, he speaks very differently from the kind of address that he gives in a synagogue (Acts 13:16) in Antioch of Pisidia, for example. Again, Peter's address here is different from the address which he gives in the house of Cornelius (Acts 10:34f). But whatever the differences, there is this in common: all of them speak of God's work in Christ, and this in a way alerts us to the limits of contextualization. When Peter welcomes the world to himself he contextualizes, he speaks in their language, according to their expectations. But the Gospel itself, God's saving work in Christ, and the need to maintain fellowship between Churches, these are the limits to contextualization, these are limits beyond which we cannot go in accommodating the Gospel and Christian life to culture.

And so from witness we come to *warning*. While Peter, on the one hand, welcomes these people to this hearing of the Gospel, he does not forget that some of them have been implicated in the recent events of the passion and crucifixion of Jesus. He reminds them that they are guilty of having caused the death of Jesus. It is true, of course, that looking at it from another way, such a passion and such a death was according to God's foreknowledge and plan. Of course God knew that if he placed his Son among sinful human beings, they would reject him, but that does not lessen the responsibility of sinful human beings in rejecting Jesus. And so he warns them that what they have done is sinful! 'This Jesus delivered up according to God's plan, you crucified and killed by the hands of lawless men . . .' that is a reference to the fact that the actual killing was done by the Romans. It is this note of judgment, warning, which leads to repentance. So we have the world present, Peter welcomes all these people, witnesses to them, warns them of judgment and then *wins* them for Christ.

As a result of his speech, they were cut to the quick and said to Peter and the rest of the Apostles, 'Brethren, what shall we do?' Peter said to them, 'Repent and be baptized everyone of you in the name of Jesus Christ for the forgiveness of your sins and you shall receive the gift of the Holy Spirit.'

I was asked recently to write a response to the Pope's Encyclical on Mission, *Redemptoris Missio*. In this Encyclical the Pope points out that witness is only the beginning of evangelization, because after witness comes the winning. Now, first, Christians, particularly Anglican Christians, are very backward about witness, and we need to repent about that, but even if we screw up courage to witness in some sort of way, we are hopeless at winning people. What do you do after you have witnessed? How do you lead people to Christ? I think we have a great deal to learn here from Christians belonging to independent evangelical Churches, for example. The Pope says that first there is witness, then conversion, baptism and the planting of a Church.[6] Of course, there must be, if that witness is to have lasting results. These things must happen. There must be winning, there must be baptism into Christ's body, sharing his joy and his suffering, and there must be the planting of the local Church in a particular place. The Church has to be truly rooted in the culture and the traditions of the place and yet, at the same time, be a Church in fellowship with all the other Churches in the world. So Peter won them for Christ and perhaps he was surprised more than anyone else. He had won 3,000 of them – perhaps he was not expecting such a great response! What happens then?

Not surprisingly, they begin to *worship* together. It is interesting that two kinds of Christian worship are mentioned here, at this nascent period. One is the breaking of the bread and the other is called the prayer. Let us take the breaking of the bread first. Wherever it occurs in the New Testament (it occurs a few chapters later on, for example, in Acts 20 where Paul breaks bread), it is always a reference to a special remembrance of Christ's death in this particular way by Christians, it is a reference to the Last Supper, to the eucharist, to holy communion, whatever you want to call it – something that quickly became central to the life of the Church. Its misuse in later years should not in any way obscure the significance of the breaking of the bread as a central aspect of Christian worship.

It was very natural, of course, for these early Christians to do this because in Jewish families this breaking of the bread is part of every mealtime, particularly of special meals, for example, at the Sabbath and the Passover. It is very interesting to read the prayers at the time of Passover that are still used by the Jews and how evocative they are of the eucharist. So they worship *together*, breaking bread *together*. The eucharist, the Last Supper, should be a way of unifying Christians and not of dividing them, as it so often has been.

And then there are the prayers. It seems that here the reference must be to the regular times of prayers the Jews have at the third, the sixth and the ninth hours. Indeed, the Christian tradition of praying at particular times arose out of this Jewish tradition. The morning and evening prayer in particular are mentioned in the New Testament and in the early history of the Church as being very special times. As the Church grew, different people evolved different ways of worshipping God, according to their culture and their language and their situation. But the centrality of the breaking of the bread remained, and remains, and the need to pray regularly and to pray daily remained and remains.[7]

But then they *worked* together. Now some of this work undoubtedly had to do with the apostles' teaching. I am sure that the apostles had a great deal to give and the people had a great deal to learn.

But work is mentioned in other places in the New Testament and there it has to do with the work of our hands: 'he who does not work should not eat', says Paul, because some, expecting the coming of the Lord, had given up work (2 Thess. 3:10). Throughout Christian history there have been various enthusiasms which have encouraged Christians to give up work and to focus on one kind of activity or one kind of life to the exclusion of the life of work. Working honestly, working for one's living, is a sign of being authentically Christian.[8] In Ephesians Paul says, 'Let the thief no longer steal, but work with his hands and give to those in need' (Eph. 5:28).

You will have heard of the Protestant work ethic and I am sure there are many things that need to be said about it which are negative, in the way that work can imprison people so that they are not liberated enough to celebrate and to enjoy family life and relationships, for example, and one *does* feel that this *has* happened in certain societies. But, on the other hand, the New Testament has a great deal to say about the need for work and for working together. *Worshipping* together, *working* together and then *witnessing* together.

The Bible says about them, 'Fear came upon every soul and many wonders and signs were done through the apostles and all who believed were together and had all things in common' (Acts 2:43, 44). They were witnesses together of how God had worked in their lives. In some cultures, where there is a very strong sense of community, it is comparatively easy for Churches to witness corporately. But in other cultures, and it may be that the cultures in Britain are among them, it is very difficult to get a sense of corporate witness by the Church. And yet if the Church is not a community itself how can it re-create community?

One of the good things about the Decade of Evangelism is that Churches are having to ask themselves whether they are defined enough in this way as a community to reach the wider community, and many are finding that they are not. Apart from going to church on the Sunday, or perhaps one other weekly activity if the church is very lively, there is often little sense of being a community, of worshipping and working and witnessing together. I have said before that I believe that the basic communities in Latin America, groups of poor people who come together to worship and to celebrate and live their lives in support of each other, have a great deal to teach the World Church in this respect.

Then, finally, there is being *willing to give* to each other. The passage says, 'All who believed were together, had all things in common, they sold their possessions and goods and distributed them to all as any had need' (Acts 2:45). Now clearly this applies first of all to Christians relieving the needs of other Christians. This is absolutely basic to the Christian life, the sharing of goods or talents, or resources in the worldwide Church. There are many examples of this in the New Testament. Paul is most concerned with organizing relief for the needs of the saints in Jerusalem. Again and again in his various letters he keeps coming back to this theme, because for him it means that the Churches are interdependent, just as the Churches of the Gentiles had received spiritual riches from the Church in Jerusalem, so they were obliged to make their wealth available for the poorer Church in Jerusalem and in Judea (e.g. 2 Cor. 8–9).

So the first thing about giving has to do with fellowship, with interdependence, with brotherhood, as the Jerusalem Bible puts it. But it is more than that because the theme of giving to the poor, not just poor Christians or poor Jews, but giving to the poor, is deeply embedded in the biblical tradition. It is found already in the formative stages of Israel's history, to welcome the stranger, to give to the stranger, to give to the widow and the orphan, to welcome them, not to discriminate, all these things are found deeply embedded in the biblical tradition (e.g. Lev. 19).

I suppose one reason for this has to do with the exercise of compassion. God is described again and again, in very feminine imagery, if I may say so, as compassionate in the Old Testament. The word used there, as you know, has to do with a mother's longing for her children (Isa. 49:15; 63:15; Jer. 31:20, Hos. 2:23). God is described as compassionate and his people are taught to be compassionate to those less fortunate.

But there is also a great sense of justice in the Old Testament, and indeed in the New, that giving to those in need has to do with righting wrongs, and we have to come to terms with this; that giving of people and material resources to the World and the Church is not just about compassion, it is not just about interdependence or fellowship but it is very deeply about justice. It is about righting past and present wrongs. But it is even more than that; it is not just fellowship, it is not just interdependence, it is not just compassion or justice, it is love.[9]

St Gregory of Nazianzus, writing about the difference between Christian and pagan charity, says that the great difference is that Christians love the poor. This love of the poor is, I think, based on Jesus's teaching about the danger of wealth, about the need for people to renounce wealth, if they are to seek the Kingdom of Heaven and to find it. It is based on his own ministry, which for the most part took place among people who were poor and deprived. And so Christian giving has to do in the end with that love of God, that *agape* of God, which brought about the incarnation, the coming of Jesus Christ to us in human form.

I believe that this speech of Peter's to the world at the very dawn of the Christian Church has a great deal to teach us today as we wrestle in trying to understand what Christian mission is about. I have said what I think there is in it. I am sure that you will find a great deal more.

Chapter 19

The Bible and Inter-faith Relations

H. D. Beeby and Lesslie Newbigin

If we turn to the Bible for guidance in the field of inter-faith relations, we must remember, in the first place, that the world religions in the sense that we know them, did not and could not then exist. Islam and Sikhism had not been born. Zoroastrian religion was certainly known by and had influence on biblical writers, but it was not discussed as such. The vast family of religious ideas and practices which the invaders of India called 'Hinduism' does not seem to have been known to the Old Testament writers, though the religious and philosophical ideas which have given birth to Hinduism and Buddhism were probably an element in the intellectual world in which the New Testament took shape.

The best way to approach the subject is by looking at the way in which the Bible speaks about 'the nations' (in the older English translations 'the heathen'). Israel was surrounded by nations, each of which worshipped their own god or gods. At some points biblical writers seem to suggest that these gods are entities with real power. When Jephtha protests to the king of the Ammonites against a threatened invasion he writes: 'Will you not possess what Chemosh your god gives you to possess? And all that Jahweh our God has dispossessed before us, we will possess' (Judg. 11:24). In the Psalms Israel's God is praised as 'king above all gods' (Ps. 95:3) and in Psalm 82 he is pictured as passing judgment on the gods of the nations because of the injustices they do. But in other places the gods of the nations are dismissed as worthless, as 'nothings'. They are identified with the idols which are the work of human hands and have no power to deliver (e.g. Ps. 115, Isa. 46).

But 'the nations' were not only at a distance. They were also the people among whom Israel lived, and their worship was a threat and a temptation to Israel. Much of the prophetic writing is devoted to warning Israel against the seduction of Canaanite worship which was concerned with wealth, power and fertility and did not make the moral demands which Jahweh made on his people. Thus, whatever may be the ontological status of the gods of the nations, and whether or not the idol is an object of worship or only the symbol of a reality beyond itself, the Bible is very clear in distinguishing between worship which is directed to the one true and living God, and that which is not. And this sharp distinction is present in the New Testament no less than in the Old Testament. Nothing could be sharper than the word of Jesus to the Samaritan woman: 'You worship what you do not know; we worship what we know, for salvation is from the Jews' (John 4:22).

But this sharp distinction which marks Israel off against 'the nations' in no way implies that Israel has some intrinsic merit or virtue, or that God's blessing is for Israel only and not for the nations. This distinctness of Israel arises from the fact that, among the nations, God has called Israel for a specific task, a task on behalf of all the nations. The opening and closing chapters of the Bible make clear how this is so.

The opening chapters of Genesis give no room for the idea (common among the mythologies of many peoples) that Israel has a special divine origin, setting Israel apart from other nations. The nations first appear in Chapter 10. They are seventy in number – a sign of perfection. They are the fruit of God's blessing given to Noah. After the awesome judgment of the Flood on the corruption of the human race, God makes a fresh start with Noah, his family, and all the animals with him. He makes a covenant of blessing which embraces not only the whole human family but also 'every living creature' (Gen. 10:8ff.), and he sets the rainbow in the sky as a sign of this universal covenant. The seventy nations are thus introduced as the fruit of God's blessing and as the object of his blessing. Nothing in the list suggests that there is anything special about any one of the families named. So the nations who will form the background for the whole story which the Bible tells, are first introduced to the reader under the sign of God's blessing. And in the very last chapters of the Bible, we see these same nations streaming through the gates into the City of God, bringing with them the treasures that they have gained in the long story of the human pilgrimage (Rev. 21:24).

The naming of the seventy nations is followed by the story of Babel. The nations seek unity and security and they set out to create a city. But the end of the effort is confusion and mutual estrangement. The nations are under the blessing of God, but they cannot create their own unity. God has another plan. One family among all the nations is chosen for a special covenant. Abraham is called to go out from his own nation, to be a pilgrim without a settled home, in order to become the one in whom all the nations will be blessed. The calling of this one people to be different from all the nations is for the sake of all the nations. Abraham is not more virtuous than the nations around him. Almost immediately after the narrative of Abraham's calling, we have the story of his taking refuge under the protection of one of the nations (Egypt), of his cowardly stratagem to save his own skin at the cost of his wife's chastity, and of the noble and generous way in which the 'heathen' king treated him. Abraham is not more godly than the nations. He is not set apart from the nations as the privileged recipient of God's blessing. He is set apart by God's calling of him for the sake of the nations.

As the biblical story unfolds, the perception of what this specific calling implies is sharpened and deepened. Over and over again Israel falls into the trap of treating the calling as privilege rather than as responsibility. Only slowly and through many shattering disasters is it learned that Israel must fulfil its calling by suffering. Right up to the time of the ministry of Jesus the illusion persists that God's special calling of Israel must mean the triumph of Israel over the nations, in spite of the prophecies which saw Israel as the servant and witness of Jahweh for the nations, a service which must entail suffering and rejection. On the road to Emmaeus the disciples of Jesus still believed that his coming must mean political liberation for Israel (Luke 24:21). Only the fact of the resurrection of Jesus could enable them to understand that the fulfilment of the calling of Israel was that which was done on a hill called Calvary.

The relation between Israel and the nations (the Church and the 'heathen') is thus a dialectical one. (That is why inter-faith dialogue is necessary.) It can be suggested by using four phrases:

1   Israel/the Church exists for the nations.
2   Israel/the Church is to live over against the nations.
3   Israel/the Church lives as debtor to the nations.
4   Israel/the Church is called to be a missionary to the nations.

Although it is obvious that the New Testament brings a perspective different from the Old in important, indeed crucial respects, nevertheless this same pattern continues through both testaments. The Church of the New Testament called itself by the name which was the name of the congregation of Israel in the Greek version of the Old Testament which was the 'Bible' of the early Church, and the same fourfold pattern of relationships remains valid for our understanding of the relationship between the Church and the religious life of the nations among whom the first Christians lived and with whom they were in daily contact.

1   ISRAEL/THE CHURCH EXISTS FOR THE NATIONS

This fundamental relationship has already been indicated in what was said above. The uniqueness of Israel's relation to God is not a ground for separation but for universality. God has made himself known, to Israel in order that Israel may be a light to the nations. The nations will come to Zion in order to find truth and justice, for this is what is revealed in God's dealing with Israel (e.g. Isa. 2:1–4). The purpose which is made known in God's dealing with his chosen people is a universal and cosmic purpose which embraces all peoples and all creation, the fulfilling of the covenant of blessing made at the beginning. And the New Testament writers pick up from the Old Testament the many passages which show that this is so. While the ministry of Jesus in the days of his flesh is directed to Israel in order to prepare Israel for the fulfilment of its calling, the horizon is all the nations who are to come from all the corners of the earth to sit down with Abraham at the heavenly banquet (Matt. 8:11). Much of St Paul's writing is dedicated to showing that God's calling of Israel was for the sake of the Gentiles (the nations), and the letter to the Ephesians gives us a picture of the Church as the visible demonstration of God's intention to gather Jews and Gentiles into one family reconciled in one body through the blood of Christ.

The specificity of this concentration on a particular people, Israel set apart from the nations, is seen as unacceptable by many. The very idea of a chosen people is offensive. On this two things may be said. First, the offence may arise because it is thought that Israel or the Church are chosen for privilege, that they are the saved as distinct from the lost. But this is a radical misunderstanding of the biblical teaching. Election is not for privilege but for an awesome responsibility. On this point it is enough to quote one representative word from the prophets. 'Hear this word that the Lord has spoken against you, O people of Israel, against the whole family which I brought up out of the land of Egypt: "You only have I known among all the families of the earth, therefore I will punish you for all your sins" ' (Amos 3:1–2). Second, the specificity is the necessary corollary of historicity. Historical events have specific times and places and people. Religious and metaphysical ideas do not. If our relation with God is a matter of ideas detached from specific happenings, then religion is a profoundly individual and private affair in which we cannot depend upon another. The Bible, by contrast, sees God's purpose of blessing for all to be fulfilled by a specific community which bears both the glory and the agony of God's work of judgment and grace.

2 ISRAEL/THE CHURCH IS TO LIVE OVER AGAINST THE NATIONS

There is no escaping the notes of conflict and hostility which run through the Bible and which come to a focus in the crucifixion of Jesus. The Cross is the ultimate sign of absolute hostility between God's elect and the world, and at the same time the ultimate action of the elect for the world. The Old Testament is full of the conflict between Israel and surrounding nations. In many cases this is interpreted as God's own action: Jahweh is using the nations to punish

Israel for her apostasy. The mighty Assyrian Empire is, according to Isaiah, only a stick to beat his stubborn people (Isa. 10:5ff.) and Jeremiah is equally sure that the Chaldeans are carrying out Jahweh's own purpose of punishment in attacking and destroying Jerusalem. In the Book of Judges we are told over and over again that God uses the surrounding nations to chastise Israel and bring her to repentance.

The nations were also a threat to Israel's faithfulness and to the faithfulness of the Church. The fertility cults of Canaanite religion offered a direct connection between their ritual performance and the abundance of harvest, and it was not obvious that the good crops were the gift of Jahweh, not of the Baals (e.g. Hosea). For Israelites who were slaves in Babylon, with its magnificent religious establishment, it took courage and faith to pour ridicule on the lifeless idols carried round in splendid processions, while it seemed that Jahweh had been unable to save his people from disaster (e.g. Isa. 46). And Christians living among the Gentiles had to be warned against the infection of the religious ideas which were part of the very air they breathed in a city like Corinth (e.g. 1 Cor. 8).

The nations could be, quite simply, the enemies. The imperial power of Egypt feels threatened by the multiplying of the immigrant labourers and tries to crush them. The nations displaced by Israel (naturally) fight back. The preaching of the Gospel provokes anger and persecution. Jesus tells his disciples that they must regard this situation as normal. Those called to be the bearers of God's revelation of himself for all the nations cannot fulfil their calling without being also against the nations. They have to be against the world in order to be for it, as Jesus was.

3   ISRAEL/THE CHURCH LIVES AS DEBTOR TO THE NATIONS

Israel is (apart from the divine calling) one nation among the nations and all its culture develops in contact with and – in important respects – dependence on the culture of other nations. Egypt, in some respects the arch-enemy, is also the nation to which Israel owes the biggest debts. Israel became a nation in Egypt. Moses was the kind of leader of the nation that he was because he was trained at the Egyptian court. It is to Egypt that Abraham, Jacob and his sons go for relief in time of famine, and it is to Egypt that the child Jesus is taken for protection. Study of the ancient history of the Middle East has shown that a very great amount of the material of the Old Testament has its origins in the myths, the legal systems and the political wisdom of the surrounding nations. It is essential to note that the material thus borrowed was reshaped in the hands of the prophets of Israel so that it became part of the pattern controlled by the self-revelation of Jahweh, but the debt remains. The names used for God in early chapters of Genesis, such as El-Shaddaai and El-Elyon, would seem to be names for God among the surrounding nations which are accepted by Israel as designations of Jahweh, the true and living God. The institution of the monarchy is something borrowed from surrounding nations, as is the construction of a temple. Those parts of the Bible which are referred to as the Wisdom literature owe a great deal to the neighbouring nations. In the New Testament also we find numerous examples of the Church's debt to those outside the Church. Paul is glad to make use of his Roman citizenship and of the justice which he expects from Roman courts. In his preaching at Athens he makes use of the work of a pagan poet. The fact that the whole New Testament is written in Greek is a reminder of the fact that it was owing to the spread of Greek culture throughout the eastern Mediterranean and West Asia that the Church was able to grow so rapidly.

The debt to the nations is especially visible in the writing of Second Isaiah (Isa. 40–55) in which the Persian ruler Cyrus is acclaimed as Messiah, God's anointed liberator who is to be the agent of a second exodus from slavery.

And finally the Bible is full of examples of people outside the covenant people who manifest a godliness and a moral excellence superior to that of the chosen people. Pharaoh's treatment of Abraham is honourable while Abraham's conduct is not. Jacob is portrayed as a cunning deceiver, while Esau is a gentleman. The prophet Jonah is a disobedient and self-centred man, whereas the sailors in his ship, pagans all, are god-fearing, generous and brave. The pagans of Nineveh repent while Jonah sulks. The ideal woman of the Old Testament is the Moabitess Ruth, who is to be the ancestor of King David. So also Jesus marvels at the faith of the Roman centurion and of the Syro-Phoenician woman and Paul contrasts the welcome which he received from the 'heathen' with his rejection at the hands of Israel. In a crucial passage of his great argument in Romans 9–11, he writes, 'There is no distinction between Jew and Greek; the same Lord is Lord of all and bestows his riches upon all who call upon him' (Rom. 10:12).

4   ISRAEL/THE CHURCH IS CALLED TO BE A MISSIONARY TO THE NATIONS

The fact that the chosen people are chosen *for* the nations must find expression in mission *to* the nations. In the Old Testament this is seen mainly in a centripetal pattern: the nations will come to Israel because they recognize that God is with her. But centrifugal patterns are not absent. Jonah, that reluctant missionary, is sent to Nineveh, and in spite of his total unworthiness, he is the one through whose mission Nineveh (the pagan world at its most formidable) is brought to repentance. The sending motif is strongest in the writings of Second Isaiah where there is a specific sending of Israel to be Jahweh's instrument of salvation 'to the ends of the earth' (Isa. 49:6). Indeed the central conviction expressed in many psalms and prophecies, that Jahweh is Lord of the whole earth, must necessarily have missionary implications. In the New Testament the centrifugal pattern is much more visible, although the other is prominent in such sayings as the word of Jesus in John 12:32: 'I, when I am lifted up from the earth, will draw all to myself.' The disciples of Jesus are sent out to 'disciple the nations' (Matt. 28:19), and they are promised the presence of the Holy Spirit who will be the witness to the world of Jesus's lordship. This sending out to all the nations is a work of the Triune God: Jesus, the Son, is the one sent by the Father – the Father whose providential governance of the world is not negated by any human sinfulness. The Church is the continuance of this sending (John 20:19–23) and is enabled to be so by the presence of the Spirit who is the Spirit of the Father and of the Son.

In reviewing the relation of Israel/the Church to the nations, in this fourfold scheme, it is important finally to note that the reality governing all these relations is the twofold relation of God to his world. God is the creator and sustainer of all things and 'his tender mercies are over all his works' (Ps. 154:9). Even among the pagans who want to treat Barnabus and Paul as gods, Paul is certain that God has not left himself without witness (Acts 14:17). There is no place in the universe from which the grace of God is absent. But, as soon as this is gladly acknowledged, there must follow the words 'But now . . .'. God has done something which goes beyond this general grace; he has acted in specific ways, ways which involve personal names such as 'Jesus' and 'Pontius Pilate', in order to fulfil the purpose which this general grace embodies. The dialectical relation between these two modes of God's working is set out classically in the prologue to the Fourth Gospel. The *logos* – the creative word of God – was in the world before Jesus came. The same *logos* is the light that illuminates every human being without exception. But this light shines in darkness, a darkness which can neither understand it nor blot it out. 'He was in the world, but the world knew him not' (John 1:10). So there had to be a sending and a coming. 'He came to his own home and his own people did not receive him' (v. 11). Here is the terrible paradox of human alienation from the source of being. It is essential to hold both sides of the paradox: the specificity of the Christian Gospel must not be used to deny the reality of God's presence in the world, among the nations, among the people outside the covenant community; likewise the reality of this presence must not be used to muffle the specificity of the Gospel. Paul at Lystra acknowledges that God has not left himself without witness among these pagans, but tells them that there is now a new action of God which it is vital for them to hear. Among the philosophers at Athens he acknowledges their religious devotion, but tells them the true name of that which they had worshipped unknowingly. God tells the pagan Roman officer that his prayers and his good works have been accepted, but then tells him to send to Joppa for something which he must hear. Peter, reluctant to accept the hospitality of a pagan home, is compelled to recognize that God has no partiality for Christians (Acts 10:34f), but then proceeds to tell the story, the story which all peoples must hear, the story through which Cornelius is brought into the company of the covenant people.

As noted at the outset, we cannot look to the Bible for detailed guidance about the relations which Christians ought to have with Muslims, Sikhs, Hindus, Buddhists. We can certainly find guidance about the relations between Jews and Christians. But for all these relations, the fourfold pattern sketched above will provide reference points for exploration, dialogue and witness.

Chapter 20

The Bible and Paradise

Rex Ambler

Our new concern with the environment is making us ask questions about ourselves and our earth which we are not finding at all easy to answer. We can handle individual environmental problems, it seems, but when we look at the picture as a whole we can easily be overwhelmed by the sheer size of the problem and its apparent insolubility. The many specific problems with water supplies, atmospheric pollution, declining forest and topsoil, growing demands for food and other natural resources all add up to one big problem: we humans are making too great an impact on the earth, and if we continue as we do, we could possibly destroy it as a basis for our own continued existence. But why are we doing this? We can point to many factors that contribute to the problem, e.g. the rapidly growing human population, new untested technologies, an unfair overly-competitive trading system, and increasing demands for individual consumption. But behind all these and driving them along is a human quest for more freedom, more power and more material wealth: the fundamental quest of modernity itself. So we find ourselves in a spiritual dilemma. We are living through a crisis which is not only of our own making, but which arises from our pursuit of the most deeply held values of our Western society. How do we handle this? What hope is there of people changing? Is it even conceivable now that human beings, with their massive numbers and sophisticated technologies, might be able to live in harmony with the earth instead of being endlessly at odds with it? Are the needs of people and the needs of the planet making inevitably for a head-on collision? Or are our perceived needs not perhaps our real needs, and if so, how did we come by this illusion and how do we get rid of it? At this point our questioning has become distinctly spiritual, and seems to require spiritual answers.

In circumstances like these we need to be able to draw on the resources of our own spiritual tradition, and in particular, of course, the tradition of the Bible. But this is already proving to be difficult.

The Bible against Nature?

One difficulty arises from the fact that the Bible seems to have rather little to say on the natural environment. It is preoccupied with human beings. It begins with the story of creation, in which each kind of creature is admittedly given attention, but which too obviously comes to a climax with the creation of human beings – 'in the image and likeness of God'. Moreover, this unique creature is then given authority over the others and ordered to 'have dominion' over them and to 'subdue' them. This has been widely interpreted to mean that human beings are thereby empowered to develop and exploit the earth and its creatures as much as they see fit. Many ecologists in recent years have seized on this as a primary source of our present crisis. Lynn White's paper of 1967 on 'the historical roots of our ecologic crisis' was the first to make this point clearly. With its rejection of all pagan beliefs in the sacredness of living things and its relegation of nature to mere servitude to human beings, Christianity, he argued, 'made it possible to exploit nature in a mood of indifference to the feelings of natural objects'.[1] It produced our distinctly modern attitude that 'we are superior to nature, contemptuous of it, willing to use it for our slightest whim'. And moreover, we 'shall continue to have a worsening ecologic crisis until we reject the Christian axiom that nature has no reason for existence save to serve man'. Similarly, Arnold Toynbee argued in 1973 that:

> some of the major maladies of the present day world – in particular the recklessly extravagant consumption of nature's irreplaceable treasures, and the pollution of those of them that man has not already devoured – can be traced back to a religious cause, and this cause is the rise of monotheism . . . Monotheism, as enunciated in the book of Genesis, has removed the old-age restraint that was once placed on man's greed by his awe. Man's greedy impulse to exploit nature used to be held in check by his pious worship of nature.[2]

If all this is true it is potentially tragic. It would mean that the very resource we might most want to turn to for healing is itself polluted.

We can add to this difficulty the thought that the Bible, having been written 2,000 years ago and more, knows nothing about environmental crises of the scale and character that we are experiencing today, and it is therefore in no position to advise us. It knows about environmental disasters of some kind, some of which threatened the survival of human beings. The great flood is the prime example, and the story about it (Gen. 6–9) is full of ecological concern. But these were 'acts of God', as we still choose to call them, and not acts of human power. And until very recently it was inconceivable that humans should be able to destroy their habitat, because they simply had not developed the material power to do so. But now of course they have that power. That marks a decisively new stage in human history. The Bruntland Report of 1987 – from the World Commission on Environment and Development – concluded with this simple, but awe-inspiring thought:

> Over the course of this century, the relationship between the human world and the planet that sustains it has undergone a profound change. When the century began, neither human numbers nor technology had the power to radically alter planetary systems. As the century closes, not only do vastly increased numbers and their activities have that power, but major, unintended changes are occurring in the atmosphere, in soils, in waters, among plants and animals, and in the relationships among all of these. The rate of change is outstripping the ability of scientific disciplines and our current capabilities to assess and advise. It is frustrating the attempts of political and economic institutions, which evolved in a different, more fragmented world, to adapt and cope.[3]

One conclusion I draw from this is that if we want to understand what this crisis is about we have to look at it historically, that is, in terms of the long story of our relationship with the earth. It is interesting that this is a characteristically biblical way of looking at things, although this approach is rarely being applied to our present environmental situation. More important, though, it tells us that if we want to benefit from the resource of the Bible it could actually be an advantage to understand how different the world was when the Bible was written. We might then find that the two difficulties I mentioned resolve each other – or nearly. The difficulty of the Bible's human-centredness might be resolved by our knowing the specific human needs of that time, and the difficulty of its remoteness from where we are now might be resolved by its helping us to know how we got to where we are.

I heard a good example of this first point when a bishop (I can't remember his name) was asked how he could possibly hold by the injunction to Adam and Eve in the Bible to 'be fruitful and multiply' when the world population was already dangerously too high. He replied that at the time when the injunction was given the total human population of the world was about two. It is an obvious point, once we think of it, however we interpret the story.

The Image of God on Earth

The same point applies equally to the whole of Genesis 1–11, which has figured so largely in recent debates about religious attitudes to nature.[4] At the time when it was written, we have to say, humans were in a very different situation from the one they are in now. They were relatively few in number, with unsophisticated means at their disposal, and they had only recently abandoned the life of hunters and gatherers for the settled but risky life of farmers and town-dwellers. To have 'dominion' over the animals meant to domesticate them for travel and work on the farm, and to 'subdue' the earth meant simply to dig it and cultivate it. Yet even for this people needed assurance that this was the right thing to do. So their new story about Adam and Eve told them that when human beings were created it was their Creator's intention that they should do just this.[5] If it appeared to them that it was a too godlike activity to interfere with the sacred earth and its creatures they had to realize that they had in fact been created to *be* like God, 'in his image and likeness'. This gave them the right to intervene and to manage. It was widely believed at that time that kings were the image of God and therefore acted as his representatives on the earth: their rule was an exercise of God's rule. In the Genesis story this idea was applied to all human beings, who all became God's representatives on earth.[6]

It is therefore far removed from the idea that human beings could dominate the earth because they were inherently superior to it. On the contrary they needed a special divine mandate to give them a right even to till the soil. It could be thought of as a rather awe-inspiring duty to be called to do this, as seems to be implied by this Psalm (8: 3–9; RSV) which echoes the Genesis story very closely:

> When I look at the heavens, the work of thy fingers,
> the moon and the stars which thou hast established;
> what is man that thou art mindful of him,
> and the son of man that thou dost care for him?
> Yet thou hast made him little less than God,
> and dost crown him with glory and honour.
> Thou hast given him dominion over the works of thy hands;
> thou hast put all things under his feet, . . .
> O Lord, our Lord,
> how majestic is thy name in all the earth!

In practice however humans did exercise their divinely given power with arrogance, first by grasping at knowledge that would have given them complete independence of God and a power to choose and do as they wish, which of course had been forbidden them. As a result the blessing which had been given them in the garden to 'be fruitful and multiply, and fill the earth and subdue it; and have dominion over . . . every thing that moves upon the earth' (Gen. 1:28) becomes a curse: 'Cursed is the ground because of you; in toil you shall eat of it all the days of your life' (Gen. 3:17). Then Cain kills his brother and Lamech avenges him 'seventy-seven fold'

(Gen. 4:24). God soon judges the human experiment to be a failure, and 'the lord was sorry that he had made man on the earth, and it grieved him to his heart' (Gen. 6:6). It is only the righteousness of Noah that persuades him not to abandon the whole project. But when God renews the project with Noah, after the great flood, and reissues the mandate to have dominion over the earth, it is given a harsh, ironical twist:

> And God blessed Noah and his sons, and said to them:
> 'Be fruitful and multiply, and fill the earth.
> The fear of you and the dread of you
> shall be upon every beast of the earth,
> and upon every bird of the air,
> upon everything that creeps on the ground
> and all the fish of the sea;
> into your hand they are delivered.
> Everything that lives shall be food for you;
> and as I gave you the green plants,
> I give you everything . . .
> Whoever sheds the blood of man,
> by man shall his blood be shed;
> for God made man in his own image (Gen. 9:1–16).

The significance of the image has been reduced to a prohibition against killing fellow humans; other animals evidently can now be killed for food, although previously that too had been forbidden. The human rule over God's peaceable kingdom has been replaced by a savage tyranny, in which every creature lives in fear of its life – 'into your hand they are delivered' is the language of conquest and enslavement. The fallenness of humans has now been accepted by God, but with obvious grief, and the divine project has been reduced to what is humanly possible.

From a biblical point of view, then, it would be more fitting to see the present exploitation of the earth by humans as a further example of their arrogance and abuse of power, than as obedience to a God-given mandate.

The Hope of Paradise

The original idea is never quite forgotten, though. The memory of paradise in Eden becomes a source of hope for the future.[7] It is a reminder of what is *really* possible for human beings, when they have learned to abandon the stupidities of their self-centred existence. When the prophets talk of the future it is often the image of paradise that inspires them:

> The wolf shall dwell with the lamb,
> and the leopard shall lie down with the kid,

and the calf and the lion and the fatling together,
and a little child shall lead them . . .
The sucking child shall play over the hole of the asp,
and the weaned child shall put his hands on the adder's
den. [A reference to the serpent in paradise?]
They shall not hurt or destroy in all my holy mountain;
For the earth shall be full of the knowledge of the Lord
as the waters cover the sea. (Isa. 11:6–9)

At the same time of course the process of learning what is possible, what is ultimately (or originally) intended by God, is extremely painful. The many ways in which humans evade their calling to act on God's behalf – their greed, search for power, tribalism, idolatry of 'things' – all lead to disaster, eventually. This may be interpreted, in the language of the time, as the judgment of God, or it may be thought (by Job, for example) that this is far too moralistic. But all suffering, whether or not it results directly from human misconduct, can purify people's insight, free them from self-centred illusions (as in the case of Job), and renew their faith in God and their calling from God. So the Bible develops a most extraordinary paradox in its account of human affairs: that the suffering and misery which come to people because of their fallen condition can also become the means of their rising above it. When Israel is made to suffer in exile because of his betrayal of God's covenant, his failure to trust – Israel is being symbolized as a man – his suffering becomes a 'ransom for money', and with his wounds 'we are healed' (Isa. 53:5, 12).

That of course is precisely the paradox which passes into the Christian tradition in the story of Christ's suffering. He is seen to renew the dream of paradise, to become God's representative on earth, 'the image of God', but then to suffer because his fellow humans simply cannot take this reminder of their own divine calling. But his suffering in turn brings insight, grief, resolve, faith. This 'second Adam' (cf. 1 Cor. 15:45, 47) brings a second chance to renew the covenant of the Garden of Eden, to bring about God's peaceable kingdom on earth, where even 'the tree of life' from the Garden will flourish once again (Rev. 22:1, 2).

Making the Dream Real

It might appear that these reflections on the Bible are subtly intended to clear it of the charge of being anti-ecological, so that we can then happily go on reading the Bible in the same old way. But whether I intended it or not, I do not think it can be inferred from these reflections that everything can remain as it is, especially in the community of Christians. On the contrary, they suggest to me that we Christians in particular, because of our preoccupation with our human selves, have lost a whole dimension of the biblical story. We have forgotten that the story begins and ends with paradise, and that much of the middle is taken up with the longing and struggle for it. Our spiritual preoccupations are shaped by the modern world of course, which is similarly insensitive to the environment. But the modern world is now being shaken by the crisis it has brought about, so that we can now look back to the pre-modern world of the Bible with fresh eyes and new expectations. Perhaps the environmental crisis, seen afresh in the light of the Bible, will reawaken the awareness of all of us, Christians and others, to what we have lost and what we still might recover. My own desire that this will happen is, if anything is, my subtle intention in writing this. I am hoping that the biblical struggle with human dreams and possibilities will be seen to provide a resource that we can and need to draw on in order to cope with the crisis itself. If and as we do this, I think we shall find that our reading of the Bible takes on a different character.

We can, for example, draw on biblical insights in order to discover how we have got into the ecological mess we are in, even though where we have got is a long way away from where the biblical writers themselves were. It gives clues about humans' lack of security, loss of home, which, as well as awakening dreams of paradise, also motivate us to build towers of Babel and great complex cities which will make us secure after all. This they may do for a time, but only for a time, because, we begin to discover, these human constructions are inherently out of harmony with the natural environment into which we are born. To outwit nature, our own nature included, we build bigger towers, bigger cities, with greatly advanced technologies, only to find sooner or later that these too prove inadequate, and nature again is allowed the last word. By now of course we are way beyond the world of the Bible, and finding it increasingly difficult to make sense of it. Yet our story is not essentially different. It is being written on a larger scale, with higher stakes, but the inner process of loss, struggle, disillusionment and recovery seems to be the same as it was.

Seeing ourselves as living through the biblical story in our own time and place can give us access to the same sources of faith and hope. We can begin to recognize the human potential (for good as well as for evil) expressed in the biblical idea that we are all created in God's image, called to represent God on earth. We can see suffering and loss, in ourselves and others, as ways to enlightenment, revelation or self-discovery. We can even see the impending disaster of ecological breakdown as a prophetic warning to break with the false gods of the modern world and to rediscover our true human calling. And we can be inspired by the possible loss of our earth to love it and cherish it, and therefore to be bold enough to believe that the dream of regaining paradise is not a mere fantasy, but even now a real human possibility.

Notes

Chapter 1   The Bible and its Versions

1 Bede, *A History of the English Church and People*, translated by E. Shirley-Price, Penguin Classics, Harmondsworth, 1955.
2 T. Fuller, *The Church History of Britain*, Book IV, sec. ii, par. 53, p. 171.
3 William Tyndale, *Tyndale's New Testament. A Modern-spelling Edition of the 1534 Translation with an Introduction by David Daniel*, Yale University Press, New Haven, 1989, p. viii.
4 D. Coggan, *The English Bible and its Versions*, British Council and National Book League, 1963, pp. 30–1.
5 Geoffrey Hunt, *About the New English Bible*, OUP and CUP, Oxford and Cambridge, 1970.
6 Roger Coleman, *New Light and Truth: The making of the Revised English Bible*, OUP and CUP, Oxford and Cambridge, 1989.

Chapter 2   The Bible and University Study

1 R. Morgan with J. Barton, *Biblical Interpretation*, Oxford Bible Series, Oxford, 1988, p. 17.
2 S. Neill and T. Wright, *The Interpretation of the New Testament 1861–1986*, 2nd edition, OUP, Oxford, 1988, p. 36.
3 J. A. T. Robinson, 'Joseph Barber Lightfoot', Durham Cathedral Lecture, Durham, 1981, pp. 8f.
4 Careers and Research Advisory Centre, *Degree Course Guide for Theology and Religious Studies*. Quotation from 1988 edition, revised by Robert P. Gordon, p. 10.
5 cf. Chaim Potok's novel (illustrating this tension), *In The Beginning*, Penguin, Harmondsworth, 1976.
6 Norman Perrin, *Jesus and the Language of the Kingdom: Symbol and Metaphor in New Testament Interpretation*, Fortress Press, Philadelphia, 1976, p. 2.
7 cf. Stephen D. Moore, *Literary Criticism and the Gospels, the Theoretical Challenge*, Yale University Press, New Haven, 1989.

Chapter 5   The Bible and the Secondary School

1 Flora Thompson, *Lark Rise to Candleford* (in three parts 1939–43, as a trilogy 1945, OUP, Oxford), Penguin, Harmondsworth, 1973.
2 George Steiner, 'The Good Books', *New Yorker*, 11 January, 1988, p. 94.
3 John Hammond, David Hay *et al.*, *New Methods in RE Teaching*, Oliver & Boyd, London, 1990, pp. 7, 15, 17.
4 Kent Curriculum Statement, Kent County Council, 1990.
5 Department of Education and Science Circular 3/89.
6 Robert Kirkwood, *Looking for Proof of God*, Longmans, Harlow, 1990.

7 *Goods News Colour New Testament*, ISBN 0564 04151 3.
8 Leslie J. Francis, Harry M. Gibson and Peter Fulljames, 'Attitudes towards Christianity, Creationism, Scientism and Interest in Science Among 11–15 Year Olds', *British Journal of Religious Education*, Autumn 1990.

Chapter 6   The Bible and Television

1 David Jones, 'A,a,a, Domine Deus'.
2 Professor Akbar Ahmed in the *Guardian*, 28 July 1990.
3 St Ignatius Loyola, *The Spiritual Exercises*, Second Week, First Day and First Contemplation.
4 The Athanasian Creed.
5 As the Very Revd Wesley Carr pointed out at a recent conference on the theology of media at the Foundation for Christian Communication.
6 Philip Larkin, 'An Arundel Tomb'.
7 Edwin Muir, *The Incarnate One*.

Chapter 7   The Bible and Broadcasting

1 David F. Strauss, *New Life of Jesus*, 1864, London, 1879, p. viii.
2 Don Cupitt and Peter Armstrong, *Who was Jesus*, BBC, London, 1977, p. 10.
3 Robert Runcie, 'Religious Broadcasting Today', *The Canterbury Papers*, Bellew, London, 1990, p. 4.
4 *Poetry New Review*, vol. 6, no. 5, 1979, p. 7.
5 Owen Chadwick, *The Victorian Church*, Part I, A. & C. Black, London, 1971, p. 530.
6 See K. M. Wolfe, *The Churches and the BBC, 1922–56, The Politics of Broadcast Religion*, SCM Press, London, 1984, ch. 1.
7 The Head of Religious Programmes at Tyne Tees TV, Maxwell Deas, is to be cited by the *Guinness Book of Records* as producing more than 10,000 Epilogues in his long career.
8 Kate Whitehead, *The Third Programme, A Literary History*, OUP, Oxford, 1989, pp. 60ff.
9 About the Gospels, CUP, Cambridge, 1950, p. 3.
10 LCC London Syllabus of Religious Education, 1947, p. 17.
11 Biographer of William Temple.
12 *The Greatest Drama Ever Staged*, Hodder & Stoughton, London, 1938, p. 6.
13 To Dorothy L. Sayers, 8 January 1942.
14 Dorothy L. Sayers, *The Man Born to be King*, Gollancz, London, 1942, p. 20.
15 See *Poetry New Review*, no. 13, 'Crisis for Cranmer and King James', vol. 6, no. 4, 1979.
16 *Illustrated*, London 3 March 1956.
17 From Elaine Greene's diary, quoted by Michael Tracey in his biography of Greene, *A Variety of Lives*, Bodley Head, London, 1983, p. 192.
18 Adrian Hastings, *A History of English Christianity, 1920–1985*, Collins, London, 1986, p. 537.
19 Quoted in J. A. T. Robinson, *Honest to God*, SCM Press, London, 1963, p. 9.
20 *Jesus Christ, History, Interpretation and Faith*, (talks to sixth-formers), SPCK, London, 1956.

21 D. E. Nineham, *A New Way of Looking at the Gospels*, SPCK, Seraph Books, London, 1962.
22 June Clayton, 'Three Broadcast Jesus Dramatisations', unpublished thesis, 1976, p. 104.
23 Quoted in *Church Times*, 5 June 1969.
24 Henry Raynor, *The Times*, 5 June 1969.
25 *The New Testament Gospels*, BBC, London, 1965, Introduction.
26 Sir Lew Grade, *Still Dancing*, Collins, London, 1987, pp. 196ff.
27 *Radio Times*, 9 April 1977, p. 4.
28 John Bowden, *Jesus: the Unanswered Questions*, SCM Press, London, 1988.
29 Trevor Beeson, *An Eye for an Ear*, SCM Press, London, 1972, p. 74.
30 Gerald Priestland, in the *Listener*, 26 April 1984.
31 Edwin H. Robertson, to the IBA, 27 April 1984.

Chapter 9   The Bible and Jungian Depth Psychology

1 This is a term that Jung borrows from the theologian Rudolf Otto, who introduced it into modern religious vocabulary in order to identify the distinctive, irreducibly religious features of religious experience. Numinous experience for Jung exercises overwhelming and unique psychological power over man's consciousness because of its distinctive features. It is mysterious and fascinating and yet terrible and even horrible, but in a way which is quite specific to religious experience.

2 Archetypes are with instincts the principal inherited contents of the collective, rather than the personal, unconscious which function completely independently of all personal experience. Although not representable in themselves, they produce numinous, feeling toned effects, often in the form of universal images, which are independent of the will of the ego. The effects of archetypes, such as the inner figures of the anima and the shadow, exercise a fascination and possess an overpowering charge of energy which it is difficult to resist. Yet, although they can arouse, affect and take possession of the will, the purpose of analysis for Jung is, through becoming aware of them, to bring them under the control of consciousness and thereby to establish two-way communication between the ego and the collective unconscious.

3 Individuation is the relatively rare, never-ending process of assimilating the contents of the collective unconscious, and thus expanding consciousness. It involves the union of consciousness with the personal and the collective unconscious, leading to the paradoxical state in which a person discards a false individuality and becomes aware that he or she is now simultaneously unique and universal or archetypal. The individuating person unites all opposites (including good and evil and spirit and matter) and is said by Jung to live 'the life in God'.

4 The shadow is the unconscious negative side of the personality, the sum of all the unpleasant qualities one wants to hide. It is the inferior, primitive and dark side of a person's nature, and its origins are to be traced partly to the personal and partly to the collective unconscious. In so far as the shadow is repressed and concealed from consciousness, it tends to stand in opposition to the conscious ego in the same way that Satan opposes Yahweh in the Book of Job.

5 The self is an archetypal (unconscious) image of the unity of the personality

as a whole, which seeks the light of consciousness and acknowledgement of its authority over the whole psyche. It 'is not only the centre, but also the whole circumference which embraces both conscious and unconscious; it is the centre of this totality, just as the ego is the centre of the conscious mind.' As such the self is able to mediate the tension of opposites, including that between good and evil, and human and divine. It is also the archetypal image of meaning, and symbols of the self typically possess a numinosity; indeed Jung argued that such symbols are indistinguishable from the most important god-images of religious traditions.

Chapter 11   The Bible and Ordinary People

1 W. Herberg, *Protestant, Catholic, Jew*, Doubleday, New York, 2nd edition, 1960, p. 2.
2 Leslie Houlden, *Truth Untold*, SPCK, London, 1991, p. 63.
3 Leonardo Boff, *Church: Charisma and Power*, SCM, London, 1985, p. 128.
4 See e.g. the SPCK series 'Taletellers', started in 1988.

Chapter 13   The Bible and Killing for Food

1 John Calvin, *Commentaries on the First Book of Moses*, vol. 1, ET by John King, Edinburgh: Calvin Translation Society, 1847, pp. 291f. Extract in Andrew Linzey and Tom Regan (eds), *Animals and Christianity: A Book of Readings*, SPCK, London, and Crossroad, New York, 1989, pp. 199–200.
2 This argument is developed at length in Andrew Linzey, *Christianity and the Rights of Animals*, SPCK, London, and Crossroad, New York, 1987, especially pp. 141–9.
3 *Where We Stand on Animal Welfare*, London: Rabbinic Conference of the Union of Liberal and Progressive Synagogues, May 1990, p. 1.
4 Karl Barth, *Church Dogmatics*, vol. III, part 4, *The Doctrine of Creation*, ET by A. T. Mackay, T. H. L. Parker, H. Knight, H. A. Kennedy and J. Marks, T. and T. Clark, Edinburgh, 1961, p. 352; extract in *Animals and Christianity*, op. cit., pp. 191–3.
5 Ibid., p. 353n.
6 Ibid., p. 354.
7 Abraham Isaac Kook, *The Lights of Penitence, The Moral Principles, Lights of Holiness, Essays, Letters, and Poems*, ET by B. Z. Bokser, preface by J. Agus and R. Schatz, The Classics of Western Spirituality, SPCK, London, 1979, pp. 317–23. I am grateful to Jonathan Sacks for this reference.
8 See *inter alia Christianity and the Rights of Animals*, op. cit., p. 148.
9 See, e.g., Geoffrey L. Rudd, *Why Kill for Food?*, The Vegetarian Society, Cheshire, 1970, pp. 78–90, and Steven Rosen, *Food for the Spirit: Vegetarianism and the World Religions*, Bala Books, New York, 1987, pp. 33–9.
10 For example, *The Gospel of the Holy Twelve* and *The Essene Humane Gospel of Jesus*, cited and discussed in Rosen, op. cit.
11 J. A. T. Robinson, 'Need Jesus have been Perfect?' in S. W. Sykes and J. P. Clayton (eds), *Christ, Faith and History*, Cambridge Studies in Christology, CUP, Cambridge, 1972, pp. 39–52.
12 'Introduction' to Andrew Linzey and Tom Regan (eds), *Compassion for Animals: Readings and Prayers*, SPCK, London, 1989, p. xv.
13 I am grateful to Richard Bauckham for his recent lecture at Essex University

on this theme and for bringing to my attention the significance of this verse.
I understand that his work will shortly be published as *Jesus and the Greening
of Christianity*.

14 St Richard of Chichester, cited in Butler's *Lives of the Saints*; also extract in
Compassion for Animals: Readings and Prayers, op. cit., p. 66.

15 *The Rule of St Benedict*, ET by Justin McCann, Spiritual Masters Series, Sheed
and Ward, London, 1976, ch. 39, p. 46.

16 See Richard D. Ryder, *Animal Revolution: Changing Attitudes Towards Species-
ism*, Blackwell, Oxford, 1989, p. 96. For a history of the Church in America
see *The History of the Philadelphia Bible-Christian Church 1817–1917*, J. B. Lippin-
cott Company, Philadelphia, 1922. I am grateful to Bernard Unti for this last
reference.

Chapter 14   An Inner City Bible

1 J. J. Vincent, *Radical Jesus*, Marshall Pickering, London, 1986. Out of print,
but obtainable from Urban Theology Unit, 210 Abbeyfield Road, Sheffield
S4 7AZ.

2 Michael Armitage, *Jesus Loves Brixton Too*, Marshall Pickering, London, 1986;
Tony Holden, *Keeping Faith*, Methodist Home Mission Division, London,
1988; Austin Smith, *Passion for the Inner City*, Sheed & Ward, London, 1983.

3 Cf. Leonardo Boff and Clodovis Boff, *Introducing Liberation Theology*, Burns
& Oates, Tunbridge Wells, 1987, pp. 32–3.

4 J. J. Vincent, 'Mark's Gospel in the Inner City', in *Bible and the Politics of
Exegesis: Essays in Honor of Norman Gottwald*, ed. David Jobling, Peggy Day
and Gerald T. Sheppard, Pilgrim Press, New York, 1991.

5 Cf. Ernesto Cardenal, *Gospel in Solentiname*, Orbis, Mary Knoll, NY, 1979.

6 The method is described, and examples given, in J. D. Davis and J. J.
Vincent, *Mark at Work*, Bible Reading Fellowship, London, 1986.

7 Cf. J. J. Vincent, 'Christian Discipleship and Politics', in *Religion in Public
Life*, ed. Dan Cohn-Sherbok and David McLellan, Macmillan, London, 1991.

8 The pattern is used as an interpretative medium for the story of the Sheffield
Inner City Ecumenical Mission in my *Into the City*, Epworth Press, London,
1982.

Chapter 16   The Bible and Peace and War

1 This is a revised version of a lecture given on 2 February 1990 at Canterbury
Cathedral Library in the series 'Using the Bible', jointly organized by the
Dean and Chapter of Canterbury and the University of Kent.

2 See G. von Rad, *Der Heilige Krieg im Alten Israel*, Zuringli Verlag, Zürich,
1951, based on lectures first given to the Old Testament Society at Bangor
in 1949.

3 H. Hendrickx, *A Time for Peace. Reflections on the Meaning of Peace and Violence
in the Bible*, SPCK, London, 1988, p. 39, based on an earlier study by Lohfink,
1983.

4 S. Z. Klausner, 'Violence', in *The Encyclopedia of Religion*, Macmillan, New
York, 1987, vol. 15, p. 271.

5 R. Gill, *Theology and Social Structure*, Mowbrays, London, 1977, p. 37.

6 For a detailed discussion of the psychological roots of war and the persuasive
arguments used to make whole populations go to war, as well as possible

ways to transcend war today by learning to make peace, see A. Stevens, *The Roots of War. A Jungian Perspective*, Paragol House, New York, 1989.

7 The Oxford English Dictionary lists the first usage of 'non-violent' for 1924, in a book associated with Gandhi. The OED Supplement gives as one of the definitions of pacifism 'the advocacy of peace at any price' and lists the first usage of the word in a French speech of 1901. For a comparative study on non-violence see P. D. Bishop, *A Technique for Loving. Non-Violence in Indian and Christian Traditions*, SCM, London, 1981. For more details on the Indian tradition of non-violence see U. Tähtinen, *Ahimsa. Non-Violence in Indian Tradition*, Rider Company, London, 1976.

8 A. Abecassis, 'Three Kinds of Peace: Shalom-Shelomot', in *SIDIC*, Rome, 1988, p. 14.

9 The differences between '*pax Romana*' and '*pax Christi*' as well as the divergent interpretations of peace put forward by different New Testament writers have been closely investigated by K. Wengst, *Pax Romana and the Peace of Jesus Christ*, SCM, London, 1987. For a detailed discussion of early Christian attitudes to war and peace see F. Young, 'The Early Church: Military Service, War and Peace', *Theology*, November 1989, pp. 491–503.

10 Quoted in H. Gordon and L. Grob, eds, *Education for Peace. Testimonies from World Religions*, Orbis Books, New York, 1988, p. 66.

11 See the earlier Church of England Report on *The Church and the Bomb – Nuclear Weapons and Christian Conscience*, London, 1982; also R. J. Bauckham and R. J. Elford, eds, *The Nuclear Weapons Debate: Theological and Ethical Issues*, SCM, London, 1989; also J. Finnis, J. M. Boyle and G. Grisez, *Nuclear Deterrence, Morality and Realism*, Clarendon Press, Oxford, 1987.

12 See Franz Alt, *Frieden ist möglich. Die Politik der Bergpredigt*, R Piper & Co., Munich, 1983, of which well over 100,000 copies were sold in Germany.

13 C. von Weizsäcker, *Die Zeit drängt*, Hanser Verlag, Munich, 1988, p. 114 (my translation).

14 This is the title of a thought-provoking study by R. Friedli, *Frieden wagen*, Universitat Verlag, Freiburg, 1981.

15 In R. J. Bauckham and R. J. Elford, eds. *The Nuclear Weapons Debate: Theological and Ethical Issues*, SCM, London, 1989, p. 62.

16 Quoted in H. Gordon and L. Grob, op. cit., p. 72.

17 Ibid., pp. 62–76.

18 P. Teilhard de Chardin, *Human Energy*, Collins, London, 1969, p. 37f. The quotation is taken from his essay 'The Spirit of the Earth', written as early as 1931.

19 Since I gave this lecture, John Macquarrie has republished his earlier study on *The Concept of Peace*, SCM Press, London, 1990, in which he argues for a vision of affirmative peace. He also includes a section on practical suggestions of what can be done towards developing the global virtue of peace.

20 R. Müller, *New Genesis. Shaping a Global Spirituality*, Doubleday, New York, 1982, p. 104. See also his two essays 'To Reach Peace, Teach Peace', ibid., pp. 84–90, and 'An Appeal to World Religions for Peace', ibid., pp. 93–100.

21 A secular perspective is presented by Birgit Brock-Utne, *Educating for Peace. A Feminist Perspective*, Pergamon Press, New York and Oxford, 1987. A Christian exploration of the same theme is found in the poems and essays by the theologian Dorothee Sölle, *Of War and Love*, Orbis Books, Maryknoll, New York, 1983.

22 H. Gordon and L. Grob, eds, op. cit.

Chapter 18 The Bible and Christian Witness

1 See further E. Haenchen, *The Acts of the Apostles*, Blackwells, Oxford, 1971 and I. Howard Marshall, *Acts*, Eerdmans, Grand Rapids, 1980.
2 H. H. Rowley, *The Missionary Message of the Old Testament*, Carey Press, London, 1944.
3 G. Vermes, *The Dead Sea Scrolls in English*, Penguin, Harmondsworth, 1962.
4 Jocelyn Murray, *Proclaim the Good News: A Short History of the Church Missionary Society*, Hodder, London, 1985.
5 C. K. Barrett, *The Gospel According to St. John*, SPCK, London, 1967.
6 John Paul II, *Redemptoris Missio*, in Catholic International, Paris, March 1991.
7 cf. Oscar Cullman, *Early Christian Worship*, SCM Press, London, 1953.
8 J. R. W. Stott, *The Message of Thessalonians*, IVP, Leicester, 1991.
9 David Sheppard, *The Other Britain*, Dimbleby Lecture, BBC, 1984.

Chapter 20 The Bible and Paradise

1 Lynn White, Jr, 'The Historical Roots of Our Ecologic Crisis', *Science*, 155, no. 3767, 10 March 1967, p. 1205.
2 Arnold Toynbee, 'The Genesis of Pollution', *Horizon*, American Heritage, New York, Summer 1973, p. 7.
3 Gro Harlem Bruntland *et al.*, *Our Common Future*, The World Commission on Environment and Development, OUP, Oxford, 1987, p. 343.
4 Cf. John Rogerson, *Genesis 1–11*, JSOT Press, Sheffield, 1991.
5 Cf. Bernard W. Anderson, 'Creation and Ecology', in his ed., *Creation in the Old Testament*, SPCK, London, 1984.
6 Cf. Walther Zimmerli, *The Old Testament and the World*, SPCK, London, 1976, pp. 40f.
7 Cf. John Austin Baker, 'Biblical Views of Nature', in Charles Birch, William Eakin, Jay B. McDaniel, eds, *Liberating Life: Contemporary Approaches to Ecological Theology*, Orbis Books, Maryknoll, New York, 1990, pp. 13–15.

Contributors

Rabbi Dr Dan Cohn-Sherbok is University Lecturer in Jewish Theology at the University of Kent, Canterbury

The Rt Rev Lord Runcie was formerly Archbishop of Canterbury

The Very Rev John Simpson is Dean of Canterbury

The Rt Rev Lord Coggan of Sissinghurst was formerly Archbishop of Canterbury

Dr John Court is Senior Lecturer in Theology and Religious Studies at The University of Kent, Canterbury.

The Rev Professor Leslie Houlden is Professor of Theology at King's College, London.

The Rt Hon Enoch Powell was formerly a member of Parliament.

Mrs Kathleen Court is Head of Religious Studies at Simon Langton Girls Grammar School, Canterbury.

Miss Angela Tilby is a writer and broadcaster.

Dr Kenneth Wolfe is Director of the Centre for the Study of Religion and Society at the University of Kent, Canterbury.

The Rev Don Cupitt is Dean of Emmanuel College, Cambridge and Lecturer in Divinity at the University of Cambridge.

Dr Leon Schlamm is Lecturer in Religious Studies at the University of Kent, Canterbury.

The Rt Hon the Earl of Longford was formerly Lord Privy Seal.

The Rev Canon Christopher Lewis is a Canon of Canterbury Cathedral.

The Very Rev Peter Baelz was formerly Dean of Durham

The Rev Dr Andrew Linzey is Director of the Centre for the Study of Theology at the University of Essex, Colchester.

The Rev Dr John Vincent is Director of the Urban Theology Unit, Sheffield.

The Most Rev John Habgood is Archbishop of York.

Professor Ursula King is Professor of Theology and Religious Studies at the University of Bristol.

Professor Geoffrey Parrinder was formerly Professor of the Comparative Study of Religions at King's College, London.

The Rt Rev Michael Nazir-Ali is General Secretary of the Church Missionary Society.

The Rev Dr H D Beeby was formerly a lecturer at Tainam Theological College, Taiwan and is Lecturer in Old Testament at Selly Oak College, Birmingham.

The Rt Rev Lesslie Newbigin was formerly Bishop in Madras.

Dr Rex Ambler is a lecturer in Theology at the University of Birmingham.